State Violence, Collusion and the Troubles

STATE VIOLENCE, COLLUSION AND THE TROUBLES

Counter Insurgency, Government Deviance and Northern Ireland

Maurice Punch

PlutoPress

www.plutobooks.com

First published 2012 by Pluto Press
345 Archway Road, London N6 5AA

www.plutobooks.com

Distributed in the United States of America exclusively by
Palgrave Macmillan, a division of St. Martin's Press LLC,
175 Fifth Avenue, New York, NY 10010

British Library Cataloguing in Publication Data
A catalogue record for this book is available from the British Library

ISBN   978 0 7453 3143 0   Hardback
ISBN   978 0 7453 3147 8   Paperback

Library of Congress Cataloging in Publication Data applied for

This book is printed on paper suitable for recycling and made from fully managed
and sustained forest sources. Logging, pulping and manufacturing processes are
expected to conform to the environmental standards of the country of origin.

10   9   8   7   6   5   4   3   2   1

Designed and produced for Pluto Press by Chase Publishing Services Ltd
Typeset from disk by Stanford DTP Services, Northampton, England
Simultaneously printed digitally by CPI Antony Rowe, Chippenham, UK and
Edwards Bros in the United States of America

*For all who have suffered, and continue to suffer,
as a result of the Troubles.*

Contents

Acknowledgements

Since I started this book a few years ago many people have been generous with their time and have aided me in various ways, by discussing the topic, commenting on drafts and/or by suggesting research material. They include some highly supportive colleagues in London at LSE and King's but especially Ben Bowling, David Downes, Janet Foster, Penny Green, Tim Newburn, Paddy Rawlinson, Robert Reiner and Paul Rock. There were academic colleagues elsewhere, as well as some 'reflective practitioners' in policing or the military, who assisted me in diverse ways including Alexis Aronowitz, Piet Deelman, Auke van Dijk, Julian Dixon, Stan Gilmour, Jim Gobert, Bob Hoogenboom, Graham Smith, Kees van der Vijver, Geert de Vries, Jim Waddington, Ron Weitzer, Hans Werdmölder and Merrick Willis, while I received sage advice from Michael Clarke. In Amsterdam I've gained much from many stimulating conversations with Derek Phillips, while he has kindly passed on *The New York Review of Books* since the late 1970s. This has been essential reading but in recent years it has carried excellent articles on the 'war on terror', Abu Ghraib and Guantanamo Bay. I am most grateful to them all. I have long drawn on the operational experience and insights on police leadership, command and control and use of force of Geoffrey Markham (former Assistant Chief Constable, Essex Police); and on the operational background in policing and expertise in Human Rights of Ralph Crawshaw (former Chief Superintendent, Essex Police). A special word of thanks has to go to them for the many valuable discussions in attractive locations throughout Essex and Suffolk. I also appreciate the professional advice and patience of Anne Beech, Will Viney and the team at Pluto. Finally, I have as ever received encouragement and affection from my dear wife Cornelia; also support from Julio, Maria, George and grandson Jimmy and from my extended family in the Netherlands, Ireland, UK and US. This network of colleagues, friends and family has been essential in the completion of this work.

Amstelveen, The Netherlands
October 2011

Paramilitary Groups

- The original Irish Republican Army (IRA) in Ireland, or Old IRA, comprised the Irish Volunteers and Irish Republican Brotherhood of the 1916 Easter Rising, and fought the British in the War of Independence (1919–21) as the Army of Ireland
- Those who resisted the 1921 Treaty with Britain fought and lost to the new Irish government in the Civil War (1922–23), called themselves the IRA and from 1922 to 1969 opposed the governments in the South and North with periodic violence to realise an independent, united (32 county) Ireland as a socialist republic
- In late 1969 a split took the new Provisional IRA (PIRA or 'Provos') out of what became known as the Official IRA, OIRA. At times there were armed clashes in feuds between PIRA and OIRA. OIRA abandoned violence in 1972. By the early 1990s PIRA was estimated to have a core of some 300 activists with about 450 in support roles (Bishop & Mallie 1988)
- Provisional *Sinn Fein* was ostensibly the political wing of PIRA, but it is assumed that it was intimately linked with PIRA; several IRA commanders probably also held leading roles within *Sinn Fein* (Moloney 2007, 2010)
- The Continuity IRA (CIRA) broke from PIRA in 1986 when PIRA recognised the authority of the Dublin government
- In 1997 the Real IRA (RIRA) split off from PIRA because RIRA was opposed to the peace process
- The Irish National Liberation Army (INLA) was the military wing of a Trotskyite splinter group, the Irish Republican Socialist Party, that had broken with OIRA
- The Irish People's Liberation Organization (IPLO) split from the INLA after a dispute. IPLO feuded with the INLA, and the IRA attacked the IPLO and disbanded it.

There were other splinter groups that might also be names used as cover for a sub-unit acting autonomously, including Republican

Reaction Force, Irish Freedom Fighters, Catholic Reaction Force and South Armagh Republican Action Force.

LOYALIST PARAMILITARY GROUPS

- Loyalist Volunteer Force (LVF): split from UVF in 1996 (and feuded with it)
- Ulster Defence Association (UDA): was set up in 1977 and was legal until 1992 after which it was proscribed for providing cover for paramilitaries
- Ulster Volunteer Force (UVF): emerged in 1965 (an earlier UVF had been launched in 1913); in the mid-1970s the UVF had around 1,500 members, with 400–500 activists that were later reduced to a core of about 80
- Loyalist Volunteer Force (LVF): split from UVF in 1996 and at times feuded with it
- Ulster Freedom Fighters (UFF): with a core of about 60 members.

The Red Hand Commandos, Red Hand Defenders, Ulster Protestant Action and Protestant Action Force were supposedly splinter groups but more often these were cover names for a sub-unit mounting an operation without authorisation.

Abbreviations and Irish Gaelic Terms

14th Int.	14th Intelligence Company (or Det for 'detached')
ACC	Assistant Chief Constable
ACPO	Association of Chief Police Officers
AIA	Anglo-Irish Agreement (1985)
APC	armoured personnel carrier
ASU	Active Service Unit (of IRA)
CAIN	Conflict Archive Internet
CIA	Central Intelligence Agency (US)
CID	Criminal Investigation Department
CIRA	Continuity Irish Republican Army
CIU	Counter-Insurgency Unit
CLF	Commander Land Forces (senior Army officer in Province)
CLMC	Combined Loyalist Military Council
CO	Commanding Officer
CT	counter-terrorism
DPP	Director of Public Prosecutions
DUP	Democratic Unionist Party (of Rev. Ian Paisley)
ECHR	European Court of Human Rights
FRU	Force Research Unit
GAL	*Grupos Antiterroristos de Liberacion*
GFA	Good Friday Agreement (1998)
GMP	Greater Manchester Police
GOC	General Officer Commanding (in charge of all armed services in Province)
GWOT	Global War on Terrorism
HMIC	Her Majesty's Inspectorate of Constabulary
HQMSU	Headquarters Mobile Support Unit
INLA	Irish National Liberation Army
IPLO	Irish People's Liberation Organization
IRA	Irish Republican Army
IRB	Irish Republican Brotherhood
JIC	Joint Intelligence Committee
JIS	Joint Irish Section
LVF	Loyalist Volunteer Force
MACP	Military Aid to the Civil Power

Met	Metropolitan Police
MoD	Ministry of Defence
MI5/MI6	The Security Service (Military Intelligence, Section 5 [domestic]/Section 6 [overseas])
MIU	Military Intelligence Unit
MP	Member of Parliament
MRF	Mobile Reconnaissance Force
NGO	non-governmental organisation
NICRA	Northern Ireland Civil Rights Association
Noraid	Irish Northern Aid Committee
OIRA	Official Irish Republican Army
OPONI	Office of Police Ombudsman for Northern Ireland
PANI	Police Authority for Northern Ireland
PC	Police Constable
PD	Peoples' Democracy
PIIC	Public Interest Immunity Certificate
PIRA	Provisional Irish Republican Army
PSNI	Police Service of Northern Ireland (2001–)
PAF	Protestant Action Force
RAF	Republican Action Force
RIRA	Real Irish Republican Army
RIC	Royal Irish Constabulary (1822–1922)
RUC	Royal Ulster Constabulary (1922–2001)
SAS	Special Air Service Regiment
SAM	surface-to-air missile
SAP	South African Police
SB	Special Branch
SDLP	Social Democratic and Labour Party
SIO	Senior Investigating Officer
SOCO	Scene of Crime Officer
SOP	Standard Operating Procedure
SPG	Special Patrol Group
TCG	Tasking and Coordinating Group
TRC	Truth and Reconciliation Committee
UDA	Ulster Defence Association
UDR	Ulster Defence Regiment
UFF	Ulster Freedom Fighters
UPA	Ulster Protestant Action
UPV	Ulster Protestant Volunteers
US	United States
UUP	Ulster Unionist Party
UVF	Ulster Volunteer Force

WMDs	weapons of mass destruction
WTC	World Trade Center
WWI	World War One
WWII	World War Two

Irish Gaelic terms:

Sinn Fein	Political wing of PIRA
Dáil	Irish Parliament
Taisoaech	Irish Prime Minister
An Garda Síochána	'Guardians of the Peace'; Ireland's Police Service

Timeline

1801	Union of Ireland with Great Britain
1822	Formation of an armed, paramilitary constabulary; became the Royal Irish Constabulary (RIC)
1858	Irish Republican Brotherhood (IRB), founded in US and later in Ireland with Fenian Brotherhood a year later
1866	First use of 'Irish Republican Army' with Fenian incursion into Canada
1867	Three Fenians, 'the Manchester Martyrs', executed in 1868 for killing a policeman; a Fenian bomb exploded outside Clerkenwell Prison killing 12 and causing immense damage; a Fenian was publicly hanged in 1868 for this attack
1883	Series of Fenian bombings on British mainland
1890	Parnell, close to Home Rule for Ireland with his Irish Parliamentary Party at Westminster, cited in a divorce case and resigns as party leader; Home Rule Bill for Ireland postponed
1912	Unionist leaders Craig and Carson mobilize 500,000 loyalist supporters to sign a covenant in Belfast to defend 'Ulster's' independence by force in the event of Home Rule; founding of militant UVF a year later with over 80,000 members
1914	30,000 rifles with ammunition smuggled into Ireland for the UVF
1916	Easter Rising in Dublin with proclamation of an Irish Republic; crushed by British troops followed by 15 executions
1919–21	Irish War of Independence against Britain commenced in 1919 with truce in 1921 and peace negotiations in London. *Sinn Fein* MPs elected to the British Parliament in 1918 refused to take their seats and an Irish Parliament, the *Dáil*, was unilaterally founded in 1919 with a declaration of independence
1920	Government of Ireland Act proposed two separate states in Ireland. Original 'Bloody Sunday' with IRA attacks on

	British agents and British soldiers killing 14 people at a Gaelic football match in Dublin
1921	Anglo-Irish Treaty; Partition of Ireland, with creation of Northern Ireland with a Parliament at Stormont; serious disturbances in North; major differences between treaty and non-treaty factions in the South led to Irish Civil War (1922–23)
1922	Founding of Royal Ulster Constabulary (RUC) in North and *An Garda Síochána* (Guardians of the Peace) in South
1923	Formal independence of South as 'Irish Free State' within British Commonwealth
1939–40	Free State remains neutral during WWII. Sporadic IRA bombing campaign on British mainland and in Northern Ireland during the war years
1948	*Eire*, Ireland, votes to become a Republic and leaves the Commonwealth (effective 1949)
1956	IRA border campaign with attacks in Northern Ireland; called off in 1962 and viewed as a failure
1964	Campaign for Social Justice founded in Dungannon
1965	First formal meeting of the prime ministers from the North and the South of Ireland in 40 years
1966	50th Anniversary of Easter Rising: shootings and bombings by new UVF which declares war on IRA
1967	Foundation of Northern Ireland Civil Rights Association (NICRA)
1968	Peoples' Democracy (PD) founded; start of civil rights marches, clashes in Derry between marchers and RUC; first RUC officer dies in Troubles
1969	PD march comes under attack by loyalists; serious disturbances in Belfast and Derry with many people fleeing their homes; British troops arrive in Province; PIRA splits from OIRA; several bombings by UVF of water and electricity facilities to discredit IRA
1970	B Specials (special constabulary) disbanded and Ulster Defence Regiment (UDR) established; founding of Social Democratic and Labour Party (SDLP). Security forces enter Falls Road area of Belfast and impose a non-statutory curfew. Labour loses Election to the Conservatives who govern 1970–74; with Labour in office 1974–79 and Conservatives 1979–97.
1971	Internment without trial; first British soldier shot dead; SDLP withdraws from Stormont Parliament

1972   Operation Motorman, 30,000 security forces enter 'no-go' areas of Belfast and Derry; high point of fatalities at hands of IRA; Bloody Friday in Belfast and Bloody Sunday in Derry; British Embassy burned down in Dublin; two unattributed car bombs in Dublin; secret talks with PIRA in London and a cease-fire; OIRA announces permanent cease-fire and relinquishes violence; direct rule over Northern Ireland from Westminster

1973   UK and Irish Republic join European Economic Community; Sunningdale Agreement announces plans to instigate a new power-sharing executive in Northern Ireland, to take account of the 'Irish dimension' with a Council of Ireland drawing representatives from North and South; Diplock courts without juries; four car-bombs in London. IRA ship with Libyan arms, the *Claudia*, intercepted

1974   Birmingham bombings by IRA; bomb explosions in Dublin and Monaghan attributed to UVF; Ulster Workers' Council calls strike, paralyses the Province and wrecks Sunningdale Agreement, collapse of Northern Ireland Assembly

1975   IRA cease-fire; end of internment, of those detained 1,874 were Catholic and 107 Protestant

1976   Special Air Service Regiment (SAS) formally active in Northern Ireland; IRA adopts strategy of 'long war'; withdrawal of special category status for republican prisoners leads to 'dirty protest', meaning refusing to wear prison clothes or use toilet facilities while smearing excrement on cell walls

1977   Second loyalist workers' strike proves ineffective

1978   IRA fire-bomb devastated the La Mon House Hotel killing twelve guests and injuring many others; European Court of Human Rights (ECHR) rules on controversial interrogation techniques

1979   Earl Mountbatten killed on vacation in the Republic; 18 soldiers blown up at Warren Point; Airey Neave killed in explosion inside the Parliamentary compound at Westminster; Conservatives win general election with Margaret Thatcher as Premier until 1990

1980   First hunger strike in Maze Prison

1981   Bobby Sands MP dies in prison during second hunger-strike; in total ten hunger-strikers die (seven from IRA and three from INLA), two of whom were elected to the British Parliament and two to the *Dáil* (Irish Parliament)

1982   Three RUC officers killed by land-mine followed by three controversial shootings by the RUC's Headquarters Mobile Support Unit (HQMSU)

1983   Mass IRA break-out from Maze Prison; 38 escaped with 19 recaptured

1984   British police officer Stalker asked to investigate RUC shootings; bombing of Brighton hotel housing Prime Minister during Conservative Party Conference (with five deaths); *Marita Ann* carrying arms for IRA intercepted

1985   All Ireland Agreement; Ireland given a say in the affairs of the North while Republic recognised legitimacy of the Northern Ireland state with its future based on majority decision making; first meeting of Anglo-Irish Intergovernmental Conference; nine RUC officers killed in mortar attack at Newry

1986   Stalker removed from investigation into RUC shootings and suspended pending an inquiry into his own conduct; *Sinn Fein* candidates allowed to take seats in *Dáil* if elected reflecting acceptance of Irish parliamentary politics

1987   Eight IRA volunteers and a bystander killed by SAS at Loughall; eleven people killed by IRA bomb at Remembrance Day Service in Enniskillen; trawler *Eksund* with Libyan arms for IRA is intercepted

1988   An unarmed three-person Active Service Unit (ASU) of the IRA is shot dead by the SAS on Gibraltar; loyalist kills three mourners at funeral of 'Gibraltar Three' in Belfast; at the funeral of those victims, two British soldiers in plain-clothes were apprehended, beaten and shot; John Hume of SDLP begins informal talks with Gerry Adams of *Sinn Fein* (seen as start of 'peace process')

1989   Pat Finucane, a solicitor for many republicans, shot dead by UVF; 'Guildford Four' released from prison after nearly 16 years following a miscarriage of justice; Northern Ireland Secretary Brooke hints at possibility of talks with *Sinn Fein* if there was a cease-fire first, refers to Cyprus and that the government must be flexible

1990   IRA bomb London Stock Exchange; Northern Ireland Secretary Brooke states that Britain has 'no selfish strategic or economic interest' in union with Northern

Ireland; John Major replaces Margaret Thatcher as Prime Minister

1991 Mortar shells fired into garden of No. 10 Downing Street; 'Birmingham Six' released from prison following miscarriage of justice

1992 UDA banned; IRA bombing of Baltic Exchange in London

1993 Downing Street Declaration indicates grounds for negotiations leading to a peace agreement, with people of Northern Ireland deciding their future; bomb attack in Warrington; explosion at Bishopsgate in London causes extensive damage; Irish President Mary Robinson shakes hands with Gerry Adams on visit to Province

1994 IRA declares complete cessation of hostilities; the Combined Loyalist Military Council (CLMC) follows suit and expresses 'abject and true remorse' to the 'loved ones of all innocent victims'; meeting between British officials and *Sinn Fein*

1995 Gerry Adams visits US and is received at White House; President Bill Clinton visits Northern Ireland and shakes hands with Adams in Belfast

1996 Cease-fire breaks down; IRA bombing of Canary Wharf in London and Manchester's Arndale Shopping Centre cause massive damage; talks begin at Stormont with *Sinn Fein*

1997 Last British soldier killed in Troubles; PIRA announces definitive cease-fire; Labour Party wins general election

1998 Omagh bombing by RIRA; RIRA and INLA announce cease-fires; Good Friday Agreement (GFA); elections for new Northern Ireland Assembly; John Hume (SDLP) and David Trimble (Ulster Unionist Party, UUP) are awarded the Nobel Peace Prize

1999 Patten Commission reports on the future of policing in Northern Ireland; IRA reveals location of six graves holding eight bodies of 'disappeared' whom it had executed; devolution of authority to Northern Ireland Assembly is restored; Republic of Ireland changes constitutional claim to Northern Ireland

2000 Office of Police Ombudsman for Northern Ireland (OPONI) operational; amnesty for many prisoners under GFA; President Clinton visits both parts of Ireland; RUC awarded the George Cross (highest British award for bravery, normally for individual civilians)

2001   RUC renamed Police Service of Northern Ireland (PSNI); a number of RIRA bombs in London

2002   *Sinn Fein* apologies for 'mistakes' made during IRA's campaign including Enniskillen bombing

2003   Mrs McConville's body was found in County Louth on a beach following erosion, 30 years after her disappearance. She had been executed with a head-shot by the IRA as an alleged informer

2005   IRA Army Council announces official end of armed campaign with formal acceptance that decommissioning of IRA weapons has been accomplished

2006   Denis Donaldson, who admitted he had infiltrated the IRA and *Sinn Fein* as a British spy, is shot dead in the Republic

2007   British Army formally leaves Northern Ireland, ending its military campaign after 38 years

2008   Ian Paisley (aged 82) announces he is stepping down as First Minister of the Northern Ireland Assembly

2009   Two soldiers shot dead outside their barracks in Antrim, attributed to RIRA, the first soldiers shot in Northern Ireland since 1997. Police officer shot dead, attributed to CIRA

2010   Car bomb explodes outside courthouse in Newry with no casualties; attributed to dissident republicans

2011   Car bomb explodes in Omagh killing PSNI officer. Queen Elizabeth II becomes first British monarch to visit Ireland since Independence; she lays a wreath at the Garden of Remembrance in Dublin for those who died for Irish freedom including the War of Independence; the Queen expresses in diplomatic terms what amounts to regret for events which have troubled the relationships between the two countries.

Main Non-Irish Insurgent Terrorist Groups

Action Directe   Marxist urban guerrilla group in France, active largely between 1976 and 1987

Al Qaeda   Radical Islamic 'jihadist' group founded in Afghanistan in the 1980s, led by the late Osama bin Laden, behind a number of highly violent attacks including the 9/11 suicide assaults with planes in the US

ANC   African National Congress, South Africa; founded in 1912, opposed the apartheid regime, militant wing (*Umkhonto we Sizwe*/Spear of the Nation) formed in 1961; ANC had formally abandoned violence by 1990

Angry Brigade   Small, left-wing, largely student group in Britain in 1970s

Aum Shinrikyo   Aum Supreme Truth: cult-like sect in Japan, used poison gas in Tokyo Metro in 1995; said to be still active in Japan (Hoffman 2006:126)

Black September   Militant Palestinian insurgent group, responsible for attack on Israeli athletes at Munich Olympics in 1972

Contras   Right-wing, anti-Sandinista group in Nicaragua supported by the US when socialist *Sandinistas* gained power in 1979

DFLP   Democratic Front for the Liberation of Palestine, militant Palestinian group, split from Popular Front for the Liberation of Palestine (PFLP)

EOKA   *Ethnikí Orgánosis Kipriakoú Agónos* (National Organisation of Cypriot Fighters), led struggle in the 1950s for independence of Cyprus from Britain

ETA   *Euskadi Ta Askatasuna* (Basque Fatherland and Liberty), striving for autonomy from Spain for the Basque region and people

FARC	*Fuerzas Armadas Revolucionarias de Colombia* (Revolutionary Armed Forces of Colombia); oldest and largest insurgent grouping in South America
FLNC	*Front de Liberation de la Corse* (Corsican National Liberation Front); group mounting sporadic campaign for autonomy from France of island of Corsica
FLQ	*Front de Liberation du Quebec* (Quebec Liberation Front); active particularly in 1970s for autonomy for French-speaking province of Quebec
FNL	*Front de Libération Nationale* (National Liberation Front); the main insurgent group formed in 1954 to fight French forces for an independent Algeria (granted in 1962)
GIA	*Groupe islamique armé* (Armed Islamic Group); extremely violent jihadist group, founded in Algeria in 1982, mounted a vicious campaign against the secular Algerian government when certain victory for the Front Islamic du Salut (FIS, Islamic Salvation Front) Party in the 1992 general election was thwarted by the Army suspending the election and declaring an emergency
Hamas	Islamic Resistance Movement; founded in 1987, strives for a Palestinian Islamic state; victorious in elections in Palestine in 2006
Hezbollah	The Party of God (also spelled 'Hizbullah'); Militant jihadist movement in Lebanon, formed in early 1980s and aimed to create a Muslim republic in Lebanon; supported by Iran and Syria, it opposed Israeli intervention in South Lebanon; engaged in hostage taking and other terrorist activities under the name Islamic Jihad; now has a number of seats in the Lebanon Parliament
Irgun	*Irgun Zvai Leumi* (National Military Organization); one of the main Zionist groups fighting the British in the Palestine Protectorate in order to found an Israeli state after British withdrawal (realised in 1948)

JRA — Japanese Red Army, small revolutionary group founded in 1970s

Muhadijeen — Holy Warriors: jihadist insurgent groups united in Afghanistan to fight Soviet invasion of 1979

NAR — *Nuclei Armati Rivoluzionari* (Armed Revolutionary Nucleus); neo-fascist terrorist group responsible for bombing at Bologna railway station in 1980

PFLP — Popular Front for the Liberation of Palestine; formed in 1967 and has opposed the Israeli–Palestinian peace process; secular and Marxist in origin

PKK — Kurdistan Workers Party; founded in 1974 it seeks an autonomous Kurdish homeland

PLO — Palestinian Liberation Organization; with militant wing Fatah, for an independent Palestinian state, led by Jassir Arafat 1969–2004

RAF — *Rote Armee Faction* (Red Army Faction) in Germany; also referred to as the Baader-Meinhof Group, active largely in 1970s

Red Brigade — *Brigate Rosse*, Italy; emerged in early 1970s partly as response to right-wing violence and provocation; stood for a revolutionary communist system; took part in bombings, abductions and assassinations; faded in 1980s due to effective police measures and internal divisions

Sandinistas — Sandinist National Liberation Front; active in Nicaragua against American-supported dictator Somoza who was deposed in 1979 with *Sandinistas* seizing power and forming a socialist junta

Tamil Tigers — Liberation Tigers of Tamil Eelam (LTTE), Sri Lanka; commenced campaign in 1976 for an independent Tamil state and fought a long and tough civil war against the Sri Lankan military but was finally defeated in 2009

The Shining Path — *Sendero Luminoso*; extremely violent Maoist group in Peru formed in late 1960s; much weakened by capture of its leadership and of its founder, Abimael Guzman, in 1992

Tupamaros

Also known as MLN, *Moviemento de Liberación Nacional* (National Liberation Movement); Uruguayan left-wing group founded in 1963, also a social movement, engaged in kidnappings, assassinations and bombings

Weathermen

Left-wing group, US; emerged from radical student movement and active largely in 1970s for a short period with sporadic bombings and shootings

1
State Crime: 'Bloody Sunday' and the Troubles

Ultimately, the struggle between democracy and terrorism is one for legitimacy and maintaining the latter is strategically more important for democratic governments than winning short-term victories through tactical 'quick fixes' which might seem effective but turn democracies into something that begins to mirror the terrorist opponent. (Schmid 1992:14)

STATE CRIME

This book recounts how the British state dramatically failed and in so doing committed crimes. In Northern Ireland it shot its own citizens, lied about it and blamed the victims. But then, states frequently misbehave when threatened, rashly choose 'quick fixes' and readily take the path of repression. This may only foster an escalation which proves counter-productive and leads the state, as Schmid intimates above, to resemble the opponent it reviles. For if insurgent terrorism provides a natural experiment in how the democratic state responds to a significant threat, with a sort of Milgram[1] for the mighty, then the British state demonstrably abandoned its expressed principles and broke the law during the 30 years of the 'Troubles' in Northern Ireland (1968–98).[2] Of interest is what this specific case conveys about state deviance more generally.

Here I shall outline the context of that bitter conflict within the UK and shall expand on the intricate strands and major incidents later. This context is necessary for readers from other societies who perhaps vaguely recall specific incidents but are unfamiliar with the background; but also for a new domestic generation for whom the Troubles are but diminishing history. And it is particularly important to use the distance since the end of hostilities with the Good Friday Agreement (GFA) of 1998 to stand back and emphasise the key role of the state. Why did a part of the UK slide into 30 years of strife with much suffering and destruction; why was the state seemingly impotent to halt this process and find a political solution; and, crucially, in what ways did the state itself play a dubious if not illicit role in the conflict? The criminological importance of this analysis is that it provides a case study of state crime as defined by Green and Ward (2004:2) as 'state organisational deviance involving the violation of human rights', and in which the British state is in the dock.

The fundamental starting point is that in its principles, values and institutions the democratic state promises legality, justice, accountability, redress for citizens, limitations to its use of force and access to power by fair means. It is precisely the blatant absence of these within a number of despotic states that sparked the current rash of rebellious insurgency in Arabic societies in North Africa and the Middle East. For decades dictatorial regimes have employed secret police, brutal incarceration, torture, execution without trial, pervasive surveillance and a constant barrage of propaganda to impose their will on the people. In early 2011, starting in Tunisia but spreading rapidly to neighbouring countries and the Middle East, mass demonstrations suddenly took to the streets demanding basic democratic rights. The initial conditioned response of such repressive regimes has been for the security forces to shoot indiscriminately at demonstrators and to use gross violence against its own citizens. Television and internet viewers have been horrified by this wanton violence as the new media afford us instant, frontline images of the carnage; and world leaders have lined up to condemn the killings by state-led forces.

Yet for many people that is effectively what happened on Sunday 30 January 1972 in Derry[3] in Northern Ireland at what became known as 'Bloody Sunday'[4], with the British state employing illegitimate violence against its own citizens.

BLOODY SUNDAY

On that day the Northern Ireland Civil Rights Association (NICRA) planned a peaceful demonstration to protest against the imposition a year before of internment without trial which had disproportionately affected 'nationalists' rather than 'loyalists'.[5] Those organising the march were not expecting any trouble although demonstrations had often turned violent in the past. The two 'republican' paramilitary organisations, the Official Irish Republican Army (OIRA) and Provisional Irish Republican Army (PIRA), had previously not mounted operations during demonstrations to avoid alienating public support if civilian casualties were attributed to them. But both would typically be present at demonstrations and be armed as 'protection'.[6] There was also no doubt that Northern Ireland was a dangerous environment for the 'security forces'; since 1969 they had faced shootings and bombings resulting in casualties and fatalities (Geraghty 2000).

I shall refer to the conventional police and army units in Northern Ireland as the 'security forces'; the intelligence units of the police and Army as the 'intelligence agencies'; the central government's Security Service (MI5) as the 'Intelligence Service'. The police and Army also made use of covert, proactive units that I call 'counter-insurgency units' (CIUs). I shall refer to the entire control apparatus as the 'security community'.

For this particular day, however, the two IRA movements stated that they would refrain from hostile activity. The march had originally been banned but was allowed to reach the outskirts of the city centre, where its path was blocked by barriers manned by army units to prevent it spreading into the centre. The estimate of the number of demonstrators is 10–20,000 according to the exhaustively documented Saville Report (2010), which is the essential mine of detail for this event. The Saville Inquiry dealt both with the Sunday itself and with the build up to it.[7] It is plain that there were complex, shifting processes at the political and security levels taking place that need to be located in the context of that period. However, the conclusions of the Inquiry ring crystal clear and are indisputable.

The Army had become the primary agency for maintaining security and public order in Northern Ireland in place of the much-troubled police force, the RUC (Ellison and Smith 2000; Weitzer 1995). The Army was not seriously trained for dealing with public order disturbances, but most units had learned to adapt to this challenging situation.[8] However, there was concern about a perceived deterioration in the security situation while the tolerance of the so-called 'no-go' areas, controlled by the IRA in Belfast and Derry, had not led to a diminution in violence.[9] The iconic mural 'You are now entering Free Derry' was, to some, an affront to the right, and duty, of the authorities to exert control anywhere. There was consequently a meeting between the military and government in London with talk of toughening the approach to the IRA. On the 6 October 1971 at 'Gen 47', the Whitehall committee dealing with Northern Ireland, the Prime Minister (Edward Heath) was reported as saying, 'the first priority was the defeat of the gunmen by military means and the inevitable political consequences must be accepted' (Saville Report 2010:Vol. I: Ch. 8: parag. 89). The Commander of Land Forces in Northern Ireland at the time, General Ford, later testified before the Saville Inquiry of a discernable 'change of gear' in that period and of adopting a 'more offensive attitude'. The military hierarchy then decided to mount a substantial arrest operation, with 300–400 arrests, in the event of disturbances. This was transmitted as an order from General Ford himself along with his choice of '1 Para' (1st Battalion, Parachute Regiment) for the arrest operation. Prior to the march, then, there were plainly several factors leading towards a robust show of strength from the Army. This was known at the highest level of government, as Prime Minister Heath later acknowledged.

The newly assertive focus to the operation led to one of the most disastrous decisions taken by the security forces during the 30 years of the Troubles. This was to employ soldiers of the Parachute Regiment in the event of an arrest operation. In tough situations in conventional warfare the 'paras' were viewed by many including Asher (2004:155), himself once a paratrooper with service in Northern Ireland and later with the Special Air Service Regiment (SAS), as the 'best and the bravest'. But he adds 'in peace-time they were *murder*' (emphasis in original). Indeed, he conveys this image of his first tour of duty as a paratrooper in Northern Ireland in the early 1970s:

> The circumstances of our training, coupled with the peculiar nature of our existence in Northern Ireland ... a blend of boredom, frustration and occasional terror ... turned us into savages. We begged and prayed for a chance to fight, to smash, to kill, to destroy: we were fire-eating beserkers, a hurricane of human brutality ready to burst forth on anyone or anything that stood in our way. We were unreligious, apolitical and remorseless, a band of warrior-janizaries who worshipped at the high altar of violence and wanted nothing more. The animal inside us had been deliberately unchained, deliberately starved and made us hungry to kill. (Asher 2004:120)

This reveals a damning portrait of what it means to send a unit geared to aggressive, proactive combat into a situation of civil strive for which it was genetically unsuited. It also seems likely that the paras were in an aggressive mood prior to Bloody Sunday (Geraghty 2000:57–66).[10]

When the march commenced on that Sunday the main body of demonstrators turned away from the barricades and followed the route to Free Derry Corner to hold a rally. But a smaller group rather predictably split off and confronted troops at what was known as 'Aggro Corner'; this had become almost a daily ritual in Derry. Stones and missiles would be thrown by youths and the Army would respond with a mix of CS gas, water cannon, baton rounds and charges. There was a peaceful demonstration going in one area while close by there was a riot that had reached its peak; people from both events were drifting away and mingling. What changed everything was that the 'Support Company', comprising paratroopers, was sent in to arrest demonstrators. The plan was to wait until the riotous youths were dispersing and had separated from the main group so that soldiers could move in with snatch squads.

In fact both groups had become intertwined, which made the swoop hazardous. Eyewitnesses recalled the sudden revving of the motors of armoured personnel carriers (APCs) and when these suddenly moved across the barriers towards the demonstrators they sensed that this was unusual; it caused concern and people started to run away. But what was unprecedented was that soldiers came out of the APCs, took aim and started to fire. By now there was blind panic and people were desperately looking for cover. This manoeuvre clearly went against the paras' instructions not to conduct a 'running battle' in the Bogside area of Derry. Moreover, the officer commanding the paras, Colonel Wilford, deviated from the plan and without authorisation dispatched two units instead of one into two areas. If this had been known, that the two fleeing crowds were mixed and that Wilford was sending in a second unit without permission, then quite probably this arrest operation would have been aborted. The soldiers were equipped with their high-velocity, 7.62 mm 'SLR' (self-loading rifle), which was the standard North Atlantic Treaty Organization (NATO) battlefield weapon, and with other handguns.

When sent into action, 'changing gear' for the paras meant opening fire and killing 13 unarmed people. A fourteenth victim died later of his wounds while twelve people were wounded by gunfire. The official account was that 21 soldiers fired 108 rounds. The soldiers of 1 Para in Derry shot unarmed civilians attempting to flee; shot people trying to tend to the wounded, including a man waving a white handkerchief; killed a man who was already wounded; shot five of the wounded in the back; and several victims were shot on the ground while soldiers stood over them. Yet there was no direct threat to these soldiers: no shots were fired at them and no nail-bombs were thrown; the Saville Report is quite resolute on this.

There are, however, several convincing accounts of occasional shots being heard and of gun-men being seen during the day. PIRA activists even removed one freelancing OIRA gunman. But any shots fired were not aimed at these paratroopers and did not hit any soldiers elsewhere. In fact, some paras had opened fired from a building just before the two para units went into action while an officer unwisely fired several warning shots. The advancing soldiers had been told that weapons were present and may have become confused by the sound of gunfire; they were in open ground and exposed to potential fire from high buildings. But in what the Saville Report refers to as a 'loss of fire discipline' the paratroopers shot people who were unarmed, posing no risk to them, running away or who were desperately seeking cover.[11]

Some soldiers continued to maintain vehemently at the Inquiry later that they had responded to incoming fire. This goes against the evidence, but it is possible that the soldiers came to believe that this 'really' was the case.[12] It is also generally recognised that there is much perceptual and auditory confusion during shootings when people see and hear things that did not happen or else did not see and hear things that did happen (Collins 2008). There is, too, considerable evidence about the unreliability of memory, especially here after a long period and with extensive media exposure. But it was evident during the Inquiry that the eyewitnesses had vivid recollections of specific events whereas the military, including senior officers, were chronically vague and suffering from memory loss. This was despite the fact that the soldiers had been offered anonymity and immunity. This reticence can be interpreted as suspect, and probably rightly so, but it could also convey that for the eyewitnesses this was an indelible, life-changing event whereas for the soldiers it was just one engagement among many. The soldiers may have initially stuck to an agreed story and became determined not to deviate from a collective version that also absolved them from blame. Several admitted that as young privates they felt intimidated by the military police questioning them and gave them the answers they thought they wanted to hear, while one said he simply signed a prepared statement. Indeed, they may eventually have come to believe in this as true and really 'real'. Vaclav Havel has referred to this as coming to 'live in the lie'; and before the South African Truth and Reconciliation Committee (TRC) the notorious former Minister of Police, Adrian Vlok, persistently denied knowledge of, and responsibility for, the extensive and well-documented brutality of the South African Police during his period of office (Cohen 2001:127). This echoes the denial of knowledge of war crimes by senior Nazi members and high-ranking German soldiers after the Second World War with the words, *ich habe es nicht gewusst* ('I was not aware of this'). A reserve police officer who in Poland in WWII had been in a command role during the shooting of 1,100–1,600 Jewish people on a single day, claimed 25 years later that he could recall 'absolutely nothing' about it (Browning 2001:117). In what appears to be an extreme form of amnesia he had completely blotted the mass murder out of his memory.

The Derry coroner, however, was quite blunt about what happened on Bloody Sunday. He was a retired major of the British Army and chaired the inquests into the deaths. He stated in 1973, 'I would say without hesitation that it was sheer, unadulterated murder. It was murder' (Conflict Archive Internet [CAIN] 2011b). The shootings were truly appalling and went against the clear legal restrictions on the use of potentially fatal force by police and military in Northern Ireland. Yet the Director of Public Prosecutions decided not to recommend prosecutions of any soldiers involved. Indeed, prior to Bloody Sunday the security forces had killed 62 people without a single prosecution of a soldier or police officer (Rolston 2006, 2010).[13]

What gravely compounded the massacre, and exposed the duplicity of the British state, was that the Lord Chief Justice, the head of the judiciary of England and Wales no less, wrote with indecent haste what most unbiased commentators acknowledge to be a blatant whitewash. The respected journalist/historian Max Hastings has called the Widgery Report (1972) a 'shameless cover-up'.[14] This inquiry effectively cloaked the crimes of the soldiers and painted out the operation's accountability trail among the military and political hierarchy. Moreover the Army 'waylaid' or destroyed evidence; the soldiers involved lied to the Inquiry about being fired on, about the victims being armed and about the presence of nail-bombs; some of them later admitted this before the Saville Inquiry (Rozenberg 2002). Reginald Maudling (Home Secretary) subsequently informed Parliament that the Army, 'returned the fire directed at them with aimed shots and inflicted a number of casualties on those who were attacking them with firearms and nail-bombs'. The Ministry of Defence (MoD), moreover, issued a statement that must have been crafted by lawyers, maintaining the soldiers had followed the legal rules on fatal force: 'Throughout the fighting that ensued, the

Army only fired at identified targets – at attacking gunmen and bombers. At all times the soldiers obeyed their standing instructions to fire only in self-defence or in defence of others threatened' (CAIN 2011b:6).[15] Both statements from high representatives of the state were untrue: there simply were no attacking gunmen and there were no bombers.

It is clear that an eminent member of the British legal establishment – the second highest judge of the courts after the Lord Chancellor and a functionary who should epitomise impartiality – neatly covered up the massacre in the interests of his political masters. Indeed, the Prime Minister reminded him that, 'we were in Northern Ireland fighting not only a military war but a propaganda war' (Geraghty 2000:66). This shameful episode was not unlike some lackey of a judge serving a despot in a rogue state who overlooks the excesses of that regime in a blatant charade of an inquiry which everyone treats with derision. Moreover, it took nigh on 40 years to produce an adequate report with a definitive description of events; this also removed the stigma adhering to the victims and survivors and by extension to their families (Saville Report 2010; McDonald 2010).

The Bloody Sunday massacre was but one of the brutal incidents in a range of 'excesses' by the British security community that took place during the Troubles. Those excesses, and the systemic failure to examine and account for them, graphically exposed not just the 'dirty hands' but, above all, the British state's 'bad faith'. One can appreciate to a degree the dirty hands dilemma; that when governing there are tough, even double-bind choices to be taken and 'rotten compromises' to be made (Margalit 2010). As Sartre expressed it, 'Well I have dirty hands. Right up to the elbows. I've plunged them in filth and blood. But what do you expect? Do you think you can govern innocently?' (Kleinig 1996:287). The key issue is when do 'dirty hands' become no longer some incidental, agonising reaction to extraordinary circumstances but are rationalised and accepted as 'SOP', Standard Operating Procedure? When do practitioners not only relish having dirty hands but also use them as justification for the unjustifiable? Indeed, for Sartre 'bad faith' was conscious and culpable (Cohen 2001:6). For instance, how does one evaluate the collective significance of internment without trial, Diplock courts, tough interrogation techniques, Bloody Sunday, the Gibraltar shootings, the RUC 'shoot-to-kill' cases and the controversial killings by the SAS, as well as the police and Army colluding with protestant paramilitaries, including the assassination of those suspected merely of association with the IRA, when nearly all the victims just happened to be Catholics, nationalists and republicans?[16] These incidents were typically accompanied by dissimulation, denial, obfuscation, discrediting of opponents, manipulation of evidence, disappearance of files, collusion, muzzling the media, leniency for those committing crimes on behalf of the state, blatant untruths by politicians and officials, obstructing the course of justice and the search for truth and by continually denying a significant section of its citizens their fundamental rights. Do these not represent far more than dirty hands and rather illustrate inbred bad faith, as something conscious and culpable at the very highest levels? It can be argued that the British state *repeatedly* failed to live up to its espoused values and expressed precepts.

In this work I shall detail a range of grimly violent incidents that took place throughout the Troubles involving both nationalist and loyalist paramilitaries; but my main focus will be on the security community. There is no shadow of doubt that the paramilitaries employed unconscionable violence but it is equally clear that the British security community – the legitimate forces of law and order – frequently, if not persistently, broke the law. It is, of course, not unusual in prolonged conflict situations for the security community to resort to excessive violence, manipulation of evidence, discrediting of opponents and widespread use of illicit covert practices. There is certainly a plethora of examples to illustrate this, including Algeria, South Africa, Vietnam, Rhodesia, Indonesia, Argentina and Chile (Lacquer 1987; Wilkinson 1985). A crucial difference in assessing these responses is whether or not we are dealing with a mature democracy; for it is clear that repressive regimes, such as Argentina under the military junta (1976–83), are not squeamish about the sordid and vile methods they employ. A credible democracy, moreover, should in theory be able to pre-empt insurgent terrorism because it can provide political avenues for dissent and for sponsoring change through consultation. In reality most western democracies have faced some form of insurgency and diverse forms of terrorism in the last half century (as we shall see below). In general, these insurgent campaigns in democratic societies, even with prolonged and highly confrontational armed struggles, have never threatened the continuity of democratic states as has happened in several Third World countries (Reich 1998).

Of the essence, according to a leading expert on insurgent terrorism, is that when faced by the threat of violent insurgency the democratic state copes with it through legal and legitimate methods (Wilkinson 1985). This was simply not the case in Northern

Ireland at some of the time and among certain security units. The accumulated evidence powerfully indicates that the political, administrative, enforcement and judicial systems were strongly skewed in favour of the majority population (predominantly loyalist, unionist and Protestant of imported 'settler' stock) and against the minority population (predominantly nationalist, republican and Catholic deriving from original Irish 'host' heredity). This meant that virtually all the principles and practices designed to ensure justice and equity were abused and negated. It was not just that the minority population endured unjustified violence, abuse and prejudice but that, intolerably, many of the perpetrators did so with virtual impunity, because their crimes were never investigated as crimes, and they were allowed to evade accountability for their deeds and carry on unhindered in their careers (Rolston 2006).

In brief, the evidence indicates that:

- police officers, including senior officers, lied under oath and falsified documents
- the coroners' courts could not function adequately
- criminal investigations, prosecutions and judicial proceedings were frequently inadequate, failed to meet the standards expected under the rule of law and due process and were all too often subordinate to the security situation
- external investigations of major deviance were obstructed and sabotaged
- oversight was ineffective, partial or absent
- human rights were abused.

These deep institutional flaws and failures in diverse agencies reflected that in responding to this conflict in an intrinsic part of the UK, successive governments of the UK too often displayed a lack of legitimacy, legality and accountability. Without these three foundations there can be no genuine democracy.

Indeed, many in the minority community in Northern Ireland felt deeply alienated from a state which not only neglected and abused them, but which displayed a wanton disregard for democratic principles and practices and for the values and implementation of the rule of law. The British state had failed them as citizens of what many view as the mother of democracy and as a beacon of enlightenment to many fledgling states. Yet its agents showed themselves to be devious, secretive, mendacious, cynical, vindictive and vicious. As these agents were acting on behalf of the state the final accountability must rest with the British state and with successive British administrations governing as the embodiment of that state. One interpretation of this gross failure, and the Troubles are plainly open to multiple interpretation from diverse disciplinary and ideological viewpoints, is that it was Britain's last major colonial conflict.

This was played out in the 'neglected colony of a decaying imperial power' (English 2004:124). But it was the wrong era, the wrong location and the state regressed to relying on the wrong practices. Geraghty (2000:29) reinforces this view:

> As Major (later Lieutenant-Colonel and Northern Ireland Minister) Michael Mates put it in an interview with the author: 'The threat evaluation in 1969 was one of civil disobedience rather than a resumption of the IRA campaign'. The doctrine governing internal security was a 'counter-insurgency philosophy from the Cyprus campaign that was not particularly sophisticated'. Intelligence about the IRA was 'pathetic'. When street violence boiled over, Northern Ireland was treated as yet another rebellious colony, to be punished accordingly.

Colonial conflicts arise in distant countries where an administration has been imported and imposed from abroad; a minority settler population holds the reigns of power and commerce; and where a majority host population of different ethnicity and religion to the settlers is treated as socially, culturally and politically subordinate while any signs of dissent are met with robust force (Pakenham 1992). Typically the colonial administrators together with the settler population construct a regime which perpetuates their control and interests by disenfranchising the majority in a manner often at odds with the norms of governance in the home country. This was the case with the French in Algeria and Vietnam, the Dutch in Indonesia, the Belgians in the Congo, the Afrikaners in South Africa and British settlers in a range of colonies including Kenya, Rhodesia and India. With just a few exceptions the post-WWII campaigns for independence by majority populations meant an armed struggle leading to negotiated independence, withdrawal of the colonial power and an exodus among the settler minority.[17] Often those struggles were bitter and prolonged with atrocities being committed by both sides as in Algeria in 1954–62 (Horne 1979), and there is no doubt about the French Army's brutality and use of torture in Algeria. It has also recently emerged from documents that British security forces used illegal methods amounting to torture during the campaign against Mau Mau insurgents in Kenya in the 1950s (Bowcott 2011a; Cobain 2011a & 2011b).

Briefly, the context of the Northern Ireland situation was as follows. Ireland was a country with a predominantly Catholic population of Celtic origin that came under loose English rule from the twelfth century. A number of rebellions and later incursions with foreign support in the sixteenth and seventeenth centuries were defeated, leading to large-scale confiscation of land and the influx of English and Scottish settlers of primarily Protestant persuasions. Ireland was incorporated into the United Kingdom in 1801 but effectively was governed as a colony, while it faced recurring rebellion with increasingly persistent demands for independence. These culminated in the abortive Easter Rising of 1916, the War of Independence of 1919–21 and a negotiated settlement with the British government in 1922. But that later much-disputed settlement divided the island in two granting independence to the South, but with administrators drawing a line across the map that effectively created a separate 'state' in the North with the settler population forming a majority. This truncated entity in the North enjoyed a measure of self-government within the UK. But the settlement shaped a distorted society that in all essential respects was based on the hegemony of the settler majority and the subordination of the host minority. And that hegemony was often expressed through brute force, crass intimidation and political chicanery (McKittrick & McVea 2001).

The key to the later conflict was that Britain failed to solve the 'Irish problem' (namely the call for independence and self-rule) in the late nineteenth century, allowed itself to be intimidated by the loyalist Protestant majority in 1912 that threatened insurrection, created a rump 'state' by sleight of pen on the map that ensured a continued majority within a contested state (which remained a constant bone of contention in the South), and thereafter effectively found itself a hostage to that majority. That 'loyalist' majority was moreover deeply conservative and systematically repressive to the minority, and had a curiously ambivalent interpretation of loyalty; they were loyal when it suited their interests and disloyal when it did not (Moloney 2010). Nevertheless, British administrations consistently supported the loyalist/Protestant cause in what amounted to a repressive, sectarian, one-party state which exercised a form of apartheid on Britain's doorstep. This unqualified support fostered a fatal duality.

On the one hand the UK persisted in the fiction that Northern Ireland was an intrinsic part of the UK, when it was indisputably governed in a fashion widely at odds with democratic practice on the British mainland and Western Europe. And on the other hand it regressed when faced with conflict in Northern Ireland by treating the Province as an unruly colony with a rebellious and obdurate host population that had to be subdued in the 'old fashioned way', by repression in collusion with the settler population. As Campbell and Connolly (2003:372) put it:

> Fractured and ineffectual civilian control facilitated a return to primordial military thinking, in which the prime consideration of the curfew [in the Catholic Falls area of Belfast in 1970] became the deployment of sufficient forces to guarantee success in the 'battle'. This untrammelled transposition of a military model to a civilian context produced a straightforwardly repressive technique ... an extreme version of the 'military-security' approach ... the Army fell back on an institutional memory of techniques employed in colonial experiences elsewhere.

That underlying duality and the impotence of Britain to resolve it led in the late 1960s, when a peaceful civil rights movement was merely demanding the rights enjoyed by citizens elsewhere in Europe, to a series of disastrous decisions that helped lead Northern Ireland into 30 years of mayhem. Precisely because it was Ireland and 'overseas', there was a reversion to a colonial style of repression in favour of the settler community and with a low regard for human rights and legality (Anderson and Killingray 1991; Weitzer 1990). And as Bowyer Bell (1973:404) remarks, 'Ireland often tends to brings out the worst in the British'. The negative and counter-productive impact of this approach was expressed unambiguously in the Saville Report (2010:Vol. I: Ch. 5: parag. 5):

> What happened on Bloody Sunday strengthened the Provisional IRA, increased [Irish] nationalist resentment and hostility towards the [British] Army and exacerbated the violent conflict of the years that followed. Bloody Sunday was a tragedy for the bereaved and the wounded, and a catastrophe for the people of Northern Ireland.

Sadly, it took some 30 years to resolve the bitter conflict and nearly 40 years to finally adjudicate on Bloody Sunday. The Saville

Inquiry also took some twelve years from when Prime Minister Tony Blair established it in 1998 and 2010 when the new Prime Minister of a Conservative-Liberal Coalition, David Cameron, commented on the Report. Not unnaturally, in Derry on 15 June 2010 there was jubilation among the family members of the victims and others watching the proceedings on a large screen when Cameron fully accepted the findings that the victims were innocent of any offence, were unarmed and that the killings were 'unjustified and unjustifiable' (Prince & Leach 2010). It was somewhat ironic that a Conservative Prime Minister was issuing an unqualified apology because for more than a century it was Conservatives who had opposed Irish independence and had displayed a close affinity with the unionist movement in Northern Ireland. Conservatism and British chauvinism were responsible for the connivance with loyalist militants in 1912 and later helped to foster and prolong the Troubles. That a Conservative Prime Minister pronounced a fulsome apology was then a highly symbolic gesture in terms of reconciliation and healing of wounds. For Rolston (2010) personally it was a 'Berlin Wall' moment. The political representative of the British state was unequivocally saying 'sorry' to the victims and their relatives for one of its most serious crimes in Northern Ireland.

It is then to the crimes of the British state and other states that I wish to turn in this book. And I mean not just to the crimes of the individual and low-level police, soldiers and intelligence agents, but to the crimes of the state itself. The policies and decisions that led to Bloody Sunday, for instance, were shaped at the highest level of government, and hence these representatives of the state were responsible for what can be viewed as the pivotal turning point in the conflict leading to an escalation in violence from the republican movements. That year, 1972, saw the highest number of casualties in the 30 years of conflict with over 10,000 shootings and nearly 2,000 bombings. In a sense no one 'planned' this massacre, but many contributed to it. And afterwards, in a form of cognitive dissonance, they became firmly committed to justifications for it despite overwhelming disconfirming evidence. Senior representatives of the state, including the head of government, defined the situation as requiring a military solution; a senior soldier wishing to illustrate this new hard line chose the toughest unit in the Army to spearhead an 'arrest' operation against demonstrators, and that tough unit collectively redefined a routine arrest swoop as being a dangerous combat situation with an armed enemy and reacted accordingly.

In unravelling this process, as is done minutely in the Saville Report, one sees the state in the flesh and its representatives at work. From close by it is almost as if nearly all states, not unlike other institutions, look rather like banana republics run by dominating despots, with no coherent vision, surrounded by willing lackeys with no conscience. Adding to this is the conditioned response in many states of manipulating the 'truth' to establish deniability, to preserve reputations and careers and to construct an official version of events which then has to be defended as the inviolable truth. A senior minister swiftly appears in public and, in a pre-emptive strike, espouses the official version which justifies the action under consideration both operationally and politically; a report by a prestigious official confirms that version which is then praised as the final reality; and the machinery of obfuscation swings into operation with a sustained effort to rewrite history. Incriminating data disappear and evidence vanishes; criminal and disciplinary investigations are rigged or preferably side-stepped; the media are gagged; no one is sanctioned and if anything those responsible are, perversely, even rewarded.[18] And there is a concerted campaign to vilify the reputations and motives of the victims, their relatives and associates and any who propagate alternative versions of events.[19]

Indeed, while the shootings on Bloody Sunday are of themselves appalling, it was to a large degree the response of the British state to them that dismayed external observers; that alienated completely the already sceptical nationalist community, and strongly advanced the cause of the republican movement. As the later Bishop Daly, who had attended the Derry demonstration in 1972 as a local priest and administered the last rites to the dying, stated: 'What really made Bloody Sunday so obscene was the fact that people afterwards, at the highest levels of British justice, justified it and I think that is the real obscenity' (*Channel 4 Television* 1992). The incontrovertible message conveyed by those events was that the state was partial, hypocritical, devious and unaccountable; and if you tweaked its tail too vigorously it killed you. Above all, it simply could not be trusted. Such a crystal clear message represents a godsend for any insurgent movement.

THE NORTHERN IRELAND TROUBLES

The Troubles in Northern Ireland reveal how the British state wrestled with the predicament of how to combat a violent and resilient campaign of domestic insurgency with the British security community pitted against the 'IRA'. The main insurgent organisation opposing the British state during the Troubles was the Provisional IRA, often referred to as 'PIRA' or the 'Provos' (Bishop & Mallie 1988; English 2004). This new wing split from a weak IRA in 1969 with PIRA developing into a well-equipped force that aggressively challenged the British state. Wilkinson (2005:112) observes that in PIRA the British authorities confronted the best armed and 'deadliest of all Western terrorist organizations in the most protracted of struggles'. Even a former head of British armed forces in the Province spoke positively of PIRA as, 'an absolutely formidable enemy' with astute leadership while some of their operations he viewed as 'brilliant in terrorist terms' (Gorman 1992). Below, in the main body of the text, I shall examine the characteristics and actions of the Provisional IRA; I shall hereafter refer to it as the 'IRA' and shall indicate when other republican movements are involved. I shall also examine in the next chapter a range of insurgent terrorist organisations in diverse countries to convey their ideologies, aims, structures and methods as a comparative backcloth to the insurgency in Northern Ireland. Drawing here on that categorisation I define the IRA as a typical, fairly traditional 'ethno-nationalist' movement.

The IRA drew on centuries-long Irish hostility to England with many acts of Irish rebellion. In a sense it was fighting old battles and especially the unfinished business of the War of Independence (1919–21), which had only led to the partition of Ireland. In a fairly traditional struggle for national independence, the insurgents asserted the moral right to rectify the wrong of partition and get the British administration and Army out of Northern Ireland leading to a united Ireland (White 1989). This drew for legitimacy on the de facto declaration of Irish independence in 1919. New to that traditional agenda, however, was that by the 1960s the activists also wanted a socialist government to replace the two administrations in Dublin and Belfast.

In a nutshell, the newly founded PIRA of 1969 had few members and almost no weapons. It was very much a home-grown movement drawing on local activists, but it went through a rapid learning curve in terms of tactics, training and equipment. In just the first seven years of the conflict from 1969 to 1976, the movement suffered 281 fatalities and saw between 8,000 and 10,000 of its alleged activists or sympathisers imprisoned. This indicates not only the willingness to die for the cause but also the breadth of support for the movement (Bishop & Mallie 1988:11). Originally it employed random violence, as in the Abercorn Restaurant bombing of 1972[20] in Belfast and the Birmingham bombings of 1974, but soon realised that this was likely to alienate public opinion among its own supporters in the North and South of Ireland but especially in the Irish Diaspora in America which was a major source of funding. In general it increasingly claimed to focus on so-called 'hard' targets (police, military and governmental targets) and tried to avoid 'collateral' damage among innocent bystanders by issuing warnings.[21] The IRA was indisputably callous and ruthless, as are all insurgent movements albeit at varying levels, but to a degree it played by a set of understood rules and within its own version of a moral code.

For example, unlike contemporary 'jihadist' groups, referring to fundamental 'salafist' Muslim insurgent terrorists, it did not seek 'mass casualties' in the hundreds or even thousands. However, it did once try to bring down a civilian plane with the Chief Constable of the RUC on board.[22] If that had succeeded it would have been the largest loss of life in any incident during the Troubles and it would have seriously raised the stakes. For it would certainly have fostered widespread revulsion at the loss of innocent lives, around 80 passengers and crew, and perhaps have been exploited to justify a savage response from the security forces. But apart from that attempt, and unlike some other insurgents, the IRA rarely attacked passengers in public transport directly; it did not hijack planes, besiege buildings, behead children before their mothers' eyes, snipe at random to kill civilians, and did not take hostages in hospitals and schools (Horgan 2005:7). The callous siege with young children, teachers and parents in a school in Beslan in North Ossetia by a Chechen rebel group, for example, was beyond the IRA's moral compass. As one IRA activist put it, 'you don't bloody well kill people just for the sake of killing them' (Hoffman 2006:239).

Over the years, the IRA became over-supplied with weapons, expert at bomb making, skilled in guerrilla tactics and able later to plant massive bombs at key targets in Britain causing immense damage (Coogan 1993).[23] The movement became highly aware of the propaganda war, became increasingly media conscious and started to develop a political strategy based on the eventual need to abandon violence and to enter constitutional politics. In the long run, the IRA did not 'win' the war, and at times was even on the verge of losing it, but it showed willingness to compromise and it emerged with a legitimate political party, *Sinn Fein*, in government and sharing power with its former enemies (Moloney 2007, 2010; Taylor 1998).

It is, indeed, part of the remarkable metamorphosis following peace that sometimes arch-enemies have to learn to work together. And that a former IRA activist, who planted bombs in London in 1973 and spent time in prison (Simpson 2010:64), could become a spokesperson on *policing* in the Legislative Assembly at Stormont. Moreover, the seemingly intractable opponent of republicanism and a rabid unionist stalwart, the Reverend Ian Paisley, was roundly praised on stepping down as First Minister of the Northern Ireland Assembly in 2008 by the two leading lights of *Sinn Fein*, which Paisley once abhorred. One has admitted to being a former member of the IRA; but now those two men, Martin McGuinness and Gerry Adams, have somewhat piously condemned violence from splinter IRA movements. Indeed, it is another by-product of peace processes that the hard-liners of insurgent movements may feel betrayed by the political compromises reached and wish to continue the struggle; this has been the pattern with the Basque *Euskadi Ta Askatasuna* (Basque Fatherland and Liberty, ETA) and with some Irish republicans (Moloney 2010).

For instance, there have been several shootings and bombings by republican dissidents in Northern Ireland since the 1998 GFA. In 2009 two British soldiers were shot dead while taking delivery of pizzas outside their barracks in Antrim; the shooting was attributed to the republican splinter group, the 'Real IRA'. These were the first soldiers killed in Northern Ireland since 1997. A PSNI police officer was shot dead in 2010 while answering an emergency call; this was attributed to the 'Continuity IRA'. In 2010 a car bomb exploded outside a courthouse in Newry but with no casualties, while in early 2011 a young Catholic police officer was blown up by a car bomb in Omagh. Both incidents were attributed to dissident republicans. The *Sinn Fein* politician Martin McGuiness said of the shooting of the two soldiers, 'I supported the IRA during the conflict, I myself was a member of the IRA but that war is over'; and *Sinn Fein* President Gerry Adams saw the shooting as an attack on the peace process stating, 'it was wrong and counter-productive' (*BBC News UK* 2009a & 2009b; Walsh 2009).

Opposing the IRA was the British state and its ostensibly formidable agents of the RUC, the Army and diverse intelligence agencies with extensive powers and resources (Geraghty 2000; Ryder 2000). These could draw on several decades of counter-insurgency experience in post-colonial, so-called 'low intensity' conflicts in Malaya, Aden, Kenya, Borneo and Cyprus (Clutterbuck 1990). These agencies, too, were forced to go through a testing process of learning in a symbiotic relationship with its adversary, the IRA. Furthermore, the number of Protestant adults, mostly males, involved in the security community and the wider loyalist movement in some way during 30 years formed a significant proportion of the Province's population. There was service in the RUC, B Specials and later the UDR, some 40,000 members of the UDA (which was legal until 1992), the paramilitary UVF and thousands of members of Orange Lodges. Most of these people were never involved actively in any way in loyalist insurgency, which was numbered only in the hundreds. But the insurgents could draw on the sympathies of many and on the active support of others in the wider loyalist/unionist fraternity, including some within the security forces. The nationalist movement had its own institutions within the minority Catholic community to back it but it never had the equivalent volume of active or passive supporters that the loyalists enjoyed in the majority community; and, of course, never had serious links to the RUC and UDR. On paper then it may have seemed no contest; here was a large, professional and resourceful security community pitted against 'amateurs' with at first almost no combat experience, no equipment and no professional leadership. But then no army in a mature, liberal democracy has ever defeated an insurgent terrorist organisation. At the same time it is also the case that no insurgent movement has defeated a stable democratic government leading to regime change. Indeed, Wilkinson (2005:22) states bluntly that, 'The overall track-record of terrorism in attaining major political objectives is abysmal'.

This prolonged and at times ferocious clash provides in retrospect, and at a distance allowing greater clarity and objectivity, two main insights. Firstly, although it never achieved its original strategic aims, the removal of the British administration from Northern Ireland leading to the unification of Ireland as a socialist state, the IRA can be viewed as a quite 'successful' insurgent movement in that it managed to campaign for some 30 years,[24] was never defeated by British forces and even entered government in the form of a legitimate political party. And secondly, and crucially, part of that success is largely and somewhat ironically due to the fact that a significant number of decisions taken by the government and security community proved to be counter-productive and hence played directly into the hands of the IRA. Indeed, the latter point conveys the main message of this work.

For what the British state and its control agents did was to fall into the trap that the leading experts on counter-terrorism (CT) insistently warn about, of abandoning the rule of law and adopting deviant means (Wilkinson 2005). Those agents indulged in dirty tricks and got their hands distinctly grubby; yet this only served further to promote the IRA's cause (Parker 2007). As Schmid (1992:14) asserts above, the danger of adopting deviant means can lead the state to lose the moral high ground and to become in some ways not dissimilar to the enemy it is demonising.

This book examines that response by democratic states to insurgency with particular regard to allegedly grave deviations from the rule of law and due process within the security community in Northern Ireland. The extensive deviance occurred not in some distant colony on another continent but in a constitutionally intrinsic part of the UK, just a short distance by boat or plane from the British mainland. And it occurred within British society, which is widely revered abroad for its democratic principles and practices.

The central issue is, then, how does the democratic state respond to the profound dilemmas faced when combating serious, threatening insurgency? Do the state and its control agencies buckle and choose deviant means to reach the formally legal and legitimate goals of tackling terrorism and of guaranteeing national security? Do they adopt the 'Jack Bauer' culture, from the American TV series '24 Hours', which was avidly viewed by US military interrogators in Guantanamo (Sands 2009), to use tough ends to get vital answers (Hoogenboom 2010b)? For Northern Ireland it is unequivocally 'yes' because there is convincing evidence that 'excesses' took place. This in turn raises several points. In what way did the agencies of law and order deviate from the rule of law and due process in combating terrorism? What was the nature and extent of that deviance, and how was the deviance from the rule of law articulated and justified? For instance, was this solely on the agencies' own initiative, or did the state in some way foster, encourage or even 'order' this deviance and covertly unleash it within the security community? Was there, indeed, an implicit, covert 'policy' on this? A full answer to this may never be known because the documentation is missing or locked in embargoed archives while some of the main actors are deceased or remain reticent. Margaret Thatcher, for instance, sat on the Joint Intelligence Committee (JIC) in Whitehall almost weekly throughout her eleven years in office as Prime Minister (1979–90), and it was the JIC which oversaw the government's response to IRA insurgency.

Yet she never once mentions the JIC in her memoirs (Thatcher & Dale 2010).

But I shall maintain on the basis of the considerable data now at our disposal that law breaking by the authorities was not incidental, individual and sporadic but prolonged, routine and systemic. The regular system of legal and accountable enforcement failed in the sense that it was unable to prevent an alternative or parallel deviant sub-system growing and thriving within it, which was sustained, camouflaged and protected from external scrutiny for many years. The checks and balances were side stepped, undermined and thwarted in ways that were starkly at odds with all the values and practices of the democratic state. In short, this was not a question of a 'few bad apples' but that the formal system failed, making it more a matter of several bad barrels or perhaps a range of rotten orchards; or even a contaminated fruit industry (Punch 2003).

And if that is the case does it convey some sense of inevitability? Do democratic states typically abandon legality and human rights, perhaps only partially and maybe even reluctantly, when challenged by a serious threat to their governing ideology and even to their existence? Many do so during wartime and it is perhaps when states perceive themselves to be effectively in an undeclared 'war' with a substate insurgency movement that they start to resort to devious means.

Finally, if 'terrorism is theatre' (Jenkins 1975:16) it implies that the *staging and choreographing of performances to influence an audience* is of the essence. The audience consists of politicians, the public, sympathisers at home and abroad, and, above all, the media. This is reflected in the definition of terrorist insurgency by Hoffman (2006:40) but echoed by others as, 'the deliberate creation and exploitation of fear through violence or threat of violence in pursuit of political change'. To create that fear, the media becomes central to terrorism (Hoffman 2006:173–96). In that sense of consciously attracting attention and assessing public and political reaction to incidents, the violence is never meant to be mindless but is designed to convey graphic, symbolic images in the media that will make people fearful and subsequently help to achieve the insurgents' political goals which are frequently focused on destabilising society to gain power. Terrorism is politics by other means.

The essence of insurgent terrorism is that it *communicates and negotiates through violence* by calculated incidents that insistently claim centre-stage. Insurgents coldly and clinically employ human suffering and physical damage as a political tool; and this involves a seemingly callous calculus of the impact of death, destruction and fear in the media and on the authorities. For example, an IRA activist, 'Donnelly', explained that killing British soldiers was ultimately more productive than planting bombs: 'Initially you would be satisfied with a good bomb but then to be effective you realised you had to stiff [kill] more Brits – that is the attitude – to the point where the Brits leave' (Bishop & Mallie 1988:182).[25] Of particular interest here is, does the state respond in kind by also communicating and negotiating through violence, but then necessarily back-stage or off-stage? The case study in this book will examine the conflict in Northern Ireland in order to explain and analyse the process of adopting deviant means and ends by the security community in their sustained counter-insurgency campaign against the IRA.

RESEARCH BACKGROUND

Much of my academic work has focused on deviance in organisations and I have written on police corruption and corporate crime (Punch 1985 & 1996). My early approach was largely based on participant observation and symbolic interactionism with analysis of the micro-processes of 'constructed realities' within groups (Punch 1979 & 1985). That has altered as, following others, I have become increasingly aware of the crimes of the powerful and of the role of the state in deviancy (Tombs & Whyte 2003). This is related to the swelling volume of research about grave state deviance in the former Soviet Union, the Nazi Empire, during the Balkan Wars of the 1990s and in repressive regimes in Africa, Asia and South America. This includes the gruesome findings of international investigatory tribunals (Bass 2001; Nollkaemper & van der Wilt 2009). The discourse from this research area has been amplified by accusations against the US of serious human rights violations in Latin America and the Middle East (Bayley 2006; Woodward 2006).

Recently I have also turned to police use of force. This was stimulated by the shooting of an innocent man at Stockwell Underground Station in London in 2005 by the police; and it raised again the emotive phrase 'shoot to kill' (Punch 2010). This had earlier been used in Northern Ireland and it aroused my curiosity as to what had actually happened during those earlier 'shoot to kill' incidents. I was drawn then to Northern Ireland by a desire to learn both more about police use of force during the Troubles. But I increasingly became aware of a much broader issue; how does the state react to a persistent terrorist threat and yet stay within the rule of law?

My background also meant that I had an interest in Ireland as my parents were Irish and I have visited the country many times. My youth in London was coloured by a romantic notion of the gallant Dublin rebels taking on perfidious Albion in the Easter Rising of 1916.[26] Later, these rosy views foundered on the grim reality of the violence in Northern Ireland during the modern Troubles. Furthermore, by the early 1970s I had become interested in policing as a research area and was with the West Midlands Police in Birmingham in 1974 when an IRA bomber blew himself up while planting a bomb (known as an 'own goal'). Just a week later the IRA returned to Birmingham and bombings took place in two pubs killing over 20 people, most of them young, in the same area I had just visited. This brought the insurgent violence of Northern Ireland more forcefully to the mainland but also elicited widespread abhorrence and condemnation. Later the subsequent miscarriage of justice against the alleged IRA bombers, the 'Birmingham Six' and in other cases against those suspected of diverse explosions, became a *cause célèbre* of police and judicial deviance in Britain (Punch 2009).

That academic focus on policing led me to becoming involved in police research in the Netherlands where I have lived since 1975. The Netherlands is not a particularly violent society and it has not faced sustained terrorist activity. In the 1970s there were several sieges and attacks including two prolonged train sieges by Malaccans as well as the occasional shoot out with the *Rote Armee Faction* (Red Army Faction) terrorists from Germany (Becker 1978). What was clear in the two Malaccan train sieges was the government's willingness to engage in prolonged negotiations along with great reluctance to employ fatal force: this has been referred to as the 'Dutch Approach' (Bootsma 2001).[27] Living abroad did mean that I observed much that was happening in the UK at a distance. However, in the early 1990s I attended a course on disasters in the UK at Bramshill Police College (later part of Centrex, National Police Training), which included several incidents dealing with terrorist violence including a presentation on the Lockerbie bombing. Also, in the Netherlands I twice heard presentations by a Dutch police officer in 'Political Intelligence' about several IRA attacks in the Netherlands on off-duty British military personnel from Germany. In one case, two Australian tourists were killed when members of an IRA ASU shot both men in the head at point-blank range. The

ASU mistakenly assumed that the young men were British soldiers on leave. It was such contacts that culminated in my turning to the events in 'Ulster'.[28]

Three other factors moved me towards studying the turbulence in Northern Ireland. Firstly, through teaching on the Strategic Command Course at Bramshill I met David Wood from the Metropolitan Police (Met) who subsequently became the first Director of Investigations for the Office of the Police Ombudsman for Northern Ireland (OPONI). Through that contact I gave seminars and contributed to a conference at OPONI; and invited the Ombudsman, Nuala (now Baroness) O'Loan, and David Wood to the Global Forum on Integrity and Combating Corruption II in The Hague in 2001. Secondly, another British police contact was (the late) Colin Cramphorn who became the Deputy Chief Constable of the RUC (later the PSNI). I made an informal visit to him in 1999 and met a range of RUC officers. And, thirdly, through my interest in police accountability I began to look at the issue of police use of firearms and fatal force.

Only recently have I been drawn to focusing on state crime. One reason is that criminology has again started to accentuate this as a crucial area of enquiry. Its roots lie in studies of 'crimes of the powerful' commencing in the 1970s (Krisberg 1975; Pearce 1976; Quinney 1970). In recent years the topic has been revisited by some of my colleagues in London, including Stan Cohen and Penny Green who are leading specialists on human rights and 'state crime'. There has also been the extensive work of Ralph Crawshaw, who has researched and published on human rights with reference to policing (Crawshaw, Cullen & Holström 2006).

There is already considerable literature on Northern Ireland and the Troubles. Some books are near definitive studies, including English (2004) on the IRA or Ryder (2000) and Mulcahy (2006) on the RUC, whereas others are more popular, journalistic accounts of varying quality. Some material is written by well-informed journalists who personally experienced the Troubles such as Dillon (1991); who examine in detail one of the paramilitary organisations, including Cusack and McDonald (2008) on the loyalist UVF and McDonald and Holland (2010) on the nationalist INLA; or who focus closely on a particular feature of the struggle, as in Geraghty's (2000) account of the military aspects. There has, too, been a stream of reports from civil liberties non-governmental organisations (NGOs) (Amnesty International, Human Rights Watch, Committee on Administration of Justice in Belfast, Irish Council for Civil

Liberties), a number of judgements from the ECHR, Hansard and newspaper archives in both Britain and Ireland, and publications from the Northern Ireland political parties as well as UK and Irish government reports on various incidents or developments. These include: the Hunt Report (1969) on policing; Compton Report (1971) on security forces brutality; Scarman Report (1972) on handling of violent disturbances; Cory Report (2004) on several cases of collusion; and the Widgery (1972) and Saville (2010) Reports on Bloody Sunday. There were also a number of inquiries and reports in Ireland including the independent Barron Reports (2003 & 2005) into loyalist paramilitary activities in the South with possible British collusion.

It does, however, appear difficult for people in this field to be completely impartial, or to escape accusations of bias. Ryder (2000:xiv), for instance, expresses his 'limitless admiration for the professionalism of the RUC'. There were doubtless courageous and highly professional officers within the RUC, but its institutional record during the Troubles is indisputably tainted and 'limitless' suggests a lack of objectivity.[29] Then a leading expert on terrorism, Wilkinson, is clear about the mistakes made by the British Army in Northern Ireland but speaks of their 'colossal achievement', their 'heroic record' and suggests that it is doubtful if 'any army in the world could have performed the tough role in Northern Ireland with such humanity, restraint and effectiveness' (2005:130, 132). But this is rather pro-army, anglophile prose which would be greeted with disbelief by many who hold strongly opposed views. These examples indicate the perceptual, cultural, ideological and interpretive divisiveness typical of much writing on the Troubles.

Initially it was mostly journalists who wrote on the conflict. Some produced informative books based on inside contacts, as by Urban (1993) on the SAS, but these are now dated. There is plainly now more openness and more data available, including some Cabinet papers of the early period, and since 2000 there have been the rigorous investigations into the police by OPONI. These include a report on the horrendous Omagh bombing (OPONI 2005; see Chapter 3). Some former participants now feel free to discuss their role in the conflict although this has not always proved to be a particularly healthy pursuit. Two illuminating and extensive interviews with frontline participants, the IRA activist Brendan Hughes ('Volunteer D Company, 2nd Battalion, Belfast Brigade') and the loyalist UVF activist David Ervine, were recently published (Moloney 2010). They are part of an oral history project at the

Boston College Center for Irish Studies in Massachusetts where participants in the Troubles are interviewed on the understanding that the material will only be published after their deaths (http://www.bc.edu/centers/irish/studies). These two published interviews, the few informal interviews I have been able to conduct and the research material garnered expose wildly contradictory discourses often conducted with hostile certitude:

- The RUC was courageous, dedicated and essentially 'clean' (and even the 'best police force in the world') or it was intrinsically biased, irredeemably repressive and deeply untrustworthy.
- The British Army was crude, trigger-happy and needlessly aggressive or it was restrained, sophisticated and performed remarkably well (better than any other army in the world).
- The SAS was a powerful, ubiquitous force of state executioners or they were merely a tiny band of disciplined soldiers who set out to arrest suspects but occasionally shot extremely violent terrorists who suddenly posed a threat.
- The IRA was an idealistic and considerate organisation with wide community support or it was a group of ruthless thugs which murdered innocent people including its own kind to the disgust of many in both communities.
- The key loyalist activists of the UDA and UVF were defenders of a righteous and just cause or they were brutal and undiscriminating sectarian killers.
- Paisley was a blustering bigot or he was a shrewd, untiring and relentless crusader for Protestant, Unionist interests.
- British governments became at first confused by the Troubles and panicked and over-reacted but not by any malice or they were typically 'English' in being coolly devious, secretive and incorrigibly conspiratorial.
- Gerry Adams was a non-violent, consummate politician or he was a slippery traitor to the armed republican movement.[30]

Continually with personalities, incidents or developments there are Rashomon-like discrepancies in interpretation with rumour, myth, confusion, layers of camouflage and downright lies. And in a conflict dominated by clandestine and secretive insurgent movements and a counter-insurgency campaign with covert units, dirty tricks and disinformation, it is difficult to discern what was really 'real' in a baffling hall of mirrors.

For example, in the murky, multiple-layered reality with deep penetration agents active inside the IRA it is difficult to discern who knew what and what 'game' was being played. In the Loughall shooting of an entire ASU (see Chapter 4), which was a severe blow to the IRA, an alleged informer was swiftly uncovered, interrogated and 'executed'. But it is likely that his 'confession' was forced out of him and that the 'real' informer was a woman who evaded sanctioning (Urban 1993:236). Indeed, Hughes in his role within the IRA Security Department became suspicious about the rapidity of some executions before he had a chance to interview the suspects (Moloney 2010). Furthermore, it is possible that the executed Loughall informer was 'thrown to the wolves' by a leak from the special branch (SB) to protect a more important source. Possibly then, internal executions were part of the clandestine game played by the two protagonists to protect their own people but for divergent reasons. Another interpretation is that some senior nationalists must have been aware that operations were being compromised by internal leaks, but allowed the Loughall operation to go ahead in order to undermine the armed struggle in the campaign and to aid in reaching a political settlement. Also, this highly active ASU was supposedly planning to split from the movement to adopt a more aggressive military campaign (Moloney 2007). It is well nigh impossible to unravel the baffling thicket of plots and counter-plots, conspiracy theories, personal vendettas, multiple motives, myths and rumour, and to decipher what is 'truth' on this particular matter and in the sinister game being played between and within the intelligence agencies and the IRA.

My main focus, however, shall be on deviancy in the security community in relation to the two sensitive and controversial areas of shoot to kill and state collusion. The publications on these topics mean that the names in this book have all been in the public arena; also, some of those mentioned are now deceased. In two cases, however, I felt it was politic to use pseudonyms, while elsewhere I have had to exercise caution on individuals for legal reasons even if their conduct has been widely portrayed in the media or through other sources. This is not an overview of the Troubles; fortunately there is a balanced account by McKittrick and McVea (2000). Delving into this area was not without emotion; some of the material is harrowing and moving, as with the volume by McKittrick, Kelters, Feeney, Thornton and McVea (2007) detailing all the deaths in the Troubles (*Lost Lives*, first published in 1999). Indeed, a legacy of the Troubles has been the forming of family-oriented interest groups, in the North but also in the South, to discover the truth about the death or disappearance of loved ones. Part of the excellent CAIN project, is designed to represent the families in their search for truth and justice in the absence of a TRC. Some relatives feel strongly that they have been 'ignored, marginalised, vilified and harassed by those same state forces which had killed their loved ones' (Rolston 2006:30).[31] CAIN is an indispensable source, as is the Pat Finucane Centre[32] for human rights issues in the name of the solicitor who supported republicans in legal matters and was murdered by the loyalist UVF.

To address the matters raised above I shall now turn to scrutinising the nature and extent of state terror, several examples of state induced violence against insurgents and others, the diverse types of insurgent terrorist organisation, and the nature and dilemmas of counter-insurgency campaigns. This will serve as essential background to the case study of the British state's response to the Troubles in Northern Ireland.

2
State Terror and Insurgent Terrorism

THE STATE AND INSURGENT TERRORISM

> In the early twenty-first century, terrorism is now the central security concern for our governments. (Xavier Raufer in Horgan 2005:vii)

When a democratic state is seriously challenged by a major external or internal insurgent threat it faces the near intractable dilemma as to whether or not it can continue to comply with the fundamental checks and balances that make it genuinely democratic (Wilkinson 1985). Following terrorist violence there is likely to be insistent pressure from public opinion, the media and from adversaries in parliament to 'get tough', 'hit back', 'teach them a lesson', to 'take the gloves off' and demonstrate firm action that elicits swift results. Presidents, politicians and control agents of the state are confronted with urgent demands to rapidly achieve tangible goals and show that they are responding adequately to the crisis (Hermann & Hermann 1998). Yet those very politicians and government agents are at the same time formally bound to adhere to the principles and practices of legality and accountability that underpin the rule of law in a democratic system. There is, however, a substantial body of evidence indicating that states resort to a range of deviant practices in such situations. These include abuse of human rights, illicit violence by covert units, systemic evasion of accountability and wide deviation from the rule of law (Richardson 2006). Furthermore, this deviance not infrequently emanates from the highest echelons of the state apparatus.

For example, when the threat is extreme as with devastating assaults on the state's own territory – say with the attacks of recent years by jihadist insurgents in Madrid, London and New York – there is a panicky tendency to push through emergency legislation and even to tolerate the suspension or selective abuse of civil and human rights. The conduct of the US since the '9/11' suicide attacks on American targets in September 2001 and other violent operations conducted by jihadist groups graphically illustrates this process of rushing to erase the restrictions on state power (as with the wide-ranging Patriot Act of 2001). The US, which ironically has been and is a vocal champion of democracy and human rights in other countries, has been exposed as a flagrant infringer of human rights and international law. This occurred notably through the gross excesses at Abu Ghraib and Guantanamo Bay (Gourevitch & Morris 2009; Sands 2009). The shocking images of prisoners being tortured and degraded by the American military in the Abu Ghraib Prison in Iraq, and the accounts of 'water-boarding' and other torture at the US military complex Guantanamo on Cuba, have been immensely damaging to the standing of the US (Human Rights Watch 2007). But the trauma of 9/11 was held to have 'produced a war mentality resembling that of the Cold War' (Bayley 2006:14), and the then American President, George W. Bush, declared a 'crusade' and a global 'war' on terrorism (known as 'GWOT') declaring, 'Either you are with us or you are with the terrorists. From this day forward, any nation that continues to harbour or support terrorism will be regarded by the United States as a hostile regime' (Richardson 2006:76). All of this can be interpreted as serving only to incite jihadist insurgents to increased violence. Furthermore, declaring 'war' on insurgents implies by definition that the opponent has been granted the status of combatant in a conflict; the 'enemy' is expected to play its role by continuing to mount an armed response (Richardson 2006). To fight a war one needs battles to achieve victory through defeating the enemy; insurgents, however, typically avoid battle, can prove remarkably hard to 'defeat' and the desired victory remains frustratingly elusive.

Importantly for the theme of this book, those disturbing images from the two American prisons abroad have proved a rich gift to America's adversaries. Their anti-American propaganda rests not only on being able to document the abuses convincingly but also, crucially, that these human rights violations were linked to the very top of government. For the two key issues remain: do the measures taken to combat terrorism simply bolster that terrorism? And how deeply is the state involved in dubious or illicit counter-insurgent strategies that can rebound on that state? For instance, in cryptic language Vice-President Cheney had spoken just after the 9/11 attacks of working the 'dark side' of intelligence. He added, 'we've got to spend time in the shadows in the intelligence world'; and also make sure that, 'we have not tied the hands of the intelligence community' (Gourevitch & Morris 2009:29). A leading official of the Central Intelligence Agency (CIA) said cryptically that the GWOT would be, 'won in large measure by forces you do not know about, in actions you will not see and in ways you may not want to know about' (Scahill 2007:254). That suggestive imagery filtered down to creating military and judicial limbos where the standard rules did not apply and torture was justified on 'security detainees', a categorisation of combat prisoners to bypass the Geneva Convention. Hardliners within the Bush Administration spoke of a 'new kind of war', of a 'new paradigm' and the limitations imposed by the Geneva Convention were seen as 'obsolete' (Sands 2009:39).

Moreover, US military prisons have extensive conduct 'codes' for qualified custodial personnel, and the military is always in charge of such prisons. At Abu Ghraib, in contrast, the prison was run by people from civilian and private intelligence agencies and the subordinate personnel were military police untrained for custodial duties. In this exceptional environment there were effectively no formal rules, instructions and supervision, only verbal orders from unidentified personnel to 'soften up' prisoners for interrogation. This context led to a deterioration of discipline with gross and persistent abuse of prisoners that was graphically photographed by the soldiers themselves and widely transmitted across the globe (Danner 2004). As one female soldier observed, 'the absence of a code was the code at Abu Ghraib. "They couldn't say we broke the rules because there were no rules"' (Gourevitch & Morris 2009:92). The audit trail for this 'rule-less', human-rights travesty ran through the military and intelligence hierarchy up to the Pentagon, and from there to the White House (Sands 2009).

Yet no one above the rank of sergeant was ever prosecuted, as was no one from the intelligence community or from the Administration in Washington. In response to this, Zimbardo (2008:21), having assessed a range of evidence about the torture, puts on 'trial' the 'command structure of the US military, CIA officials, and top government leaders for their combined complicity in creating a dysfunctional system that spawned the torture and abuses of Abu Ghraib'. But typically deviance on behalf of the state rarely leads to prosecution and even then seldom ends in a conviction;[1] and we shall certainly witness that pattern in the case study of Northern Ireland.

These two US cases also illustrate how a government can shape policies and send out messages that indirectly foster deviance at the 'sharp end' yet while relying on *deniability* to protect the initiators at the top from any direct implication in that conduct. As the legal Counsel to the White House Gonzalez put it:

[T]he US did not torture; it acted with deliberation; everything was vetted; none of the approved interrogation techniques amounted to torture ... the decisions taken were reasonable, restrained and lawful. Finally, *there was no connection between Administration policy and Abu Ghraib*. (Sands 2009:21, my emphasis)

This 'state of denial' that characterised the Bush administration according to Woodward (2006) clashes with the fact that what occurred in these US establishments in Iraq and Cuba can be clearly linked to the Administration and to an inner group around the President (Sands 2009). Furthermore, this high-level activity fits the definition of 'state crime', which is generally taken to mean the state breaking domestic and international law and infringing human rights (Barak 1991; Doig 2010).

The 'state' is of course an abstraction, representing a set of fundamental values and norms that persist when governments change (Benn & Peters 1959). Those values and norms are, in a democracy, rooted in the sovereignty of parliament, free elections, an independent judiciary, free speech and a free press, rights of association, right to privacy, restraint in the use of violence against citizens, and channels for redress with transparent and accountable institutions. Above all in a healthy democracy the citizens should feel that the state is not repressive and possibly even benign, but never itself above the law. In particular, control agencies such as the police and criminal justice systems should be trustworthy and legitimate. All this should foster in citizens a sense of living in a 'just world' (Lerner 1980).

There will, however, always be 'agency' in the sense of a group of individuals combined in a specific government that determines particular policy in the name of that state. In certain sensitive areas including combating insurgents, moreover, there may well be covert, robust but legal and legitimate counter-insurgency policies and practices. But there can also be a kind of shadow state, or 'deep' state (Green & Ward 2004), where in the name of the state a number of clandestine and illicit policies and practices are formulated and implemented. There are always grey areas especially in the intelligence and security areas; say with ghost units that formally do not exist and that explore the boundaries of legality with prolonged infiltration by participating informants in undercover roles or functioning as 'agents provocateurs' (Marx 1988). But there can also be deeper and darker areas of assassination, abductions by non-government agents, secret flights and hidden torture centres

(Human Rights Watch 2007; Scahill 2007).[2] In the murky world of national security, espionage, counter-espionage, surveillance and counter-insurgency the state, state-agents, hired hands of the state and the state's willing or unwilling volunteers can readily slip, slide, be pushed or consciously step from the grey area into that black area of the shadowy, deep and dirty state. This can manifest itself in extremis as terror by the state.

STATE TERROR

Tyrants, dictators and leaders of one-party states with unlimited power, a subservient political and judicial apparatus and no effective mechanisms of accountability need have no qualms about human rights and civilian redress. The autocrats can answer a threat (real or fabricated) with little or no concern for the rights of their enemies or, indeed, their own citizens. However, there is evidence that democratic states have also engaged in excesses of violence and other human rights abuses during external threats in conventional war situations or colonial conflicts related to national independence (Collins 2008). The US, UK, France and the Netherlands are examples of democratic states that have all resorted to illegal behaviour, and even what could be judged war crimes during WWII and/or in post-colonial strife. However, the scale of state terror in dictatorial regimes can outweigh the excesses in many conventional armed conflicts while insurgent terrorism is puny in comparison to state violence.[3] Stalin's Soviet Union and Hitler's Nazi Empire, for example, both constructed a vast apparatus of terror against dissidents and out-groups. In the Soviet Union there was a complex network of labour work and punishment camps, the 'Gulag' (Appelbaum 2006); but the gulag has also come to represent the entire apparatus of repression with secret police, extensive torture, mass expulsions and murders, arbitrary arrests, show trials with forced confessions and periods of often arbitrary terror. The scale is almost beyond comprehension and it created a society based on pervasive fear, suspicion, arbitrary repression, covert surveillance, informing, denunciations and systemic state lawlessness (Montefiore 2003). The total number of victims from terror and induced famine during Stalin's dictatorship (1928–53) has been estimated by Conquest (2008) at not less than 15 million deaths.

Alongside the mega-examples of Stalin's and Hitler's repressive empires there has also been mass terror in certain dictatorial, ethnically or religiously divided, failed and rogue states in the form of genocide, war crimes and crimes against humanity including expulsion, mutilation and rape. The collapse of the Soviet Union, the disintegration of Yugoslavia and the political and ethnic divisions in a number of African states have also unleashed new and vicious separatist wars of ethno-nationalist and ethno-religious origin in recent decades. These are conducted with immense savagery and widespread dislocation. Again the number of victims is staggering and the terror was at times unleashed by leading members of the government and conducted by government or state supported forces (Nollkaemper & van der Wilt 2009; Roth 2001).

A further important dimension of state terror was and is the *export* of terror and training of other terrorists. Since the 1970s, insurgent groups could readily seek training in camps abroad and also seek to buy or be given weapons and explosives. The various wings and derivative groups of the Palestine Liberation Organization (PLO) are said to have helped train and equip some 40 insurgent movements including the Red Army Faction in West Germany (Hoffman 2006:28). Furthermore certain states – notably Cuba, China, Soviet Union, Libya, Iran, Jordan, Sudan, North Korea and the US – have promoted terrorism in other countries with training and the supply of military equipment. The US, for instance, supported the right-wing 'Contras' in Nicaragua who opposed the socialist government of the former *Sandinista* guerrilla movement (Sandinist National Liberation Front).[4] Of major importance has been the role of the late Colonel Gaddafi of Libya who supplied the IRA and several other insurgent groups with large amounts of weapons and explosives. For the IRA, these included five to ten tonnes of semtex-H plastic explosives and some 120 tonnes of material including anti-tank guns, rocket-propelled grenades and even surface-to-air (SAM) SA-7 missiles (Hoffman 2006:264).[5] Gaddafi had become the implacable enemy of America and its allies and was especially willing to support insurgents active in the countries he held responsible for a US bombing with UK assistance on his headquarters in Libya. In 1988, as a reprisal for the US attack, a bomb was planted on an American plane departing from London, which blew up and disintegrated over Lockerbie in Scotland causing 270 deaths.[6] This remains the largest loss of life in a single terrorist incident in Europe.

Furthermore, in some societies it is precisely the state's security agencies that engage in gross violence and other abuses against ordinary citizens, but particularly against those defined as enemies of the state. There is the nightmare scenario of failed, rogue or totalitarian states where such agencies are repressive, violent and unaccountable (Hinton 2005; Huggins 1991). A number of right-wing regimes – including at various times Chile, Brazil, Argentina and Greece – have implemented repressive measures emanating from military and police agencies but also from units of paramilitaries, vigilantes and agents provocateurs. In Chile and Argentina there was extensive covert violence such as abductions, torture, rape, murder and with some victims simply disappearing; a number were drugged and thrown out of aircraft into the sea. There are, moreover, in several societies diverse examples of formally unacknowledged and covert practices which are informally encouraged, evade mechanisms of formal accountability and amount to a kind of 'shadow' policy with varying measures of collusion from the authorities. I shall touch on four examples:

- State violence during the apartheid regime in South Africa (Boraine 2000).
- State violence in democratic Spain was conducted by a covert unit, GAL, aimed at Basque ETA activists (*de Volkskrant* 1998a & 1998b; Woodworth 2002).
- Police violence in India was and is aimed at eliminating dangerous criminals and Naxalite insurgents by blatantly illegal means. Although this is a form of 'grass-roots', practitioner generated deviance it also receives wide popular approval and even informal political support (Belur 2010).
- Extra-judicial executions by police, military and intelligence agencies.

Police Violence and the 'Third Force' in South Africa

The conflict between the racist South African state and the African National Congress (ANC) lasted more than 30 years, 1961–94. From the early 1960s, the right-wing government of the all-white National Party faced growing militancy from the majority black population along with a declaration of war by the armed wing of the ANC (*Umkhonto we Sizwe*). The government and its followers perceived themselves to be in a war if not a crusade against an external, allegedly communist-led onslaught against their Christian way of life (Ellis 1998:264). In response, an elite of key figures began to organise an alternative structure alongside the established governmental system to implement a covert policy. This utilised special units to conduct a 'dirty war'.

The efforts of the Security Branch of the South African Police (SAP) and of the National Security Service (the notorious BOSS) were combined. This wide-reaching security apparatus was constructed to conduct the ensuing de facto war and became effectively an alternative government apparatus implementing a shadow, parallel policy which can even be seen as the state's 'real' policy. The cover of secrecy in relation to 'national security' kept this substantial apparatus outside of formal decision making and scrutiny. SAP had combat experience in neighbouring states where it was used in a military, counter-insurgency role. These police units drew from the techniques and experience of other counter-insurgency forces in Algeria, Israel, Chile and Argentina. The 'Selous Scouts' in Rhodesia, for example, had been trained to operate behind enemy lines pretending to be guerrillas, to engage in reconnaissance and sabotage, to capture guerrillas and 'turn them' rapidly through torture and to use that intelligence quickly to attack guerrilla camps. There was also the *Koevoet* Unit of highly mobile 'hunter-killers' that endeavoured to fulfil the 'kill-rates' demanded by superiors.

There is no doubt that encouragement for these covert practices came from very senior figures in government. These set a tone, fostered expectations, gave off signals wreathed in ambiguity and euphemisms, tried to avoid an accountability trail but also pressurised subordinates. One police general said that President Botha himself 'gave us hell' and he was told to 'take the gloves off' (Ellis 1998:273). Everyone understood what 'taking the gloves off' or 'remove from society' meant. The bag of dirty tricks stimulated by this pressure from above was carried out by special units referred to collectively as the 'Third Force'. Ellis (1998:278) states:

> They enjoyed great prestige within the security services. They developed a distinctive culture which was aggressive, arrogant and utterly contemptuous of the law and of civilians and even of other soldiers or policemen. Such units tended to attract officers with disordered personalities, and long service in them brutalised otherwise unremarkable people.

There was the SAP covert unit C10, which was a 'general purpose death squad'. Members of it formed a brutal, ruthless warrior caste and for them 'total war meant simply war without rules'. This grisly, no-holds-barred approach could even be viewed as the highest of duties for one's country and people. C10 engaged in systematic murder, torture, bombings and subversion.

But of the essence is that those murky techniques learned on battlefields abroad were used in the domestic campaign within South Africa against communists and members of the ANC. The government reacted to the growing turbulence verging on insurrection in the 1980s by unleashing a concerted battery of dirty tricks. But even during the four years of transition towards democratic elections under President De Klerk, 1990–94, the killings continued with 14,000 deaths in that period. This was despite the fact that the ANC had officially ended its campaign of violence. But the horrendous practices of these covert units came to light with the regime change of 1994 and the election to the presidency of Nelson Mandela. There were the revelations of the TRC as well as inquests, trials, journalism and research (Boraine 2000; Wilson 2001).

What is crystal clear is that a campaign of murder and mayhem was unleashed at the highest levels of government, with an alternative apparatus of covert police and military units that engaged in murder, abductions, torture, bombings, massacres, sabotage, subversion and propaganda. There is no doubt that the most senior officials were aware of this parallel apparatus of illegal repression; some not only gave direct encouragement but also attended celebratory drinking sessions after 'successful' operations at the secret location of the C10 unit at Vlakplaas (Ellis 1998:278). The state, albeit through a hidden shadow of the deep state, was directing the violence through covert police and military activity and turning a blind eye to crime by government operatives. Ellis (1998) comments that until the transitional period the entire government including the President:

> ... was willing to allow covert war to be waged on a substantial scale provided only that ministers could not be held personally responsible. They did not wish to be informed precisely about what happened on the ground. It did not require much imagination to suppose a connection between secret projects, no matter how bland their formal description, and the waging of war at ground level. Ellis (1998:287)

The case of South Africa and the Third Force illustrates clearly how a state under threat was able to mobilise and stimulate a long campaign of repression and subversion; how certain units and certain people rise to the task of organising the delivery of violent means without scruple; and of how politicians, who are deeply involved in these clandestine processes, endeavour to evade accountability. South Africa's conduct during the repressive and widely condemned apartheid regime can be viewed as a systemic example of 'state terror'. Yet within an ostensibly legally compliant democratic state in Europe we can also witness recourse to state-sponsored violence in response to a substantial threat.

State and Police Violence in Spain: GAL and ETA

What separates a democratic society from repressive ones is that there are no death-squads or covert military units acting as vigilantes, plying their grisly trade with the passive or active collusion of the state. We tend therefore to associate 'death-squads' with pernicious regimes in South America. Yet in Spain, a democratic country and member of the EU, and signatory to its treaties, there was a covert unit that engaged in murder and torture in the 1980s. The Basques in Northern Spain saw themselves as a separate people with their own language and culture. They were strongly opposed to the centralist policies of Madrid under the dictatorial regime of General Franco, the victor in the Spanish Civil War of 1936–39 who was antagonistic to the autonomy of ethnic minority provinces. Resistance to this led in 1959 in the Basque region to the formation of a militant insurgent group, ETA, striving for an independent Basque state. ETA commenced a campaign of violence that led to some 800 deaths through shootings and bombings while there were also numerous kidnappings; the late 1970s were especially violent.

There was a formal response of banning ETA and mounting conventional counter-insurgency measures; ETA was and is banned as a terrorist organisation in Spain and also within the EU and US. Next to this formal policy there also emerged a covert policy, developed by several officials and ministers, which was to set up a secret unit, *Grupos Antiterroristos de Liberacion* (GAL), a paramilitary group for counter-insurgency activities. There had earlier been suspicions in the 1970s of 'death-squads' formed from elements of the security and secret services; but GAL, which operated between 1983 and 1987, was publicly exposed as a unit set up to eliminate suspected ETA activists. A number of its members and several politicians subsequently went on trial.

In short, politicians and senior police officers constructed a 'death squad' – which engaged in abductions, torture, death-threats, letter-bombs and assassinations both in Spain and across the border in France – as part of a covert, counter-insurgency strategy. GAL drew from the security services, but particularly from the paramilitary Guardia Civil, and it was held responsible for at least 28 murders. Among the victims were a number of innocent people with no ETA connections whatsoever. GAL was secretly financed by government funds that were used to mount clandestine operations but also to hire common criminals for some killings. It was a media campaign by the respected newspaper *El Mundo* that uncovered the activities of GAL and this exposure ended with a judicial inquiry and several court cases (*de Volkskrant* 1998c).

A number of senior officials were involved and the proceedings brought ministers, leading civil servants and high-ranking military officers to court. Three generals from the Guardia Civil and the Army, two ex-Ministers of Home Affairs, a provincial governor, and an under-Minister for Security were summoned to appear in court in 1995. Earlier, two senior police officers were convicted of funding GAL operations and of recruiting hitmen. But after initial silence the two pointed higher up the hierarchy. This sponsored a judicial inquiry in 1994 and subsequently trials in which an under-minister for Security received a ten-year sentence, as did a former Minister of Home Affairs, while nine former police officers were jailed for the abductions (*de Volkskrant* 1998c).

The GAL affair indicates that, when faced by a resilient and violent threat from Basque activists, a number of senior people in the then socialist government mounted a conspiracy to start a 'dirty war' against ETA. This involved ministers, officials and members of the Secret Service, Army and Guardia Civil. This informal policy of counter-terror when exposed did lead to inquiries, trials and some stiff sentences. There have been no examples of similar activities since 1987 and it does seem that a free press, democratic processes and an independent judiciary have effectively tackled these abuses and excesses. There does remain the question as to how it was possible for senior government members to mount this considerable operation without the Prime Minister and his Cabinet being aware of it. And this was under the democratic premiership of the progressive socialist and widely esteemed Felipe Gonzalez. Who knew what, and how was 'deniability' in the upper levels of government arranged? Here we have elements within a democratic government choosing illegal violence as a 'justifiable' means of dealing with a serious threat to the state.

Police Violence and 'Encounters' in India

The example of 'encounters' in parts of India illustrates not so much a state initiative but more practitioner-generated practice, but which elicits wide support within and outside the police. Encounters are confrontations between the police and serious criminals or insurgents, who are considered highly dangerous and/or successful at evading conviction, and which lead to the deaths of the criminals in shootouts with the police. Belur (2010), a former Indian police officer, examines this practice in detail for Mumbai and elsewhere. These encounters are ostensibly spontaneous shootouts. But police and others often make a distinction between genuine and fake encounters. Typically the latter take place in isolated places and/ or at night and usually there are fatalities among the criminals, considerable firepower, no injuries to the police, no witnesses and remarkably similar if not identical cover stories. In effect these are extra-judicial executions, but they bring out broad public, media and even official approval. Certain police officers gain popular status from their role in both types of encounters, which are seen as a justified means of tackling burgeoning violent crime and rampant drug dealing, and as a way of retaliating against violent Maoist Naxalite insurgents (Belur 2010:vi–vii). There is generally wide support for the elimination of those serious criminals seen as 'folk devils' in the context of a cumbersome judicial system. Of interest is that the officers concerned are quite open about the practice and some become public heroes with considerable status within the force and outside. For example, Inspector Pradeep Sharma is the 'encounter king, having killed more than 120 Bombay gangsters in shoot-outs' (Glenny 2009:167).

India is ostensibly a country that abides by the rule of law and encounters are condemned by civil-liberties groups. But it is clear that some politicians effectively give the practice their blessing as a necessary if 'temporary' measure in the face of a severe crime wave; the media are mostly positive, and senior officers encourage and reward it with recommendations for bravery, medals and promotions. The police culture tends to view them in terms of the 'Dirty Harry Problem' of having to use dirty means for good ends (Belur 2010:80–1; Klockars 2005). It is clear that police and societal culture in India is not strongly rooted in notions of legality and there is wide acceptance of police deviance within a populist notion of 'rough justice' or 'just deserts'.

Extra-judicial Executions

A related concept to encounters is that of 'extra-judicial executions', which are particularly associated with societies where the police, military or semi-official 'death squads' engage in killing criminals, members of perceived oppositional or out-groups and the political rivals of the government. In its fake form, the 'encounters' mentioned above are also a form of extra-judicial execution. In parts of India, Belur (2010) refers to police and paramilitary units, on duty or functioning as vigilantes off duty, in Punjab, Assam and Kashmir engaging in assassinations and torture including the murder of prisoners in custody. These criminal practices by the forces of 'law and order' – which may include kidnappings, torture, rape and mutilation – can flourish because the agencies involved are effectively unaccountable. In some societies they gain immunity because they function in collusion with organised crime, the judiciary and leading politicians (Hinton & Newburn 2009; Penglase 1996).

At times the state itself is involved actively or passively and rewards it formally or informally. Of India, for example, Grossman (2002:268) states that the 'government practice of providing cash rewards for police who eliminated wanted militants encouraged the police to engage in extra-judicial killings'. Societies where this practice of informal executions and illegal shootings take place include Jamaica, Guyana, Brazil, Argentina, Nigeria, Pakistan, Guatemala and Congo. Typically these practices are accompanied by a lack of serious investigation, weak oversight and very few prosecutions so that the 'executioners' enjoy a form of immunity (Glenny 2009; United Nations 2010).

TYPES OF INSURGENT TERRORIST ORGANISATIONS

Terrorism is aimed at the people watching, not at the actual victims. (Jenkins 1975:16)

There is no settled definition of insurgent terrorism, which takes many diverse forms. Furthermore, the multiple definitions of 'terrorist', with some speaking of over 100 (Schmid & Jongman 1988), does mean that the extent of terrorism cannot be accurately calculated (Horgan 2005:4). There is, however, some evidence that terrorist style attacks have been on the increase during the last two decades, in number and intensity (Wilkinson 2005:3). It is debatable as to what extent an insurgent group forms a structured *organisation*. Insurgent groups vary widely in structure, style and culture from being simply a tiny coterie (Angry Brigade); a strongly hierarchical, well-armed, military-style institution (Tamil Tigers); a fluid, international network (*Al Qaeda*); or part of a wider social movement with many functions, as with Hezbollah in Lebanon (Farida 2010).[7]

In general the leading authors agree that terrorism is essentially a *method*. It is also agreed that terrorism is a value-laden, pejorative term used to negatively label opponents.[8] Indeed, 'one woman's terrorist is another woman's freedom fighter', to use an old saying. And that terrorism is most often taken to mean the deliberate creation of fear through violence or threat of violence to achieve political ends (Hoffman 2006:40; Horgan 2005:1). Some authors add that the violence is aimed specifically at civilians.[9] For example, Richardson (2006) sees that as one of the seven characteristics of terrorist acts. These are for her: politically inspired; violent; communicating a message; having symbolic significance; involving sub-state groups; the victims and the audience are not necessarily the same; and the 'final and most important defining characteristic of terrorism is the deliberate targeting of civilians' (Richardson 2006:20–1). As mentioned, the most extensive users of terrorism have been states and some refer to this as 'state *terror*' to distinguish it from sub-state *terrorism*. This is also why I speak of *insurgency* rather than only terrorism. This is in no way meant as a euphemism, but is partly because insurgent movements tend to use a pallet of methods that include terrorist violence as but one feature, however dominant that feature may become. It could be argued as well that those who employ terror on behalf of the state could equally be dubbed 'terrorists'. Insurgency is used here then as a 'relatively value-neutral concept' denoting a 'rebellion or rising against any government in power or the civil authorities' (Wilkinson 2005:1).

I shall now briefly outline six main types of terrorist organisation.

International, 'Middle-East', Arab Terrorism

The advent of international terrorist movements has been traced to 1968 (Hoffman 2006:19); and they were typically Arab groups drawing on the Palestinian problem. There began a range of terrorist attacks outside of their homelands that gained world-wide publicity and sometimes significant concessions from governments. The insurgent groups included the PLO and its militant wing Fatah, Black September, Democratic Front for the Liberation of Palestine (DFLP) and Popular Front for the Liberation of Palestine (PFLP). Later there was an emphasis not just on liberation but also on turning the new state into an Islamic society with the emergence of Hamas in Palestine and Hezbollah in Lebanon. Starting in 1968 there was a spate of plane hijackings, shootouts at airports and attacks on embassies. Especially dramatic was the assault on Israeli athletes during the Olympic Games in Munich in 1972. The images of masked and armed insurgents from Black September holding Israelis hostage in the Olympic Village transfixed audiences across the world (Hoffman 2006:68). The ability of these movements to dominate the headlines with an increasingly global media sent a powerful signal to other insurgents. And it proved fruitful:

> Within four years, a handful of Palestinian terrorists had overcome a quarter century of neglect and obscurity. They had achieved what diplomats and statesmen, lobbyists and humanitarian workers had persistently failed to do: focusing attention on the Palestinian people and their plight. (Hoffman 2006:70)

Large-scale, Rebellious Movements

These generally left-wing (Marxist, Maoist) insurgent organisations in 'third world' countries forcefully challenge the state and can end up controlling large areas of a country. They can mount substantial, well-trained units with considerable firepower to contest government forces as with The Shining Path (*Sendero Luminoso*) in Peru, the *Sandinistas* in Nicaragua and the *Fuerzas Armadas Revolucionarias de Colombia* (Revolutionary Armed Forces of Colombia, FARC) in Colombia. In the territory they control, they often function as a form of 'proto-government' (Green & Ward 2004). They can also 'degenerate' to becoming hybrid agencies engaging largely in criminal activity such as kidnapping and drug smuggling, while in the territory they control they resort to intimidation, assassination and destruction of property (Glenny 2008:294f; Betancourt 2011).

Urban Guerrillas

In the second half of the 1960s and the 1970s there arose a number of small, left-wing insurgent groups in western societies that tended to attract intellectuals with middle-class backgrounds who had become attracted to Marxism and militancy. There were, for example, the Red Brigades in Italy (*Brigate Rosse*) and Japan, the Angry Brigade in Britain, the Weathermen in the US, *Action Directe* in France, and the Red Army Faction founded in 1970 in Germany (Becker 1978; Sprinzak 1998). Those attracted to the Red Army Faction, for example, had often studied at German universities at a time of radicalisation and challenging of authority. They identified with the oppressed in Palestine and Vietnam, rejected western capitalism and American imperialism, and moved from theory to action with ruthless violence. The techniques of terrorism were learned from the PFLP in a Jordanian training camp. In West Germany and occasionally abroad they subsequently indulged in arson, assassinations, bombings and kidnappings, and their targets tended to be shops, embassies, bars frequented by American soldiers, US military establishments and leading figures in German society. The violence caused an intense moral panic in German society (Kellen 1998) but its role diminished after the leading players were imprisoned, following which several committed suicide (Becker 1978).

These underground 'urban guerrilla' groups rarely mounted long-term campaigns with coherent and well-organised operations while they were vulnerable to internal dissent, to dissolution on losing their leadership, and concerted police campaigns and legal measures (Ferracuti 1998).

Ethno-nationalism and Movements for National Independence

In general, the experts in the terrorism area maintain that ethno-nationalism has been the main cause of insurgency in recent decades up to the start of this century. They also conclude that such insurgent terrorist organisations rarely achieve their strategic goals (Wilkinson 2005:13). The exceptions are several movements for national independence which faced democratic societies that emerged war-weary from WWII. They often fielded a more powerful security presence than the insurgents, but the control agents in these colonial societies often found themselves in a spiral of violence as they responded to insurgent 'atrocities' by employing themselves illicit violence against civilians and activists. The dilemma of the French in Algeria, for instance, was that the more ruthless and 'successful' they were in counter-insurgency operations, including wide use of torture, against *Front de Libération Nationale* insurgents (National Liberation Front, FNL) the more they hardened resistance while facing an increasingly hostile press and public opinion in France (Horne 1979).

A number of former imperial and ostensibly democratic countries withdrew in the face of determined insurgent movements from their colonies. Of importance was the acknowledged right to self-determination of nations enshrined in the UN Charter of 1945. An abiding image for IRA leaders was of Archbishop Makarios, who had been closely associated with the *Ethnikí Orgánosis Kipriakoú Agónos* (National Organization of Cypriot Fighters, EOKA) insurgency movement for the independence of Cyprus, standing on the steps of 10 Downing Street in London in 1961 as the first president of an independent Cyprus. One IRA leader carried press cuttings of the progression of Makarios from outlaw to statesman saying 'that will be us one day' (Ryder 2000:438). Indeed, umpteen leaders of insurgency movements against the 'occupiers' subsequently entered government following regime change. These include Menachem Begin of the *Irgun Zvai Leumi* in Palestine (National Military Organization, a Zionist group that attacked the British and Arabs) and Nelson Mandela of the ANC in South Africa. Both went on to lead their countries and both were awarded the Nobel Peace Prize, which was also later awarded to Yassir Arafat of the PLO. This encouragingly conveyed that leading activists in insurgency and even violence could nevertheless transform themselves into statesmen of international acclaim.

Right-wing Extremists

Although the dominant insurgent movements of the last half-century have been mostly left-wing in ideology or ethno-religious in orientation, two right-wing movements were remarkably successful between the Two World Wars. These were the fascists of Mussolini, who gained power in Italy in 1922, and Hitler's Nazis in Germany in 1933. In addition there has been a spate of right-wing and neo-Nazi groups in western and eastern European countries in recent decades that can be violent (Wilkinson 2005:56). Groups from both ends of the political spectrum employing terrorist methods want to destabilise society, but for diametrically opposed ends (Hoffman 2006:101–18). There have also been right-wing, anti-insurgent groups in Turkey, the Balkans and throughout Latin America that have matched, or even out-matched, left-wing groups in violence. The anti-Communist Contras in Nicaragua kidnapped, tortured and mutilated civilians; burned houses in captured towns; abused women; and their form of combat was 'one of consistent and bloody abuse of human rights' (Reed 1985).

In the US, moreover, there are various right-wing groups including militias, rural survivalists and Christian white followers who are often vehemently opposed to the federal government in Washington DC (Hoffman 2006:101). The army veteran Timothy McVeigh, for instance, sympathised with these movements and placed a huge car bomb outside a federal building in Oklahoma City in 1995. The explosion caused immense damage and killed 168 people including 19 young children. Indeed, until the 9/11 attacks the largest loss of life due to terrorism in America came not from abroad but from the domestic far-right in Oklahoma City.

Fundamentalist Jihadist Organisations

In the last decade the discourse on terrorism has been dominated by the rise of radical and extremely violent jihadist insurgents. However, of considerable significance earlier was the extended occupation of the American Embassy in Teheran in 1979 following the Islamic Revolution in Iran. The public display of the blind-folded American hostages was an intense humiliation for the US, which seemed impotent until the matter was resolved but only after a year of captivity for the hostages. The contemporary jihadist groups have mounted well-prepared, spectacular attacks aimed at highly symbolic targets and geared to creating mass casualties. The attacks have been against hotels, embassies, war-ships, public transport, places of entertainment and government buildings. The 9/11 assaults using aircraft as missiles against four targets in North America in 2001 brought dramatically to the world the grim images of the Twin Towers of the World Trade Center (WTC) in New York, icons of American capitalism, collapsing in flames. The planes had been hijacked by well-prepared teams who were prepared to die in the conflagration. Indeed, jihadist insurgency has become closely associated with suicide missions, symbolic targets, martyrdom, mass casualties and extreme cruelty (Hoffman 2006:131–72). In Algeria, the *Groupe islamique armé* (Armed Islamic Group, GIA) has been utterly ruthless and quite vicious in its attacks on civilians and security forces (Horgan 2005). In the Caucasus there have been well-equipped and determined groups that have mounted large-scale attacks within the Russian Federation including a theatre in Moscow and a school in Beslan, North Ossetia, that ended in a bloodbath with 331 deaths among the hostages including some 170 children (Hoffman 2006:30). Certain jihadist insurgents have murdered their hostages in cold blood and beheaded them with knives, and this gruesome ritual has been filmed and distributed through internet sites.

These new style insurgents have created highly flexible, almost virtual organisations of considerable resilience, sophistication and with extensive funding and have used modern communication methods to great effect. The more substantial groups form a kind of loosely coordinated jihadist 'crusade' against the West (Merari 1998) and compared with the largely politically motivated insurgent groups are clearly dominated by the religious imperative.

METHODS, CHARACTERISTICS AND MOTIVATIONS OF INSURGENTS

Insurgent Methods

Insurgents may be revolutionaries but they remain remarkably conservative in their methods. Until fairly recently they have relied primarily on the gun and the bomb. This is because these are simple, cheap, easy to use and frequently quite effective. Most insurgent groups are small compared with the forces pitted against them while they often have to rely initially on members with little or no military experience and no familiarity with weapons. This usually makes them adopt the principles of guerrilla warfare, with Marighela's (1970) *Mini-manual of the Urban Guerrilla* as the bible for many. In general, insurgents in western societies have relied on assassinations, arson, abductions, ambushes and various types of bombing, and casualties have generally been relatively 'low'. Handguns have always been relatively easy to acquire or manufacture and a basic use is fairly straightforward to learn; even the use of specialist sniping weapons can be learned with patience.[10] Bomb-making can be a straightforward matter with instructions on manufacture directly accessible nowadays to all from the internet. The devastating bomb in Oklahoma City in 1995 was constructed from readily available materials, mainly high-nitrate agricultural fertilisers; while the operation cost only about $5,000, it caused some $700 million of damage in addition to the horrendous human casualties (Hamm 2002). The IRA went through a rapid learning experience in bomb-making after some early mistakes. By the time of the Brighton bomb in 1984, which was aimed at killing Prime Minister Thatcher during a conference, the IRA had been able to place it in the hotel three weeks in advance and with a long-delay timer adapted from a video-recorder. However, some of the most telling IRA explosions in Britain were also made like the Oklahoma City bomb from easily available, over-the-counter, agricultural products (Horgan 2005:9).

But with insurgent movements it is usually not so much the number of casualties or explosions that matter but the impact of them on public and political opinion. They mostly do not want 'lots of people dead' but prefer 'lots of people watching' (Jenkins 1975). In relation to casualties the major contemporary fear is of chemical, biological or nuclear attacks and of insurgents acquiring weapons of mass destruction (WMDs). There is also the possibility of insurgent groups gaining access to a nuclear device or more easily manufacturing a 'dirty bomb', which uses a conventional explosion to distribute radioactive materials (Richardson 2006:201).

But often insurgency has been on a small scale, using light weapons and easily made bombs. These are relatively simple to use, effective and cheap. The same is true of suicide bombing, which is remarkably 'cheap' (Richardson 2006:158).[11] It plainly requires no plans for an escape route and has proved highly effective: 'There are only two operational requirements ... a willingness to kill and a willingness to die' (Hoffman 2006:165). The tactic has been employed particularly by the Tamil Tigers (LTTE, Liberation Tigers of Tamil Eelam), Hamas and *Al Qaeda*.

In western insurgent groups the 'human-bomb' type of attack is almost unknown, but the hunger strike has often proved highly effective in drawing attention to a cause. There is a tradition of hunger strikes in Irish republicanism and it is a powerful means of displaying the ultimate personal sacrifice yet without causing other casualties (Merari 1998:196). The martyrdom status of the hunger striker and the subsequent funeral can be a powerful psychological weapon for insurgent movements. Bobby Sands, for example, was apparently a fairly ordinary young man, but he joined the IRA and became transformed in prison through his hunger strike, which turned him from a 'terrorist' into a martyred victim to be admired. His death attracted worldwide attention with sympathy for his dedication and willingness to die for the republican cause; an estimated 100,000 people attended Sands' funeral in Belfast (Richardson 2006:147).

But the methods adopted by insurgents are typically those of the weaker player in the armed struggle, so they adopt the 'war of the flea' familiar in guerrilla warfare. This includes ambush with killing at close range; abductions and assassinations; random bombings of civilian targets; remote control or delayed fuse explosions; and killing members of the security services and others when vulnerable such as when they are off duty (Horgan 2005:9; Wilkinson 2005:10). These tactics typically violate the rules of conventional warfare and are, in addition, a gross infringement of the human rights of the victims. They may well foster great anger among politicians, the public and security forces, igniting a desire for retaliation and revenge.

Characteristics of Insurgents

Most sources strongly emphasise the 'normal' character of insurgent terrorists. Richardson (2006:32), who has interviewed a number of insurgent terrorists, concludes that they are not insane or 'deranged psychopaths' while the 'primary characteristic of terrorists is their normalcy'.

This has been reinforced by those who have taken a psychological or psychiatric approach to terrorism; rarely is paranoia, psychopathology or another psychotic condition found in those who have been clinically examined or interviewed (Reich 1998). There was, for example, little evidence of personality disorders or psychological abnormality among the members of the Italian Red Brigades. They were not the stereotypical 'bloodthirsty desperadoes', but were seriously reflective, conscious of the choices, 'well-prepared' and with 'great intelligence, great openness and great generosity, with sometimes a bit of exhibitionism' (Horgan 2005:63–4). Others have stressed the 'rational' choice of adopting terrorism and see that choice as collective, contextual and strategic rather than individual. As Crenshaw puts it,

> The wide range of terrorist activity cannot be dismissed as 'irrational' and thus pathological, unreasonable, or inexplicable. The resort to terrorism need not be an aberration. It may be a reasonable and calculated response to circumstances ... a reasonably informed choice among available alternatives. (Crenshaw 1998:10, 11)

Activists in most insurgent movements are typically young males between 20 and 40 years old. This is also the usual age-range for active military service so that typically young males are pitted against young males. But a number of movements such as the Tamil Tigers in Sri Lanka and rebel groups in Chechnya, with the 'Black Widows' who have lost their partners in the struggle with Russia, have conspicuously employed women in violent activities including assassinations and suicide bombings. The violence of the movements may well attract some with psychopathic or sadistic tendencies who 'enjoy' the violence, but that could equally be said of the military and of irregular paramilitary groups. In contrast, the authorities in this area accentuate that insurgent activists tend to be stable, rational and altruistic in their thinking and fully conscious of the choice made in entering a movement (White 1989). Typically an insurgent group run on disciplined lines will want recruits who are stable and dependable in order to carry out military style operations including suicide bombing.

A psychiatrist who interviewed many IRA members during the Troubles saw them as 'resilient, relaxed, stable' and with little hindrance from guilt (Bishop & Mallie 1988:15). In prison, moreover, many IRA activists engaged in self-education and read the classics of socialism and of national liberation, began to learn Irish Gaelic and often attended Mass. The Maze Prison became a kind of college, 'our Eton' as one of them quipped, and there were serious debates that surprisingly also included loyalist prisoners.[12] These images of soberness, discipline, reflection and an eagerness to learn are far from the stereotype of wild gunmen and ruthless bombers (White 1989). But there is also evidence from some groups of negative personality characteristics, disrupted backgrounds and social marginality (Kellen 1998; Post 1998).

At some stage, however, they embrace a 'career' that pursues violence (Bandura 1998). There are diverse paths to arriving at that position. It may be through religious conversion or radicalisation; through cultural and family background; or it may be through some specific incident or triggering event that changes a conventional and law-abiding person into a terrorist recruit. That event could be violent and illegal conduct by the security forces against a collective, such as Bloody Sunday; or an incident of violence or humiliation against an individual, close relatives or friends. Collins (1998:50–3), for example, gives a graphic account of how when he was a schoolboy, he and his family had been terrorised by British paratroopers during a raid for explosives in their home in 1974. This was one of the factors that led him to becoming active in the IRA.[13] The willingness to turn to bombing and murdering assumes a process of becoming committed to a cause, stepping over a psychological hurdle to abandon one's previous self to take on the identity of 'insurgent', being initiated into the movement, and learning to apply and justify violence. This is typically accompanied by routinisation, depersonalisation and rationalisation in relation to violence and killing. There has to be an initiation process, a step by step involvement, an acceptance of violence, a justification for it and eventually a hardening to death and suffering (Grossmann 1995).

A member of the IRA, for example, with severe qualms about the first murder he was involved in, stated that he steeled himself and from then on 'each subsequent death meant less to me than the previous one'. He further stated:

> I had become a cold, killing automaton ... I had become hardened to death ... Death had become my way of life, my everyday mission, my business, my reason for being ... I never lost sight of the awfulness of what I was doing, yet I felt this savagery was

the necessary price of our struggle to create a more just society. We were involved in a war of attrition and even then I knew that my participation in that war had changed me. I knew I no longer existed as a normal human being. Every aspect of my life was dedicated to the purpose of death. I knew that a change had taken place within me but at the time I felt I had changed *for the better*: I was becoming a true revolutionary. I had almost rid myself of any sympathy for my victims ... I kept telling myself that compassion for the oppressor was a debilitating legacy of the bourgeois mentality of my upbringing. (Collins 1998:20, 148 & 191, emphasis in original)

This routinisation and rationalisation process is typical of professions associated with violence including concentration camp guards, torturers, hitmen, executioners and soldiers detailed to mass killing (Browning 2001; Katz 1988; Polk 1994).

Next to this 'dulling' effect it is also clear from some accounts that a number of insurgents revelled in violence and some activists from all combat groups in Northern Ireland – IRA, INLA, UVF but also in the security forces – relished the 'buzz' of action with jubilation, celebrations, hooting and cheering, sexual arousal, mutual con-gratulations and jocular banter with much near hysterical laughing following operations including killings (Collins 2008).[14] One highly violent IRA activist admitted that he liked to get close to his victims to see the fear in their eyes, and after the operation he was aroused and had to masturbate.[15] A number of IRA members spoke of involvement in terrorism as becoming addictive and some of the loyalist groups operated more like criminal gangs, or even serial killers, whose murders were lubricated by alcohol and drugs (Moloney 2010:260).

It is perhaps difficult to perceive of another 'career' after that violent insurgent world and away from that callous mentality. How did people step off from what the former UVF activist, Ervine, called 'the hamster wheel to hell'? Once you are on it, he said, 'not only does there seem even with hindsight no way off, [but] I didn't want to get off' (Moloney 2010:346). Ironically, some of the most violent offenders became most in favour of a settlement (Moloney 2010). Gusty Spence, for instance, was a highly active member of the UVF and its commander in the Maze Prison, but he later turned against violence and became influential in the peace process leading to the GFA, as did Ervine. Indeed, many of those insurgents who have survived the struggle or have been released from prison have returned to a conventional existence, resumed family life, attended university, entered public life and held office, given interviews, written memoirs and some have strongly renounced violence. In fact you can now invite the 'Brighton bomber', Patrick Magee, who almost obliterated a British Prime Minister and Cabinet, to lecture in your classroom.

Motivations of Insurgents

In general insurgents think in terms of altruism, fighting for a just cause, promoting the greater good and from a sense of honour. There can of course be mixed motives including mercenary ones. Hoffman (2006:243, 255) sees them as seeking attention, acknowledgement, recognition, authority and governance. Richardson (2006:95–132) summarises their motives around the 'three Rs' of 'revenge, renown, reaction'. There may be many underlying individual and group motives for taking the path to insurgency: for instance ideological zeal, religious conviction, chauvinism and ethnic identity, a deep sense of injustice and humiliation, feelings of victimisation, new standing in a group or community, a sense of purpose and a feeling of excitement from taking part in violent action. Like frontline soldiers, the individual insurgent may experience an intense camaraderie with his or her activist peer-group that is never found in civilian life. Inclusion in the insurgent group may well be the 'first time they truly belonged, the first time they felt truly significant, the first time they felt that what they did counted' (Post 1998:31).

The social and ideological mix will of course vary according to the group. Gurr (1970), in his pioneering work, argued that 'relative deprivation' was a prime motive. Behind many insurgent movements, he maintained, was a sense of being unjustly deprived of something that was their right, but which others were monopolising and denying to them. Revenge is for some a powerful motivator with actions planned on the anniversaries of humiliating defeats or of the executions of activists or at significant locations in the movement's institutional memory. Joining and taking part in the struggle can bring a powerful if not addictive sense of mission, glory and honour, and of being involved in an heroic enterprise. Some suicide bombers go to their deaths with a smile on their face; this is the *bassamat al-farah* or 'smile of joy, prompted by one's impending martyrdom' (Rapoport 1998:117; Richardson 2006:163).

For some insurgents, involvement in a clandestine and action-oriented group can be exciting, fulfilling and even erotic. Andreas Baader of the German Red Army Faction, for example, was fascinated with weapons and equated shooting with sex (Hoffman 2006:246). For some it gives a new identity that confers enhanced status while a few even become global celebrities, such as the iconic Che Guevara in the Cuban Revolution. The Red Army Faction insurgents during their campaign, trials and imprisonment were violent bandits to some, but they also attracted the sympathy and attention of progressive intellectuals including Gunther Grass, Herbert Marcuse and Jean Paul Sartre. Astrid Proll of the Red Army Faction stated, 'You must understand that then the most fantastic thing in the world was not to be a rock star, but a revolutionary' (Hoffman 2006:75).

SUMMARY OF FEATURES OF INSURGENT TERRORISM

We have seen that insurgent terrorist groups, organisations, networks and movements vary greatly in ideology, aims, size, structure, operating style, extent and nature of violence, the territorial range of operations, legitimacy in a community or constituency and the continuity and level of success (Horgan 2005:vii–ix). What all these diverse institutions require are short- and long-term goals, a legitimising ideology, leadership, resources (funds and equipment), recruitment, training and skills, access to targets and support and approval from a constituency. In general, they are against something; they want political and societal change; they are impatient and not prepared to go through constitutional processes; and they turn to violence. They tend to be action-oriented rather than reflective; to think in inclusive-exclusive terms of 'them' and 'us'; to speak of being involved in a 'war' if not a 'crusade'; and to focus on bringing enough physical and psychological damage to the 'enemy' to force through political change (Post 1998). Given the imbalance of resources compared with governmental agencies, they typically gear their activities to gaining publicity by scoring points through symbolic and psychologically effective warfare which impacts on the media and public opinion and which tests how much damage and injury the 'enemy' is prepared to take.

But clearly what essentially binds them all is the resort to violence. And then largely violence to induce terror aimed at innocent civilians whom the conventional rules of war explicitly protect as non-combatants. For insurgents civilians are prime targets:

Enthusiasm for inflicting pain on their enemies, making them suffer before killing them, is a common feature of ethnic or religious conflicts. The loyalists of Northern Ireland are guilty of this, as are republicans ... If the avowed aim was to terrorise the Catholic population, which supported the [IRA] terrorists, in some people's eyes the more horrible the violence, the more terror you inflicted. (Cusack & McDonald 2008:171)

It can, however, also be violence against its own members or those under their control in communities. Given the covert, secretive, solidaristic and sometimes precarious nature of insurgency, there can be prevalent suspicion if not paranoia, leadership struggles, infighting, ideological disputes, factionalisms, distrust, pervasive fear of infiltration and of informing and severe sanctions against those who are exposed as informers or traitors or those who fall under suspicion. If they are fighting for civil and human rights to be gained externally, they do not always comply with those same rights internally. With the IRA, for example, internal discipline measures, and so-called punishment beatings in the community, could be vicious, sadistic and fatal (Horgan 2005:50).

Furthermore, like nearly all who deviate from societal norms they feel obliged to justify and rationalise their conduct (Downes & Rock 2007). One rationalising device, or vocabulary of motive, is to perceive the violence as a justifiable part of a morally righteous cause; this conveys that the ends can always be held to justify the means. A de-legitimating device furthering this is to reverse the aggressor-victim dichotomy with the insurgents becoming the real victims (Sprinzak 1998:82). The founder of the Palestinian Hamas denied that his members were the aggressors; that was 'the number-one misunderstanding' because 'we are the victims' (Richardson 2006:65). Another reversion technique occurs almost universally among insurgents who vehemently reject the terrorist label but apply it instead to their enemy. The late Osama bin Laden stated in 1998, 'We believe the worst thieves in the world today and the worst terrorists are the Americans'. That enabled him to classify *all* Americans as the enemy and as justifiable targets, 'We do not differentiate between those dressed in military uniforms and civilians; they are all targets' (Hoffman 2006:97).

It is, then, the use of violence against innocent civilians, and others, which is the distinguishing mark of insurgent terrorism. Insurgents coldly and clinically employ human suffering and physical damage as a political tool, with a calculation on how many deaths and what sort of damage will serve the cause by reaching the media and influencing the authorities. Gerry Adams has said that he would have preferred no armed struggle, but that was precisely what provided '"the vital cutting edge. Without it the issue of Ireland would not be an issue". *Violence is what gives the IRA its importance*' (Bishop & Mallie 1998:449, my emphasis). And sometimes that armed struggle has effect and even 'astonishing success' as in Lebanon in the early 1980s (Kramer 1998:140); as Bloomfield puts it, 'Violence never pays? Cant' (Brock 2008). In short, insurgents kill, maim and destroy to get their way.

THE STATE AND COUNTER-INSURGENCY

A democratic state confronted with aggressive and determined insurgent terrorism faces a tough if not insuperable dilemma. Effectively, the insurgents have declared a form of civil war on the state and their goal is no less than regime change if not significant societal reform. However, during a counter-insurgency campaign there is the acute dilemma of a severe security threat demanding an immediate response yet having to remain within the rule of law. That many states fail and fall into abuses is clear. This illicit response may be understandable, but it conflicts with the conventional wisdom of the terrorism aficionados. In essence, their message is threefold:

- Learn as much as possible about your adversary because at some stage there will have to be a *political* solution.
- There can never be a purely military solution. But again, the state will almost inevitably react, if only initially, with a military response probably out of desperation in seeking swift measures to combat the insurgents.
- The key message is: if the state combats its adversary with illicit means it is abandoning the values, principles and practices of the democratic state, which is precisely what the insurgents want; it will play into their hands and prove counter-productive. The worst thing the representatives of the state can do, according to Richardson (2006 15), is to declare a 'war' on terrorism; '... given everything we know about the causes of terrorism and the motives of terrorists, the declaration of a global war on terrorism is a terrible mistake and a policy doomed to failure'.

In short, the historical evidence is that no insurgent movement has defeated and removed a well-established, democratic government. Attempts to do so have proved 'an almost total failure', but then no army in a democracy has brought about a military defeat against insurgents (Wilkinson 2005:25). This argues for a long-term, patient, multifaceted strategy; yet the politicians defending the state frequently feel obliged to react rapidly and with short-term, tough measures. They face the reality that insurgent terrorist movements can be smart, creative, resilient and tenacious adversaries. A relatively small and determined group can maintain a violent campaign for years that ties down a much larger conventional army.[16] The insurgent group can also win the political 'hearts and minds' battle among a population that remains or becomes sympathetic to its cause. And crucially it can maintain a relatively 'small' level of physical and psychological damage that nevertheless persuades a significant part of society that a solution has to be found to end the combat. Insurgents helped to remove two imperial powers, France and Britain, from several of their colonies; defeated the despotic rulers in Russia and China; overthrew right-wing regimes in Cuba, Nicaragua and Vietnam; forced the Americans and French to pull their forces out of Lebanon in 1983; brought the one-party, racist government in South Africa to the negotiating table; made Israeli forces withdraw from Southern Lebanon; pushed the invading Soviet forces out of Afghanistan; and forced the fall of the Shah in Iran, occupied the American Embassy in Teheran and held a group of Americans hostage for over a year.

In the last four decades, moreover, insurgents have drawn world-wide attention through sometimes spectacular operations with assassinations, abductions, skyjackings, sieges with hostage taking, suicide bombing, arson, kidnapping, sabotage and massive explosions. Insurgent groups always have the element of surprise and, even if they do not often achieve strategic goals, they can readily grab the headlines. Their tactics can achieve more than publicity alone. Insurgents have elicited concessions with sometimes-free passage out of a country following an operation or particularly the release of prisoners. Governments frequently state that they will never negotiate with terrorists but often do so covertly. This is perfectly illustrated by the Iran-Contra scandal. The American government was opposed to the Islamic regime in Iran and adamant about not doing deals with regimes held to be supportive of terrorism. And yet it was trying to transfer funds to groups in Iran that might persuade Islamic Jihad in Lebanon to release American hostages. The overriding argument used against this conduct is that a concession to insurgents by one government will work as encouragement to other insurgents. Yet of all nations the US gamekeeper was paying poachers to return the game.

Finally, there is another strong signal emanating from the material which is of relevance here and that is the vital role given to intelligence:

> But the key to success against terrorism in a democracy is winning the intelligence war and mobilising the political will and democratic support for a multi-pronged strategy, carefully calibrated to the specific threat posed by a particular campaign. (Wilkinson 2005:207)

Insurgent organisations are covert entities that cloak their activities in secrecy and are well aware of the efforts to penetrate them. Consequently they instruct their operatives in retaining secrecy and can also often rely on a strict rule of silence in the community that supports them (Wilkinson 2005:25). This forces security agencies to rely on SIGINT (signals intelligence), data from technical surveillance, but crucially on HUMINT (human intelligence) from informants, infiltration and undercover work. These are similar to the techniques employed in tackling serious organised crime or political crimes. And this opens up a notoriously murky area which is ripe for manipulation and dirty tricks (Marx 1988; Brodeur 1981, 1983).

This is important because the struggle in Northern Ireland was fought at diverse but interlinked levels. There was the political battle between the insurgents and the government, which was covert, vacillating and mostly not visible. There was the battle between the IRA and the conventional security forces, the RUC and the Green Army, which was to a degree visible. But there was also the battle between the IRA and the 'spooks' of the intelligence services and their proactive CIUs; this has been partly unravelled since the end of hostilities. The 'war' between the British state and the IRA was largely an intelligence war fought with the full gamut of dirty tricks, grubby hands and unfortunate victims.

This background can only convey that there is no 'magic bullet' and no quick fix when it comes to coping with insurgent terrorism. In brief, the message is for states to think long term, to anticipate a political solution, not to rely solely on a military strategy, to focus on sound intelligence and solid police work, to seek out the vulnerabilities of the opponent, to mount a sophisticated counter-campaign at diverse levels and keep channels of communication open for possible negotiations. And, above all, *abide by the law*. In effect that last powerful message is reflected in the remainder of this book. Did Britain abandon those principles of the liberal democratic state during the Troubles in Northern Ireland; and if so, to what effect and with what consequences?

3
Roots of the Troubles:
Emergency Context: Conspiracy?

We are NOT British, WE ARE IRISH. We will not willingly serve under British rule. England for the English and Ireland for the Irish. Is that unreasonable? (IRA spokesperson). (English 2004:126)

During a 30-year period (1968–98), Northern Ireland experienced prolonged turbulence and extensive violence in a form of civil strife. The Troubles cost some 3,800 lives with an estimated 40,000 people injured (McKittrick & McVea 2001). Many families – of police officers, soldiers, members of the emergency services, politicians, judges, paramilitary activists and of ordinary people with no involvement in the conflict – suffered variously from death or injury to a relative or close acquaintance, to having a relative incarcerated, to being forced to move home and/or to experiencing long-term psychological problems. In this chapter I shall examine the roots of that grim conflict, which caused so much suffering and physical damage, to pose what precipitated it; how did the Province became in effect a 'war zone'; and what was behind a disturbing range of incidents with persistent reports of state deviance and violence?

Those incidents involved especially the fatal shooting in highly suspicious circumstances of suspected IRA insurgents, alleged insurgents and republican/nationalist sympathisers by the police and military together with violence by loyalist paramilitaries against nationalists and Catholics. The phrase 'shoot to kill' entered the Northern Ireland political lexicon and was used to refer to the possibility of illegal actions including effectively extra-judicial executions with state collusion. This will be examined in the following chapters. Here I wish to sketch the context in which those controversial incidents took place and raise the issue as to whether or not there is evidence of some form of conspiracy to explain them.

HISTORICAL ROOTS

I wonder who *does* understand the place? Not the natives, certainly, for the two parties so hate each other that neither can view the simplest proceedings of the other without distrusting, falsifying and abusing it. To have an opinion about Ireland one must begin by getting at the truth; and where is that to be had in this country? Or rather, there are two truths, the Catholic truth and the Protestant truth. (Thackeray in 1843; Johnson 1980:83)

The key element in explaining the intensity and duration of the Troubles has to be found in the nature of the socio-political context shaped by deep historical forces. And the Irish, it is said, have a preoccupation with the past (Mulcahy 2006:48). This undeclared, ethno-religious, post-colonial, near civil war remains a painful and poignant memory. And many of the insurgents were not professional soldiers fighting in uniform abroad at the legitimate behest of their state but were ordinary citizens of the UK, or Ireland, killing fellow citizens, and members of the UK security forces, on UK soil. So how did the situation deteriorate to such an extent that normal democratic and political processes failed and that the members of diverse groups set out to kill one another?

The roots lie deep in the history of the island, reaching back some 700 years, with the key themes being poverty and hunger, religion, immigration, disdain for the English, rebellion and martyrdom. There is a pattern of Irish revolt against English rule from Elizabethan times and of forceful repression from the mainland. Oliver Cromwell figures prominently as an Irish folk demon for his violent campaign of 1649 and ruthless sacking of Drogheda. The subjugation of the Irish nobility and the confiscation of their lands, moreover, led to the 'planting' of English and Scottish Protestants, especially in the Northern counties, and this brought two widely divided ethnic and religious groups to live uneasily cheek by jowl. Catholic Ireland was also seen as the 'back door' for foreign intervention – as Castro's Communist Cuba became to the US – by the French, Spanish and 'Papists'; and later militant Irishmen sought support from England's enemy, Germany, in two world wars. A defining moment was the defeat of the Catholic King James II, who had fled abroad and returned with foreign supporters, at the Battle of the Boyne in 1690 by the Protestant William III, the Dutch Prince of Orange and King of England. That date has become the defining moment for Protestants and it is annually celebrated in Northern Ireland with much bombast. The defeat also led to further incursions by Protestant settlers and to discriminatory laws against Catholics. This created what became the 'Irish problem' of a Catholic peasantry, a

Protestant ruling class, with a Protestant enclave in Ulster and with separate communities divided by religion, race and culture; 'they learned different poetry, sang different songs, celebrated different victories, mourned different calamities' (Johnson 1980: 54).

Furthermore, the island witnessed a number of attempts at armed insurrection. Wolfe Tone brought the ideas of the French Revolution to Ireland and led a rebellion with French support; he stated, 'the truth is, I hate the very name of England. I hated her before my exile and I will hate her always' (Johnson 1980:68). The hostility was accentuated by the imposition of union with Britain in 1801, which abolished a form of de facto independence. This ignited support for nationalism and fanned the desire for independence. The nineteenth and early twentieth centuries also saw several parliamentary efforts to gain 'Home Rule' for Ireland fail when at times independence seemed almost within Ireland's grasp. Later, Home Rule was again postponed with the advent of World War I (WWI) in 1914, leaving the Irish to think that independence was only a matter of time.

But Irishmen have turned periodically to violence in the past. There was the founding of the Irish Republican Brotherhood or 'Fenians' in 1858 in the US and the movement also sprang up in Ireland. Irish-based Fenians then conducted attacks on the British mainland. British politicians became distraught about coping with the intransigent Irish and the intractable Irish problem. The Lord Lieutenant of Ireland lamented to Prime Minister Disraeli after the Fenian scare of the 1880s, 'Ireland is an infernal country to manage ... I wish you would send me to India. Ireland is the grave of every reputation' (Johnson 1980:113).

Frustration at the failure to bring about Home Rule eventually sparked off the Easter Rising of 1916 in Dublin and, after the end of WWI, the War of Independence against the English of 1919–21. The poorly supported Rising in 1916 was swiftly crushed and its leaders executed, becoming instant martyrs. The subsequent guerrilla war aimed at British forces elicited some vicious reprisals by the infamous Black and Tans and the Auxiliaries, two irregular British units recruited for the Irish campaign. A particularly serious incident occurred when English soldiers shot into the crowd at a Gaelic football match in Dublin killing 14 as a reprisal for attacks on English secret agents (English 2004:19). This period promoted a romantic legacy of tiny Ireland courageously taking on the mighty British Empire with its vicious soldiers and forcing Albion to negotiate. Ireland's Declaration of Independence following the 1918 elections, when the electorate overwhelmingly supported *Sinn*

Fein candidates, was a fervent expression of national identity and a pledge to fight for independence:

> In the name of the Irish people, we humbly commit our destiny to Almighty God, Who gave our fathers the courage and determination to persevere through long centuries of ruthless tyranny, and, strong in the justice of the cause ... we ask his Divine Blessing on this the last stage of the struggle we have pledged ourselves to carry through to freedom. (Solomons 1966:5)

Following the truce of 1921, an Irish delegation negotiated in London on the assumption of withdrawal of British troops and full independence for an Ireland of all 32 counties. The Government of Ireland Act (1920), however, proposed partition into two home rule entities in the North and South; but this was ostensibly only temporary while the border had yet to be drawn. The unionists in the North saw this as de facto recognition but the republican-minded South rejected it. The British negotiators were acutely aware of the possibility of armed resistance to Home Rule from the Protestant loyalists; and were mindful of losing the industry in the North and access to the Atlantic. The loyalist leaders Craig and Carson had led some 500,000 Protestant unionists in 1912 in signing a Covenant in Belfast to defend the union, had raised some 80,000 members of the paramilitary UVF a year later, and had large quantities of arms and ammunition smuggled into the Province. There was also vociferous support from Conservatives on the mainland and a clear willingness to come to the aid of the unionist cause. Effectively the UVF was an 'army' which would have taken 'even the British Imperial army years and rivers of bloodshed to defeat' (Cusack & McDonald 2008:37). Faced by this groundswell of opposition to a united Ireland the Boundary Commission drew a line which preserved six of the nine counties of Ulster in the North and ensured a solid, permanent Protestant majority. This dubious administrative exercise bequeathed Ireland a volatile post-colonial legacy with an inbuilt potential for conflict.

The London treaty led to the formal founding of the 'Irish Free State' within the British Commonwealth in 1923. But there emerged strong dissatisfaction with this compromise which divided Ireland and created a separate 'state' in the North. Civil War broke out between the treaty and anti-treaty factions and although the anti-treaty faction lost the Civil War it later regained ground though the politically dominating Eamonn De Valera and his new

Fianna Fail party created in 1926. Under his powerful influence in government from 1932 onwards, there emerged a strongly nationalist, republican society that effectively became a republic in 1935 (formally in 1949). It drew on the myths and icons of the Easter Rising, the War of Independence, on Catholicism and on Irish culture, sports and language; in short, 'Irishness' with a strong antipathy to 'Englishness' (Solomons 1966:5).

Importantly, there was a firm determination never to recognise the legitimacy of the Northern Ireland rump 'state'. Indeed, Article 3 of the Irish constitution claimed sovereignty over a united Ireland and this long remained a bone of contention in the North (Boyle & Hadden 1985). There remained, too, the continued albeit sporadic threat of armed insurgents mounting cross-border raids from the Republic. The last IRA campaign before the Troubles began in the late 1950s, but was called off by the IRA in 1962 – just a few years from the start of the Troubles. It was lamentably ineffective, with Bowyer Bell (1973:399) speaking of an 'almost unbroken record' of IRA failure.

START OF THE TROUBLES

Northern Ireland is at war with the Irish Republican Army Provisionals.
(Chichester-Clark, Prime Minister of Northern Ireland, speaking on television in 1971) (Geraghty 2000:40)

In the North, there was then effectively a one-party state since the early 1920s based on Protestant, unionist dominance. Its first Prime Minister, Sir James Craig, had boldly pronounced, 'We are a Protestant Parliament and Protestant state'. Many Catholics felt that they were second-class citizens due to forms of official and unofficial 'apartheid'. Yet the Protestant majority displayed a constant fear of being abandoned by Britain and developed a defensiveness based on the prospect of becoming a beleaguered and vulnerable minority should the Province ever be absorbed within a united Ireland. 'Doomsday' for them was to witness a British withdrawal (Ryder 2000:12); and 'in their heart of hearts' they increasingly sensed that Britain had an exit strategy (Cusack & McDonald 2008:227). The culture and identity of the loyalists was, then, defensive and backward looking, rather like the Afrikaners in South Africa or the white supremacists in the Deep South of the US. Their rhetoric drew on:

- *Unswerving loyalty* to the Protestant, unionist cause through the institutions of the Orange Lodges and the rituals of dominance in the annual Marching Season.
- *Demonisation* of the Catholic government in Dublin, the Pope in the Vatican, while any enemy of unionism was vilified.
- *Sacrifice*: The Reverend Ian Paisley, a preacher and hard-line unionist with considerable political power, would often recall the blood sacrifice of 'Ulstermen' in wars on behalf of Britain.
- *Pride*: in their particular 'Irish' identity along with identification with 'Britishness' and its totemic symbols (the Crown and Union Jack).

But in this dichotomous world of inclusion and exclusion – 'us and them' and 'if you are not for us you are against us' – the loyalists were rather dour and uncompromising. Their mindset was rooted in terms of blind loyalty or treacherous betrayal. In the 'zero-sum' game of Northern Ireland politics, any concession to one of the parties could only be seen as disadvantageous to the other and hence to be opposed virulently, with blustering, verbal venom and threats of violence which could spill over into real violence (Mulcahy 2006:159).

This was not the soil for compromise and reconciliation. Moreover, the divisions within the unionist/loyalist cause itself always meant that the moderates would have to battle with the die-hards. When Margaret Thatcher signed the Anglo-Irish Agreement in 1985, proposing that the South would have a say in the affairs of the North, the unionists were furious. The Prime Minister was a committed opponent of the IRA but nevertheless became 'Mrs Traitor' overnight. And the RUC, seen traditionally as 'our' police force by the unionists, became vilified and even subject to physical attack when it endeavoured to intervene impartially between the warring factions. Chief Constable Hermon came in for much abuse from loyalists and was referred to as an 'enemy of Ulster' (Ryder 2000:257). Paisley's inflammatory rhetoric, bordering on subversion, can be judged by his reaction to the RUC blocking of Orange marches:

> If the RUC are going to push the tricolour [flag of the Irish Republic] and Dublin down our necks and be used as the stooges of Dublin, then the whole might of Protestant resistance will be brought against them. If they are going to put us in the Free State in a clandestine way, and the RUC is going to be the weapon,

then the RUC and anyone who stands in our way is going to be opposed. *It's going to be a battle to the death.* (Ryder 2000:320, my emphasis)

This one-party state, representing primarily the interests of the Protestant majority, with security forces used to doing its bidding in repressing dissent and with an implacable hostility to its southern neighbour, was hardly the soil for compromise in 1968. But there was a window of opportunity when the Campaign for Social Justice and then the NICRA began to lobby for reforms. NICRA was initially not radical in its demands and did not openly propagate a united Ireland. There could have been negotiations, compromise and gradual change; after all, many demands were to bring the Province in line with the rights long established on the mainland and elsewhere in Europe, such as 'one person, one vote'. But the unionists view was that 'giving in' would lead to radical change to their permanent disadvantage and saw NICRA as a front for nationalist, republican elements. And there is evidence that the IRA played a significant role in promoting NICRA and providing protection for it. Furthermore, a number of UVF shootings and bombings had taken place in 1966, two years before the acknowledged start of the Troubles to coincide with the 50th anniversary of the Easter Rising, and again in 1969. But these were falsely attributed to the IRA so that loyalists already helped to destabilise the situation by planting the spectre of a newly active IRA (Cusack & McDonald 2008).

What took Northern Ireland into the abyss was, then, a cumulative number of savage hammer blows:

- The first was the attacks on civil rights demonstrators in 1968 with the RUC clubbing crowds in Derry during a banned march and later at Burntollet Bridge in 1969 with off-duty B Specials assaulting peaceful marchers. The Cameron Inquiry into the Derry disturbances concluded that, 'while an extremist section of the crowd wished to provoke violence with the police, the baton charge was premature, uncontrolled and ill-conducted' with damaging pictures of RUC violence seen throughout the UK and abroad' (Ryder 2000 105). These included oft-repeated images of a senior officer laying into people 'uninhibitedly' with a long blackthorn stick, 'wild-eyed and almost out of control' (McKittrick & McVea 2001:41).
- The second was when Protestant mobs attacked Catholic homes in Belfast in the summer of 1969, with assistance

from B Specials and sometimes with RUC officers as passive spectators.

- The third was when the British Army proclaimed a non-statutory 'curfew' in the Falls area of Belfast in 1970, which almost amounted to imposing martial law (Campbell & Connolly 2003:344).
- The fourth was when the IRA re-armed and went on the offensive with appalling casualties in the early years when both OIRA and PIRA were involved; the peak year for violence was 1972.
- The fifth was internment without trial, which was clumsily implemented and ineffective, and at first limited entirely to republicans while many of those lifted had no active involvement with the IRA. Also, some detainees were 'subjected to sleep and food deprivation, wall-standing, hooding, and "white-noise"' (Campbell & Connolly 2003:360). The use of internment rebounded on the authorities and greatly benefited the IRA; it 'barely damaged the IRA's command structure and led to a flood of recruits, money and weapons' (Parker 2007:160).
- The sixth was Bloody Sunday when the British Army shot dead unarmed civilians during a demonstration in Derry. It worked as a fund-raiser and recruiting sergeant for the IRA, according to Gerry Adams.
- The seventh was when in 1972 the Army entered the so-called 'no-go' areas of Derry and Belfast with some 30,000 troops in 'Operation Motorman'. There were amphibious craft, helicopters, two armoured units and 27 infantry battalions in the largest deployment of troops since WWII: (Smith & Neumann 2005). This show of strength with much gunfire, liberal use of CS gas, mass house searches and 337 arrests was focused almost exclusively on Catholic/nationalist areas.
- The eighth was related to the deaths of unarmed IRA insurgents at the hands of the RUC or SAS where it appeared they had been 'executed' in Northern Ireland, but also on Gibraltar in 1988 (Moysey 2007; Punch 2010:15–19). There was a wave of violence against republicans and Catholics by loyalist paramilitaries.

The selective, heavy-handed imposition of order largely through a military solution helped sour the 'previously good relations' with the Army and alienated the Catholic/nationalist community from the military (Campbell & Connolly 2003:343). It very quickly became legitimate, if not an obligation, for young Catholic men to take up arms against what many viewed as this cruel army of occupation.

The impact of these eight factors meant that the already slender legitimacy of the state was totally undermined by these events as far as the Catholic minority was concerned. But this disillusionment drew on some seven centuries of friction and strife between the Irish and England. Although republicans drew variously on left-wing ideologies, a prime motivator was simply a feeling of national identity and cultural heritage; and for Catholics in the North being stuck in the wrong state, cut off from their own people in the South. In republican circles, this fed from the 1920s onwards a longing for a fully independent Ireland with withdrawal from the North of the British administration and its armed forces. Boyle and Hadden are clear that the failure to deal with the Northern Ireland problem between Partition and the commencement of the Troubles with reforms to bring the Province in line with the rest of the UK, was crucial to creating an inflammable situation:

> The abandonment of control over part of the UK to a local majority with minimal safeguards for the minority and the failure over more than fifty years to correct the ensuing abuses together justify a grave indictment of British policy for which Britain has always borne the ultimate responsibility. (Boyle & Hadden 1985:28)

That long legacy of suspicion, distrust and disappointment then aided in launching a campaign of death and destruction by nationalist, republican groups. In response to that violence some elements of the British security community resorted to systemic deviance with collusion from above but also from across the Irish Sea in Whitehall.

EMERGENCY SITUATION

> I never had to go looking for power. This is where Northern Ireland is different. You had more than you could use. If I thought the Security Forces needed an extra £10 millions, I could give it to them. That's power. I had power to let prisoners out of prison; power to keep them in; power to stop their visits and change their conditions ... I didn't have to go to Parliament for these ... There's no bloody democracy over there. That's why it works so well. I've never been happier. I had power. But one keeps very

quiet about it. (Michael Mates on his period as Northern Ireland Secretary, 1991–92; Geraghty 2000:132)

Although Northern Ireland was and is an intrinsic part of the UK, it has always had special significance since partition in the early 1920s. To many Irish nationalists and republicans this partition was viewed as illegitimate and stood in the way of a united Ireland. Underlying the violence, intimidation and discrimination against Catholics prior to and following partition the violence of the later Troubles was, then, a fundamental societal schism on the legitimacy of the Northern Ireland state. As Mulcahy (2006:5) puts it:

> Unionists and loyalists – overwhelmingly Protestant – assert that the state is a legitimate political entity that properly expresses the political outlook of the majority of the Northern Ireland population. Nationalists and republicans – overwhelmingly Catholic – claim that the Northern Ireland state is a malign and artificial creation based on the political expediencies of imperial retreat, and dependent for its survival on the dominance of the unionist community.

In many ways Northern Ireland was a 'tribal', sectarian society with deeply rooted divisions between Catholics and Protestants with regard to politics, religion, identity, culture, education and sport. There was a measure of devolved self-rule that the unionists dominated in the Parliament at Stormont, holding power continually since 1921. And, significantly, the police force of Northern Ireland, the RUC, was overwhelmingly Protestant; Catholics viewed it as the 'coercive arm of the Unionist Party' (Farrel 1980). Most of the B Specials (Reserve Constabulary) and its successor the UDR were Protestant. Membership of the UDR moreover was held to be compatible with membership of the Ulster Defence Association (UDA) that promoted unionist and Protestant interests until it was banned in 1992. Officers in the RUC could also join unionist 'Orange' lodges and RUC buildings displayed the Union flag on the 12th July which initiated the start of the 'marching season'. This marching season is concentrated in July and August, and in a year might reach 3,000 parades of which the majority were and are 'orange' (Ryder 2000:319). The predominantly Protestant and unionist Orange Order had long expressed its supremacy through large and intimidating marches, often provocatively through Catholic, nationalist areas and not infrequently setting off disturbances.

Resulting from this political imbalance the Catholics/nationalists in the North increasingly felt that there was discrimination against them but especially in employment, voting regulations, housing allocation and through the manipulation of electoral boundaries to preserve Protestant majorities. The latter was known as 'gerrymandering' and it kept unionists in power in Derry despite a Catholic majority. And for nationalists there were restrictions on displaying Ireland's national tricolour flag in public under the Flags and Emblems Act 1954 and on giving streets Irish names. In the second half of the 1960s, stimulated by the demands for social reform emanating from social movements in the US, on the Continent and in Britain, a largely but not exclusively Catholic civil rights movement, NICRA, emerged in 1967. Along with the Campaign for Social Justice and PD, NICRA called for an end to the discriminative practices. This broad movement for civil rights met fierce Protestant opposition and police obstruction during peaceful demonstrations, with some off-duty B Specials taking part in aggressive confrontations. During the PD march from Belfast to Derry in January 1969, for example, the marchers were savagely ambushed by loyalists at Burntollet Bridge.

This pushed matters 'over the edge', according to Conor Cruise O'Brien (the Irish politician and writer). For this was a defining moment when an ostensibly moderate movement, that included some Protestants and did not openly propagate Irish unity, was met with loyalist violence, police baton charges and water cannon. Yet each over-reaction by the authorities simply elicited a larger turnout the next time. One of the movement's leaders understood this and admitted the aim was, 'to provoke the police into an overreaction and thus spark off a mass reaction': the Cameron Report (1969) spoke of 'calculated martyrdom' (Geraghty 2000:366). But this is a dangerous game and the leader had overestimated the 'animal brutality' of the RUC (Bishop & Mallie 1988:76).

English (2004:90–1), furthermore, argues that there is evidence that NICRA drew on republican roots and was implicitly anti-unionist; 'there was a direct, causal, practical and ideological connection between the 1960s IRA and the civil rights initiative'. And the *Sinn Fein* leader Gerry Adams stated that republicans were 'central to the formation of NICRA' and the movement was 'a creation of the republican leadership', which might be overstating the case (McKittrick & McVea 2001:44). But the marches can be viewed as potentially provocative and even counter-productive; 'despite the reasonable intentions of most of its supporters, the civil rights movement of the north unintentionally helped to produce a descent into awful and lasting violence' (English 2004:99). Derry and Burntollet ignited the conflict.

There was a long tradition of Protestant reprisals at moments of turbulence to intimidate the Catholics (Cusack & McDonald 2008). But in this inflammatory situation in the summer of 1969 many Catholic families faced especially violent harassment in Belfast from Protestant gangs. Some 1,600 Catholic families were forced out of their homes, as indeed were 350 Protestant families, and with entire streets burning there were seven deaths and 750 injuries resulting from the violence. Some observers maintained that B Specials were involved in the collective violence and that RUC officers conspicuously did not hasten to intervene:

> In 1968–9 men within both the RUC and B Specials not only demonstrated a hatred of the nationalist community but showed exactly where their loyalties lay. This was no more clearly illustrated than in West Belfast, where Loyalist mobs were allowed and even assisted by some members of the RUC and B Specials to burn Catholic homes and loot shops. I remember as a journalist watching policemen stand idly by while Loyalists set alight Catholic-owned business premises in North Belfast. (Dillon 1991:209)

The Irish government moved troops to the North with the possibility of crossing the border to protect Catholic enclaves, Irish soldiers gave weapons training to IRA members and Irish field hospitals were established. But much of this was posturing because the Irish Army of the time was impoverished, badly equipped and poorly clad (McKittrick & McVea 2001:59). If it had come to a confrontation the Irish soldiers – in worn-out great-coats and carrying vintage Lee Enfield rifles inherited from the British (according to two former British soldiers I spoke to) – would have been out-matched by the British Army.

These turbulent events accentuated the territorial divisiveness in a number of towns with the RUC increasingly facing hostile 'no-go' areas in Catholic communities such as the self-proclaimed 'Free Derry'. The British government agreed in August 1969 to send in the Army once law and order were deemed to have broken down. This made it legally different to 'military aid to the civil power', known as ' MACP', when military aid is requested by the police for a specific incident and limited period (Punch 2010). Also, the Police Service in Britain had turned down a request to send British 'Bobbies' to the Province. But in this turbulent situation the Army could also be seen to have an independent right under common law to intervene to restore order. Indeed, a Belfast magistrate ruled, in adjudicating on cases arising from the Falls Road curfew in Belfast in 1970, that every soldier had a common law duty to suppress riot 'by every means in his power'. But martial law had not been declared and the soldiers did not enjoy the legal immunity of the battlefield, so they could be prosecuted for crimes arising from their actions. This ambiguity became a major source of frustration among soldiers and, according to Geraghty (2000:39–40), set the scene for Bloody Sunday.

Initially the Army was welcomed by Catholics, because the overstretched and demoralised RUC was widely distrusted and deeply resented by many in nationalist areas. For example, the RUC had overreacted to what they saw as an incipient republican uprising by mounting machine-guns on Shorland armoured cars and firing indiscriminately; some tracer bullets hit the Divis flats in a Catholic area of Belfast killing a nine-year-old boy. In Derry the RUC had withdrawn to recuperate from sustained rioting and had allowed the B Specials to move in wielding pick-handles. British troops from the mainland, it was hoped, would be restrained and impartial. The 'entire Stormont security system had been discredited' and for a time the British Army was perceived as the 'only legitimate authority' (Bowyer Bell 1973:408). But having British soldiers policing the streets was a highly emotive issue for some nationalists and the relationship between the military and the Catholic population soon deteriorated.

At first the Army was fairly neutral and pragmatic, but when the soldiers went on the offensive in republican no-go areas they did so in force. There followed 'axeing down doors, ripping up floorboards, disembowelling chairs, sofas, beds and smashing the garish plaster statues of the Madonna, the Infant of Prague and Saint Bernadette that adorned the tiny front parlours' (Bishop & Mallie 1988:159). Soldiers from Scottish regiments in particular were thought to be anti-Catholic while paratroopers were especially disliked for their perceived aggression and heavy-handedness. Moreover, Collins' (1999) account of paratroopers raiding his family home with much verbal abuse and damage, mentioned in Chapter 2, makes the important point that this helped convert him to the IRA movement. IRA recruitment was enhanced by the roughness of parts of the Army and by the abuses attributed to the military (Ryder 2000:157; Smith & Neumann 2005).

The grim developments of 1969 also led to the almost defunct IRA splitting. Its new activist wing, the Provisional IRA, took up arms to defend Catholic areas against further attacks from Protestant mobs. The other remaining wing became known as the Official IRA. Indeed, if the 1968 marches were initially instrumental in igniting the conflagration then Belfast in August 1969 signalled the real opening of hostilities:

> It can be said that the civil war started on the 14th [August 1969]. That night extremists of both sides and B-specials, an auxiliary – largely Protestant police force, went on a spree of shooting and arson ... The spectacle of Bombay Street, between the Protestant Shankill and the Catholic Falls Roads, burning from end to end, signalled the total inability of Stormont to enforce law and order or to protect the citizenry ... In 1969 the Official IRA in the north was advocating political change and eschewing violence. Yet the very violence of 1969 undermined its authority; out of the ashes of Bombay Street arose the Provisional IRA. (McWhinney, British politician from the Province, quoted in English 2004:108)

The IRA first openly brandished weapons during the PD/NICRA march from Belfast to Derry in January 1969 (Dillon 1991:4). But loyalists definitely began the chain of violence in the second half of the 1960s, declaring 'war' on the IRA in 1966 and declaiming, 'Known IRA men will be executed mercilessly and without hesitation ... We are heavily armed Protestants dedicated to this cause' (Bishop & Mallie 1988:62).

Before the split, the IRA was poorly armed and badly prepared; some referred to it disparagingly as 'I Ran Away' after the failure to parry the attacks on Catholics in Belfast. It had become geared to avoiding confrontations with the military and was determined not to resort to sectarianism. This stance initially paralysed the movement but in reality the IRA leaders could hardly mount a defence with only about 60 members in Belfast in 1969 and ten in Derry. Most no longer took part in military training and there were only about six old weapons in the Northern Ireland arsenal (Bishop & Mallie 1988:106f).[1] Furthermore OIRA abandoned its campaign of violence in 1972, making PIRA the main terrorist organisation taking on the security forces.

There began a state of persistent and violent civil strife. In the bloodiest year, 1972, some 500 people died and the IRA killed around 100 soldiers and wounded 500. The largest number of fatalities of any incident in Northern Ireland occurred, however, after the GFA had formally ended hostilities. On a busy Saturday in 1998 in Omagh, a car bomb exploded in the main street: 29 people were killed, including two Spanish tourists (OPONI 2005). This atrocity was attributed to the dissident Real IRA. During the Troubles there was no sustained loyalist campaign in the South, but in 1974 in the Republic 33 people died during bomb attacks by the UVF in Dublin and Monaghan; with nearly 300 injured, this was the highest number of casualties in a single day throughout the Troubles (Barron Report 2003). The British armed forces, moreover, were to lose over 700 personnel with more than 6,000 injured during the Troubles; combined with police fatalities, including on the mainland, this put all security agencies deaths at 1,048 (CAIN:2011c).[2] The Army bore the brunt of these casualties in the longest running campaign in its history (Operation Banner), officially leaving the Province in 2007 after 38 years.

Throughout the Troubles there were protests and riots, inter-community violence, hunger strikes, arson attacks against commercial premises, pubs and private houses, torture, kidnappings, armed robberies and many assassinations and bomb explosions, primarily in Northern Ireland but also in the Republic, mainland Britain (including Birmingham, Warrington, Manchester and London) and occasionally on Continental Europe. There were three main protagonists on the ground; the RUC along with the British Army and the Security Service; the IRA; and a number of Protestant paramilitary groups including the UVF and UDA.

WAR ZONE

Although Northern Ireland was and is an integral part of the UK, it was clear that quite different rules applied than on the mainland. In terms of the law and police procedures it was almost like a foreign country according to Stalker (1988), the British police officer who carried out an inquiry into controversial shootings by the RUC (see Chapters 4 and 6). Indeed, police officers from the mainland carried no legal authority in the Province. This exceptional situation was plain in the formal arrangements with draconian emergency legislation under the Civil Authorities (Special Powers) Act of 1922, which remained permanently on the statute book (Hillyard 1987).

The Act allowed arrests without warrant, internment without trial, unlimited search powers, bans on meetings and publications with some 'catch-all' phrases to cover other eventualities (McKittrick & McVea 2001:11). There were, moreover, 'Diplock' courts with single judges and no juries from 1973; internment without trial; the use of 'super-grasses',[3] informants with considerable inside knowledge of insurgency and a willingness to name names in return for a deal with the authorities (such as immunity from prosecution); and legislation (Emergency Provisions Act 1973) granting soldiers powers of arrest for certain offences; and a constant security situation during almost three decades. At one point nearly 30,000 military personnel were on duty in the Province, along with an RUC which peaked at nearly 13,000 personnel (including reserve officers). This made the RUC the second largest force in the UK after the Met in London, and this in an area that would fit about 16 times within Great Britain (England, Scotland and Wales) and with a population of only 1.6 million.[4]

All of this was in stark contrast to the rest of the UK. For example, when I first flew to Northern Ireland to visit Belfast in the late 1970s from a peaceful and rampantly tolerant Netherlands, the situation I encountered was as follows. The plane landed at the then Aldergrove Airport, an RAF military airfield with a section set aside for civil flights and policed by the RAF Regiment. There was high wire netting to protect the airfield against missiles and the perimeter road was blocked to traffic. On the road into Belfast there was a permanent checkpoint with concrete guard-houses manned by soldiers and police. The much-bombed Europa Hotel in the centre of Belfast was surrounded by a fence and everyone had to enter a hut where their luggage was carefully searched. There was an Army surveillance helicopter constantly hovering over the city, and heavily armed police and army units patrolled the city streets in armoured vehicles. Police stations looked like fortresses with pill-boxes, reinforced gates and wire-netting against missiles. There were many gaps in commercial buildings following arson attacks. Every pub, place of entertainment and commerce had doormen searching bags on entry. The Belfast city-centre was fenced off, with shoppers entering through iron gates where their bags were inspected. On that first visit I drove to the Devil's Causeway and stopped in a town for lunch; the car had to be parked outside the town because there were obstacles along the main street as a measure against car bombs in the shopping area. This was plainly a society under siege and on a constant, pervasive security alert.

In effect, there was an unacknowledged 'war' going on. And it was a dirty war. War is of itself intrinsically dirty in that it is regulated barbarity and legalised slaughter (Ellis 1982). Yet it can be fought according to agreed rules of engagement and even with a measure of mutual respect. The rules are embodied in the laws of war, such as the four Geneva Conventions of 1949 and their two additional protocols of 1977; these are designed primarily to protect victims of war and in the main those fighters who are *hors de combat* and civilians. They also regulate the conduct of hostilities by, for instance, prohibiting certain forms of warfare and some types of weaponry as did the Hague Convention of 1899. These provisions apply only in international armed conflicts; that is to say, in formally declared wars between signatory states. This was not the case in Northern Ireland because this was an internal conflict in which the insurgents did not have combatant status and were, in the eyes of the law, committing common crimes. This also meant that the British state could not be accused of war crimes; but it could be held to account under human rights law, and particularly Article 2 of the European Convention on Human Rights espousing the right to life. And, of course, the UK had to abide by international laws on sovereignty.

It is then somewhat disturbing but most revealing that the British Cabinet in 1972 was proposing not only illegal incursions into a sovereign state, Ireland, but also a form of 'shoot to kill' policy that was at odds with British law. It was on Field Marshall Lord Carver's first day as Chief of the General Staff when a senior member of the Cabinet and a 'legal luminary', the Lord Chancellor (Lord Hailsham) no less, was suggesting he should order his forces to break both international law with incursions into Ireland and the criminal law by shooting rioters. Carver was 'appalled' and asked Premier Heath if he was prepared to stand in court to defend soldiers on a murder charge (Harding 2002). It indicates how bullish, or perhaps poorly informed or even panicky, the Conservative Cabinet then was and how the military had to deter them from rash action (Geraghty 2000:44).

But the sort of guerrilla-style warfare indulged in by many insurgents employing terrorism is played by other rules than the Geneva Convention. It uses both indiscriminate and/or selective violence against civilians – but also security forces, government officials, politicians and property – to create a climate of fear in society which is intended to bring about political change. Soldiers in contrast are supposed never purposely to target civilians directly in war situations (Luban 2011). This means the methods adopted by insurgents clearly do not comply with the conventional rules as formulated in international law and protocols. Acts of terrorism are, in fact, prohibited by the laws of war in international and non-international armed conflict. They are, furthermore, serious crimes under the national laws of states and gravely infringe people's human rights.

In the armed struggle under consideration, for instance, the IRA engaged in the following terrorist activities (I will indicate if PIRA was not involved):

- In the beginning of the campaign there were unannounced, random bomb attacks on innocent civilians with horrendous casualties, as in the Birmingham bombings of 1974 where two busy pubs frequented by young people were targeted. Some bombs had nails, bolts, jagged pieces of scrap metal and ammunition attached to them to cause severe wounds. The targets tended to be busy public places frequented by ordinary people, or else pubs often used by soldiers as in the Guildford and Woolwich bombings.
- Later attacks shifted largely to so-called 'hard' targets, related in some way to the security or political apparatus, or to symbolically important buildings (the Old Bailey Courts and the Houses of Parliament in London, the Criminal Courts in Belfast, Army Headquarters in Northern Ireland) and more often a warning was issued for other targets. There were, however, constant problems with warnings arriving too late, or not at all, confusion about the message, code words or location and also technical problems with timing devices.[5] Sometimes activists were nervous and in their panic neglected to phone the message (Collins 1998).
- Security forces personnel were especially targeted and soldiers were shot by snipers or police officers might be shot at home in their bed, in front of their children, on the church steps after a religious service or be blown to bits or severely mutilated by a bomb under their car; part-time members of the UDR were shot on their farms or in tractors while working the land. When the IRA began to target RUC and UDR members more than regular soldiers they were mostly attacked when they were off duty and presented easier targets.
- Some soldiers became victims of 'honey-pot' operations when enticed by young women to enter private houses where they

were apprehended and later murdered; or they were seemingly befriended by people in pubs who invited them to other premises only to kill them elsewhere.

- A member of the British royal family, Earl Mountbatten, was blown up on vacation in Ireland ('executed' according to the IRA).
- A Member of Parliament was blown up at Westminster within the Parliamentary precinct (by the INLA).
- A number of foreign business executives who represented welcome investment from abroad and the much-needed provision of jobs in the Province were killed.
- Prime Minister Thatcher and members of her Cabinet narrowly escaped death in a bomb attack on the Conservative Party's conference hotel in Brighton which killed five people; the IRA stated, 'Today we were lucky, but remember ... we only have to be lucky once; you have to be lucky always' (Taylor 2001:265).
- A number of mortar shells landed in the garden of 10 Downing Street in Whitehall while the Cabinet was in session inside the building.
- Then, when the security services started to have increasing success in the cities, the IRA escalated operations in the border area, especially 'bandit country' in South Armagh, and their tactics comprised long-range ambushes with modern firearms and remotely detonated road-side bombs, on occasion detonated from across the border, with booby traps or secondary explosions directed against security personnel attending to the casualties of the original explosion.
- Sometimes, by mistake, innocent people – the young, the old, the infirm, mothers with children and foreigners – became casualties. Civilians were forced to drive cars with 'proxy bombs' in them to places targeted for attack, on occasion dying in the subsequent explosion. Faulty intelligence or wrong identification could lead to 'mistakes', like shooting an innocent Catholic man mistaken for a member of the UDR (Collins 1998) or killing two Australian tourists in the Netherlands because they had short-hair and a British registered car, leading the IRA ASU to believe they were British soldiers.
- Then the IRA tortured and murdered its own members accused of informing[6] and other offences and dumped their bodies on the road-side (although a few were secretly buried). Of all the

paramilitaries, the IRA killed the largest number of its own members, 66 out a total of 74 for all paramilitary groups, and most of them were suspected informers (Mulcahy 2006:74). Following an internal 'trial' the victim's body would usually be left on the road naked, the hands bound, with tape around the eyes and several bullet wounds in the head: a folded bank-note would clearly indicate an informer. Audiotapes of 'confessions' were often sent to the victims' families.

- They also enforced 'civil administration' in the communities they controlled through banishment, punishment beatings and knee-capping with a pistol shot, electric drill or baseball bat. Certain people, like young women suspected of associating with the enemy – say through *collaboration horizontale* – were paraded around before being tarred and feathered and tied to a lamp-post with a warning message around their neck. A Belfast teenager was nailed to a wooden fence with metal spikes through his knees and elbows and one criminal gang member was shot in the arms, legs and ankles, and warned that further offences would lead to 'more serious' punishment (Dillon 1991:465). There are estimates of some 2,000 punishment shootings and beatings between 1973 and 1997 (English 2004:275).

For many years, then, this largely rural and scenic province, with ironically the lowest common crime rate in the UK, witnessed carnage and butchery which devastated many people's lives, scarred cities and impacted negatively on economic and social activity. There was an estimate of £25 billion damage to property. If the conflict had occurred on the same scale throughout the UK, this would have meant some 110,000 fatalities and around *one million* injured (Geraghty 2000:v). The impact on the much-targeted police was tangible when I visited the RUC in 1999, which was then facing re-branding including a name change following the GFA. There was a defiant poster on the wall in almost every office with the portraits of the over 300 RUC officers who had died in the Troubles. The list was 301 serving officers and 18 who had retired; some 9,000 had been injured. In the Met of London, that would have meant around 1000 officers killed or over 30 deaths a year. Indeed, figures published by Interpol in 1983 indicated that Northern Ireland was the most dangerous place in the world for police officers (Ryder 2000:2). In addition, some 70 RUC officers committed suicide during the Troubles. It is difficult to know how related these suicides were to work and the security situation, but there was clearly much stress and trauma (Mulcahy 2006:54; Simpson 2010).

There were many violent incidents by the IRA that deeply affected public opinion and I shall mention just a few to convey the scale of violence, how it overshadowed public life and, particularly, how it may have fostered feelings of revenge and retaliation among loyalist militants and the security forces. Some of the defining incidents can be attributed to the IRA but also to the security forces while others were the work of loyalist paramilitaries.

For instance, the 1975 UVF attack on the Miami Showband from the Republic, when three popular Irish musicians were shot dead, caused outrage throughout all Ireland and elicited a unique joint-statement from the Prime Ministers of Ireland and the UK expressing horror at the atrocity.[7] The violence was also often blatantly sectarian with Catholics deliberately targeted, as with the bombing of McGurks Bar in Belfast killing 15 people, but also extremely cruel. The beheading of victims may have become associated with jihadist groups but the notorious 'Shankill Butchers' in Belfast displayed comparable barbarity (Dillon 1990). One elderly victim of the 'Butchers' had been stabbed superficially about 150 times during a five-hour ordeal; his naked body was kept upright with a rope that eventually strangled him. Other victims had their throats cut (Cusack & McDonald 2008:175f). They have been described as behaving like serial killers and, usually following drink and drug sessions, they chose victims they simply assumed were Catholics (Moloney 2010).

However, my main focus shall be on IRA attacks as a backdrop to the climate sponsoring a violent response from the security services and the loyalist paramilitaries and aiding them in 'justifying' that response.

- In a 1972 attack by OIRA on the Parachute Regiment in Aldershot in retaliation for Bloody Sunday, there were seven fatalities; not soldiers but five female caterers, a gardener and a Catholic padre.
- On 'Bloody Friday' in 1972, the IRA set off 22 bombs in Belfast within a short space of time, killing 9 and wounding over 130 people.[8]
- In 1974 a bomb on a bus carrying military personnel and their families exploded on the M62 motorway in Britain, killing twelve people including an entire family (a soldier, his wife and two young children).

- In 1978 a fire-bomb devastated the La Mon House Hotel outside Belfast killing twelve guests including seven women and injuring many others, some with serious burns as the bomb formed a fire-ball after ignition
- In 1982 two attacks on one day in London killed seven army bandsmen giving a concert in Regents Park, and four members of the Household Cavalry and eight horses in Hyde Park.
- Also in 1982, a bomb at the Droppin Well disco in County Derry killed 17 people, including eleven off-duty soldiers.
- In 1983 an explosion at the Harrods store in London during the Christmas period killed five people, including two police officers.
- Nine RUC officers were killed when a mortar round hit the police station at Newry in 1985.
- An explosion on a mini-bus at Ballygawley killed eight soldiers; and six soldiers were blown up in their vehicle following a charity run in Lisburn.
- In Deal in Kent in 1989 eleven bandsmen of the Royal Marines were blown up.
- In 1993 an abortive attack on a supposed UDA meeting above a fish shop on the Shankill Road in Belfast killed nine Protestants in the shop as well as the bomber in a premature explosion.
- At Enniskillen in 1988, eleven people – ten civilians and an RUC officer (and all of them Protestants) – died following an explosion on Memorial Sunday, when people were gathering to honour the fallen of the Two World Wars. The IRA claimed its target was members of the security services who were to parade later, but the device had been prematurely activated by Army radio-signals.
- Although the IRA maintained that its campaign was non-sectarian, it appeared that their violence was often sectarian and aimed at Protestants. In 1976 ten Protestant workers were shot dead on their way from work (the Catholic driver of the van was allowed to leave the scene), and eight Protestants were blown up in 1992. In both cases they were targeted because they were allegedly involved in work for the military.

The importance of itemising these 'outrages' to some, but 'legitimate operations' to others, is threefold:[9]

- Firstly, they deeply offended notions held by many of some form of common decency or moral boundary when nationalists pursued legitimate and widely-shared political aims but then achieved them through unacceptable violence. Indeed, the IRA largely abandoned random attacks and selected what were considered 'legitimate' targets while making distinctions about the nature and timing of violence and issuing warnings. There were even occasional excuses from *Sinn Fein* for 'mistakes', including an apology for the Memorial Day bombing at Enniskillen.

- Within the security services, moreover, there probably was the understanding that police and soldiers were effectively on active service against insurgents with the risk of being killed in combating the IRA. But this informal awareness of the risk of suffering 'combat' casualties could hardly be extended to the deaths of innocent victims of random bombings or 'mistakes'. There was the Enniskillen bombing on Memorial Sunday, killing the ageing Mountbatten along with two youths and an elderly woman on the boat; and bombing a bus with military personnel including their spouses and children. These were rarely accepted by majority opinion in the UK and abroad as 'legitimate' targets; rather they generated widespread revulsion while among some people they fostered virulent hatred for the killers and a thirst for revenge.

- Secondly, this violence was aimed at changing a way of life held precious by many. This was a battle to force through a different society to that which the Protestant majority wanted to retain and for many loyalists they were engaged in a righteous struggle to protect a way of life threatened by pernicious forces that used evil means. To lose to them would deprive them of 'their state' and deliver them into the hands of a despised Catholic society. Part of the motivation for loyalists – in the paramilitaries, B Specials, UDR and RUC – was they were fighting a 'legitimate' war to preserve their society. This relates to the collusion that will be examined later.

- For, thirdly, there was a perception that however repulsive to many this gross violence was, it was also slowly winning concessions with the sour likelihood that it would eventually pay off. One former RUC SB officer states that he saw the writing on the wall when New Labour entered office in 1997; and 'Labour's victory ensured the IRA's victory' (Barker 2006:233). This reflects the feeling that so many concessions had been made to the IRA that it had come out on top in the struggle.

In fact the British government was prepared from early on to enter secret negotiations with the IRA insurgents, who in turn were ready to call occasional cease-fires. The Labour government of Harold Wilson (1964–70) was plainly anti-Unionist. Later in opposition Wilson met representatives of the IRA in Dublin in 1972 and also proposed a British withdrawal from Northern Ireland within 15 years (McKittrick & McVea 2001). Irish history is replete with 'almost there' moments that end in independence delayed or settlement postponed and with failures to capitalise on windows of opportunity. Perhaps a re-elected Labour government in 1970 would have cracked the nut and reached a settlement. But even a Conservative government was prepared to fly an IRA delegation in a Royal Air Force plane to London for talks in 1972. Amazingly, Gerry Adams was temporarily released from prison for the trip and Martin McGuinness was included although he was on the run. The IRA overplayed its hand in London with brash demands and left feeling the British were offering more than in fact they could in reality ever deliver. Attempts to find a political solution in the Sunningdale Agreement of 1973 and the Anglo–Irish Agreement of 1985 did, however, contain concessions to the 'Irish' dimension and the right of Ireland's government to be consulted on the future of the island. This in itself was anathema to many hard-line unionists. Indeed, Sunningdale was swiftly undermined by massive industrial action from unionists.

For many unionists, locked into their reactionary belief in the *status quo ante* fuelled by fear of abandonment by Britain, the writing was already on the wall with that first cease-fire, when it emerged that IRA leaders had been flown to London for talks. That angst was reinforced with the imposition of direct rule from London in 1972 with the Stormont Parliament in abeyance; and this was 'their' Parliament as no Catholic party had ever shared in government. From 1972 onwards, their affairs and even their police would come under the direction of Whitehall. And concern grew with what was seen not only as a slowly escalating stream of concessions to Dublin but also to the republican movement. The IRA's armed campaign gradually shifted to more of a focus on political ends as *Sinn Fein* became more prominent, took part in local elections, recognised the *Dáil* (Irish Parliament), stood in elections in Ireland and sought election to Westminster. The hunger-striker Bobby Sands won a seat in the British Parliament from his prison cell; but no nationalist would ever enter Westminster and swear allegiance to the Crown. However, the hunger strikes provided a turning point as nationalists realised they could be successful at the polls (Collins 1998:210). Although the hunger-strikes were abandoned, Geraghty (2000:101) views them as a 'brilliant political success' exemplifying the IRA's use of a 'varied arsenal ... psychological and political warfare as well as urban terrorism and guerrilla warfare ... in a loosely orchestrated, extemporised fashion that always kept its opponents off balance'. Eventually the republicans of *Sinn Fein* even took part in governing the Province. This culmination of the armed struggle and its accompanying political campaign led to yet another division within the IRA, between the hardliners and those willing to negotiate, as it had done in the 1920s, between the men of action and the 'politicians' (Moloney 2010).

The bitter pill for many loyalist and British hardliners was, then, that the terrorists could be seen to be gradually winning ground through their campaign with the car bomb, semtex, Armalite and ballot box, and would eventually share power as elected politicians in a devolved government. Following the GFA, the RUC was replaced with the PSNI; convicted terrorists (from both sides) were released from prison with an amnesty; and former republican activists were sitting down to govern among their former enemies at Stormont, once the bastion of Protestant hegemony. There was an unpalatable and galling truth for those who saw themselves as the 'losers' in this struggle; that sometimes insurgent violence gains significant concessions even if the sought after 'victory' eluded the nationalists. Many loyalists considered that British governments had proved to be appeasers and that they had allowed violence to succeed; this was an incentive for them to defend their way of life by resorting to violence.

CONSPIRACY?

The historical roots in Ireland and contributing factors in Northern Ireland outlined above shaped the context in which the Troubles ignited and were sustained. There emerged a vicious circle of escalation in which IRA violence nourished unionist intransigence and loyalist reprisals; and security forces excesses 'justified' an even more daring and damaging response from the IRA. Indeed, a persistent theme throughout the Troubles was accusations of deviance within the security community. 'Shoot to kill', for instance, was used to refer to the possibility of illegal actions including effectively extra-judicial executions with state collusion. A key related matter was how these illicit activities were articulated, and if there was some form of conspiratorial 'policy' on this and, if so, how high did it reach?

A much used metaphor when describing an individual's pathway into deviance or crime is the 'slippery slope' (Downes & Rock 2007). This conveys imagery that, once on the slope, the individual will go on irreversibly 'sliding'. This starts a process where what was initially deviant, and troublesome to the conscience, becomes routine as the person passes a psychological point of no return. This slide into routinisation and rationalisation has been noted among many deviant groups including corrupt police officers where illicit practices become engrained and accepted (Punch 2009). Here I apply the imagery of the slippery slope also to institutions. Of course, individuals within a collective have to take ostensibly autonomous decisions; but within institutions there is collective behaviour with pressure to conform according to common understandings. Each individual has to acquiesce in this, but compliance is powerfully influenced by group processes and organisational pressures. Examples of this collective immersion and acceptance of illegal conduct were given above for South Africa, Spain and India. 'Extra-judicial executions', for instance, are abhorrent to western eyes and are antithetical to the espoused philosophy and practice in democratic societies where the state's monopoly of violence is embedded in the rule of law. A central pillar of the democratic state is, indeed, the promise that it will only employ violence against its own citizens which is legitimate, justifiable, proportional and, above all, subject to judicial accountability.

Yet we know from a wealth of evidence that in practice both governments and their official agencies deviate from the rule of law and from agreed procedures to engage, occasionally or frequently, in deviant or illicit behaviour while also endeavouring to evade accountability (Ermann & Lundman 1982). Behind what Reisman (1979) calls the 'myth system', the formal façade of the responsible and accountable state, there exists an 'operational code' as to how rule-bending and rule-breaking is covertly constructed, justified and managed. And it appears difficult for any government, however 'clean' in its intentions, not to get 'dirty hands' at some stage. An illuminating example of very dirty hands, accentuated by persistent denials, is that of France sending secret agents in 1985 to disable the Greenpeace ship the 'Rainbow Warrior' in the waters of a friendly nation, New Zealand.

Teams from the French secret service mounted an operation in Auckland Harbour to plant bombs on the ship to prevent it being used to protest French nuclear tests in the Pacific. The operation went badly wrong when a crew member drowned in the half-submerged vessel. The conspiracy began to unravel, however, with the apprehension of two of the French agents leading to questions being raised on who had ordered the covert mission and, indeed, who else knew about it. In reaction to such a damaging scandal it is often part of the defensive institutional processes of secrecy, evasion, track covering, manipulation of evidence and the mechanisms of *deniability*, that it may long remain unclear who precisely was involved, who knew of it and who was ultimately responsible. Typically, the tell-tale footprints in the sand are erased and highly-placed officials are shielded. However, following leaks from members of the security service it emerged that Minister of Defence Hernu had ordered the operation and he resigned; later, however, it was revealed that President Mitterand himself had approved the plot (King 1986; Bremner 2005). This case exemplifies a carefully fabricated and fully intended conspiracy at the highest level of the state.

Was this, then, the case in Northern Ireland that the British government engaged in a *deliberate* conspiracy to kill suspected insurgents? We may never know the full story or will have to wait some time to gain access to key documents. Some of these are embargoed forever because of 'national security' reasons, while some have simply disappeared in the shredding machine. Some participants have passed on and many of those questioned later have highly selective recollections or chronic amnesia. Was it perhaps not so much a fully articulated conspiracy in Northern Ireland, but more a constellation of factors taking certain actors down an institutional 'slippery slope' to what can be interpreted as extra judicial executions within the security forces and collusion with violent paramilitaries within the UK?

For example, I refer elsewhere (Punch 2003) to the miscarriages of justice in the UK and to the Dutroux affair in Belgium as examples of *system failure*. In both cases a number of actors and agencies bent and broke rules, or simply malfunctioned, to the extent that the broader system of justice failed through an unarticulated but cumulative collusion with grave consequences. With regard to the miscarriages of justice in the UK in relation to suspected IRA bombers, for example, there were multiple failures leading to long prison sentences for innocent people (Walker & Starmer 1999). It is doubtful if this was systematically coordinated although there may have been elements of implicit collusion between various segments. To a large extent the system failed because the checks and balances did not function or were sidestepped; but the convictions were doubtless what many (government, media, criminal justice community, families of victims and so on) wanted to see. So, here we can speak of a cumulative but not closely articulated failure leading to a collectively desired outcome.

In contrast, in the Dutroux affair in Belgium there was a cumulative failure within the police-justice system related to incompetence, institutional rivalry, shortcomings in professional conduct and operational standards, and to culpable miscommunication. This led to consequences which no one wished or intended, namely the death of four young girls held in captivity under appalling circumstances by the convicted rapist Dutroux (Punch 2005).

In short, there can be system failure based on:

- a covertly shared and desired outcome through semi-conscious 'reinforcing collusion'
- or to an undesired outcome by fragmented 'negative collusion'.

In Northern Ireland, negative collusion can almost certainly be ruled out because there is little evidence that the excesses extending over 30 years were a result of cumulative negligence leading to undesired consequences. Some speak of the ripe tradition of 'The Great British Cock-up' and there were doubtless serious mistakes and grave blunders made; but it is stretching matters considerably to believe that this could have persisted in the Province for 30 years. The choice is, then, in deciding whether or not the evidence at our disposal indicates a fully intended and articulated conspiracy – and perhaps from the very top as with the French sabotage of the 'Rainbow Warrior' – or a form of 'reinforcing collusion' as with the miscarriages of justice in Britain. This is what I shall explore in the following chapters.

4
Security Units: Firearms Policy: Rough Justice

RUC, ARMY, INTELLIGENCE AND CIUS

As mentioned earlier, I refer to the combined RUC and Army as the 'security forces'; the diverse intelligence units as the 'intelligence agencies' with among them MI5 as the 'Security Service'; the proactive counter-insurgency units (for undercover work, surveillance and covert operations) as 'CIUs'; and all of these together as the 'security community'.

Within the RUC

- *Special Branch* (SB): played a key role throughout the Troubles.[1] Early on it was small in number and primarily focused on the OIRA, with poor intelligence on the new PIRA. This deficiency was clear when internment turned into a fiasco because of lack of accurate information. SB also suffered initially from lack of sophistication and resources (Barker 2004:164). SB grew to over 200 dedicated staff handling informants and intelligence gathering.
- The *E4 Department* was for person-to-person surveillance and undercover operations (E4A) and the three other E4 sections were for various forms of technical surveillance. This in turn came under SB and MI5 supervision.
- The *Special Patrol Group* (SPG) Bronze Section was for 'executive operations' meaning covert operations by armed, uniformed officers.
- The *Headquarters Mobile Support Unit* (HQMSU) supplanted the SPG for covert operations by uniformed officers.

British Intelligence Agencies and Institutional Arrangements

- *MI5*, Section 5 of the Intelligence Agency for domestic security, was responsible for the *Joint Irish Section* (JIS), which brought all the agencies together to keep everyone informed of on-going activities (MI5 and MI6, RUC and RUC SB, Force Research Unit [FRU], 14th Int., Military Intelligence Unit [MIU]).

- The JIS would report weekly to the JIC in London within the Cabinet Office in Whitehall, routinely attended by the Prime Minister.
- MI5 had close links with certain government officials and ministers in London and Belfast. In Northern Ireland it assisted the operational units with technical support, including bugging devices, and informant handling.
- In the early 1980s MI5 was tasked by Margaret Thatcher to reinforce the role of JIS. JIS was run by a senior civil servant with several political assistants along with MI5 officers and staff personnel. There were MI5 officers at Army Head Quarters Northern Ireland in Lisburn, at RUC Headquarters at Knock and with the RUC's SB at Castlereagh (both in Belfast). A MI5 officer was always present in the FRU operations room. MI5 agents also worked covertly in the South (Davies 1999). JIS collated information but passed this on to London for the final decision and to make sure operations did not lead to any political repercussions in the UK, Ireland or abroad.
- *MI6*, the UK's Intelligence Agency for external security, was initially involved because the Republic of Ireland was a separate, sovereign state but in a turf war it lost out to MI5. It made sense, according to MI5 and its supporters, to coordinate the security response throughout Ireland with a single agency although MI6 would still have been involved in some activities.

Army Intelligence and Covert Operations Units

- *Mobile Reconnaissance Force* (MRF). This was trained by the SAS; set up early on for covert operations and undercover work. The Home Office and MI5 wanted the Army to become more active in intelligence work as the RUC was at first seen as lacking skills and resources. The MRF soon came to be seen as somewhat amateur and roughshod, coming under suspicion for the random shooting of Catholics, and was disbanded (Davies 1999:40).
- *14th Intelligence Company* ('14th Int.' or 'Det' for 'detached'); this comprised 50 operatives under an SAS officer; intended for surveillance and covert operations and set up in 1978 to succeed the MRF.
- *Force Research Unit* (FRU): this officially did not exist and was not mentioned in reports or budgets; ostensibly it

functioned as part of 14th Int. but was a self-sufficient unit with 80 operatives and 100 staff (Davies 1999). An MI5 officer was always present in the operations room and would have been informed of all actions undertaken. It was set up as an aggressive, well-resourced, proactive unit and enjoyed elite status.

- There was the the *Tasking and Coordinating Group* (TCG), of about 40 officers; it liaised between the Army and RUC to ensure there was clarity around operations, to avoid duplication or unintended contamination and coordinate joint action.
- There were units of *22 SAS Regiment* for 'executive action'. It is clear that the SAS also played a key role in training all the RUC and Army undercover and intelligence units as well as leading some of them. 14th Int. had an SAS officer commanding it while a number of SAS soldiers were seconded to it for two years (Davies 1999:47).
- The MIU comprised about 40 soldiers whose task it was to liaise with the RUC on intelligence gathering and analysis.

FIREARMS POLICY AND 'SHOOT TO KILL'

There is a great deal of confusion about the term 'shoot to kill' and firearms policy. Traditionally the British police service has not routinely been armed, unlike Northern Ireland, and has a reputation for minimal use of fatal force. But then, during the Troubles the emotive phrase 'shoot to kill' was raised, which colloquially refers to situations where it appears that police or military set out with the deliberate intention to kill the assailants, as with some of the 'encounters' in India (Belur 2010). This 'shoot to kill' theme requires some explanation about policy on police use of firearms in Britain to unravel the accusations in Northern Ireland and I shall discuss three categories.

- Firstly, there is *shoot to prevent*. The British policy and practice regarding firearms was based on restraint. However, standard firearms practice became to 'incapacitate' the target by shooting at the body mass which always carries the chance of a fatal injury. But the expressed policy was that it was not the specific intention to kill someone. Underpinning this is that each officer remains *individually responsible* for the use of force and has to show restraint, use of 'reasonable' force and accountability for *each single shot*. If there is doubt about this they can be subject to disciplinary and criminal charges, including murder. For example, in Sussex in 1998 a firearms officer on an authorised raid to arrest a possibly armed suspect shot dead another man who was not that suspect; he was naked and unarmed but in the dark he had made a sudden movement towards the officer. The officer then faced a charge of *murder* (Markham and Punch 2007a & 2007b). Officers cannot then easily use a plea of self-defence and have to convince a court there were grounds for suspecting life-threatening danger. Officers can also not claim they were under 'orders' as that is not legally acceptable.

- In brief, police firearms policy and practice in Britain was based on issuing a warning; exhausting non-violent possibilities; minimum force; accounting for each bullet; individual accountability; no 'acting under orders' defence; and each officer being subject to the law. This is appropriate to 'civil' policing where officers do not often face armed opponents. But if officers do encounter opponents posing an immediate threat to life – for example, during an armed robbery where the suspects are ignoring warnings or have already opened fire – then officers can keep firing at any part of the body in order to eliminate the danger; this is highly likely to kill the assailants. But they would have to justify the level of force in relation to the risk. This may seem like semantics but formally there is no express intention in advance to shoot to kill. Indeed, most people hit by police bullets in Britain do survive (Punch 2010).

- Secondly, there is *shoot to eliminate*. In serious situations beyond the range of police capabilities, the military may be called in to assist the police in carrying out an operation. For instance, in London in 1980 an SAS unit was filmed spectacularly entering the Iranian Embassy to rescue hostages being held by a group demanding the release of prisoners in Iran (Asher 2008:1–21). From reconstructions we can discern that the SAS' aim was first to eliminate the hostage takers, even if they had put down their weapons and were trying to surrender, and second to rescue the hostages (*Thames Television* 1988). The thinking was that these were armed and dangerous 'terrorists' who had killed and were threatening to kill again and who had to be eliminated to erase any possible risk to the soldiers and hostages. The SAS unit clearly went in intending to 'take out' the hostage takers in a close-combat, battlefield style of shooting with multiple rounds at close range to the head and/or vital organs. This is more than shoot to kill: it is shoot to eliminate (Punch 2010).

- Thirdly, there is *shoot to kill/Kratos*. On an underground train at Stockwell Station in London in 2005, in the wake of the July bombings on public transport that had caused many casualties, officers from the Met fired seven bullets at close range into the head of Jean Charles de Menezes. This was a radical departure from traditional practice, based on the 'Kratos' policy, as the officers were clearly 'shooting to kill' (Punch 2010). This dramatic shift in policy with Kratos had arisen with the new threat that suicide bombers pose and it had been established between the Association of Chief Police Officers (ACPO) in consultation with the government. Since the 9/11 attacks in the US, police in countries with a risk of terrorist attack had examined the CT options including dealing with a 'walking bomb'. In brief, the thinking was that under Kratos a senior officer in charge of an operation with an identified suicide bomber on foot and among the public should issue an authorisation for a 'critical head-shot'. This would be delivered with no warning, firing at point-blank range, aiming at the brainstem, and there should be multiple shots to ensure the suspect was dead. The purpose was to prevent the bomber from setting off an explosion. Tragically, Mr de Menezes was innocent, was not carrying a bomb, and with this style of shooting there is plainly no question of recovery.

The Stockwell shooting conveyed a massive shift in British policing from 'shoot to prevent' to 'shoot to eliminate' as used by Special Forces, and obviously to be used only under specific circumstances. In effect, this was also the style sometimes adopted in Northern Ireland by CIUs when they assumed they were dealing with identified terrorists who were on an active service mission and posing a direct danger to others through their intended use of firearms or explosives. The problem was that formally and legally in Northern Ireland, the police and military were dealing with criminal 'suspects' who should have been dealt with under the restraint and prevent paradigm with arrest prior to engaging in criminal activity or else issuing a warning and applying minimum force. In practice, the CIUs considered they were dealing with imminent danger and this justified immediate armed intervention using close-quarter combat techniques. The difficulty was that there may have been no direct danger to the soldiers while there could have been an arrest attempt; to cover this discrepancy, between the formal rules and the operational code employed, required fabrication of accounts, interfering with evidence, making a proper investigation difficult and prompting conspiracy to pervert the course of justice by lying in court. The police and soldiers concerned would doubtless have argued that this was all part and parcel of fighting the dirty war; and the courts were simply part of the battlefield. This was the ambiguity running through the Troubles, that it was an undeclared war situation being fought with inappropriate rules. The practitioners, with no one resolving that ambiguity for them, rather predictably broke those rules and equally predictably lied about it.

There are two further developments of considerable importance in this area that need to be considered in holding up a template with which to judge the shootings in Northern Ireland:

- Firstly, the police service in Britain has tried since the 1980s to support the frontline officer by constructing a command-and-control structure around major incidents and especially firearms operations because these are always potentially fatal. In set-piece operations there will typically be a command-and-control structure based on three command levels; namely, Gold (setting strategy), Silver (implementation of strategy) and Bronze (carrying out strategy). In spontaneous firearms situations attended to by frontline officers, the contemporary institutional effort is to get a Silver commander to the scene is fast as possible and to mobilise a Gold Commander to oversee the operation. This is very much an accountability model based on senior officer involvement and supervision but also on transparency through an operational dossier in anticipation of external scrutiny and oversight (Markham & Punch 2007a & 2007b). Clearly this structural and cultural change in British policing from the 1980s was outside of the operational style of many operations in Northern Ireland but it was visible and available from the mid-1980s.
- Secondly, a landmark human rights case with important implications for police and CT operations and accountability is *McCann and Others v United Kingdom* (1995). This arose from the killing of three suspected IRA insurgents by soldiers of the SAS in 1988 on Gibraltar. Although military personnel were deployed, it was initially a police operation to arrest and

detain the suspects. A three-person IRA ASU was thought to be preparing a remote-controlled explosion with a car bomb to coincide with a military parade on Gibraltar (Crawshaw, Cullen & Holmström 2006:86–104). The ASU had split into a male and female pair, Mairead Farrell and Danny McCann, and a single male, Sean Savage, and were walking away from a car they had parked. The couple were alleged to have noticed the SAS unit trailing them and made a sudden movement. Both were shot and firing continued after they had fallen to the ground while the third member of the unit was shot elsewhere shortly afterwards. It turned out that all three were unarmed; had no remote-control device on them to explode a bomb; there was no bomb in the car; and there was no military parade planned for that day. Farrell was shot at close range in the face and back; McCann was shot in the head and back; Savage was hit by 16 bullets (Waddington 1991:94). There was no warning given and there was no attempt at an arrest. There was subsequently no prosecution of the soldiers but at an inquest the soldiers maintained they were briefed about a 'button-job' (a remote-control device). They perceived the sudden movement of the couple as a sign of imminent danger requiring immediate use of fatal force.

- In the name of McCann, the case was referred to the ECHR in Strasbourg. The ECHR scrutinised not only whether the force used by the soldiers was strictly proportionate but also whether the anti-terrorist operation was planned by the authorities to minimise recourse to lethal force (Crawshaw, Cullen & Holmström 2006). The reasoning behind the Court's decision is noteworthy; it placed the responsibility for violations of the right to life *squarely on those in command of the operation.* The Court accepted that the soldiers honestly believed, given the briefing, that it was necessary to shoot the suspects to prevent them from detonating a bomb and causing serious loss of life. It followed that regarding the dilemma confronting the authorities, the actions of the soldiers in the eyes of the judges did not in themselves give rise to a violation of Article 2.

- The question arose, however, as to whether or not the operation was controlled and organised in respect of the requirements of Article 2. Given that nearly all the assumptions proved to be erroneous, the Court observed that insufficient allowances had been made for alternatives. For example, the ceremony was to take place several days later, so this was possibly a reconnaissance mission. But in the absence of sufficient allowances for alternative possibilities, the assumptions were conveyed to the soldiers as certainties, making the use of lethal force almost unavoidable. Furthermore, the soldiers were trained to continue shooting until the suspect was clearly dead. The soldiers' reflex action lacked the degree of caution to be expected from law-enforcement personnel in a democratic society, even when dealing with dangerous terrorist suspects. This failure by the authorities suggested a lack of appropriate care in the control and organisation of the arrest operation.

- In sum, the Court was not persuaded that the killing of the three suspects constituted the use of force not more than absolutely necessary in defence of persons from unlawful violence within the meaning of Article 2, paragraph 2(a), of the Convention. Accordingly, the Court held by majority votes that there had been a violation of Article 2 of the Convention.
- Another important ECHR case was related to a shooting in Northern Ireland, *McKerr v the United Kingdom* (2002). The McKerr case drew on one of the three controversial 'Lurgan' shootings involving the HQMSU in which the unarmed McKerr was shot dead (see below). The Court ruled that there had been a violation of the right to life because the state had failed to mount an *adequate investigation*. Under Article 2 there had to be investigations capable of leading to the identification of those allegedly responsible for unlawful killings (Punch 2010:128–9).

Putting these two features together – and it should be stressed that much of this took place after the commencement of the Troubles – one can see a conventional professional wisdom allied to judicial pronouncements developing. Its foundations are:

- Incidents involving use of potentially lethal force should be well organised and planned with the right to life as the guiding light; alternative approaches should be considered and care should be taken in briefings.
- In principle, operations will be conducted within the restraint paradigm appropriate to civil policing in a democratic society; in the McCann case, the ECHR recognised that soldiers are trained to continue shooting until all possible danger is eliminated.

- Operations will be encapsulated in a command-and-control model of supervision, implementation and accountability that is also geared to external oversight.
- An adequate investigation will be conducted in relation to possible illegal conduct; and where appropriate compensation will be paid.
- Attention to the right to life should be paramount. Allied to this are international protocols and UN guidelines regarding the responsibility for ensuring swift and adequate medical treatment following a shooting.
- Crucially, the McCann case placed accountability for the operation *squarely on those in command of it.*

The various developments, guidelines and judicial human rights pronouncements provide an outline of a growing body of restraints that, along with the development of best practice on use of firearms, can be used in assessing the material that follows. The traditional British restraint paradigm based on shoot to prevent was of course long prevalent on the mainland and was ostensibly applicable in Northern Ireland. But there was an armed police force, the RUC, which had faced periodic emergency situations and operated with a different operational style that was evident in public order situations and use of firearms. Employing armoured cars with machine guns against civilians, for instance, was unthinkable in Britain. There may well be extreme circumstances, say in response to a concerted terrorist attack, where they might be employed but then they would have had to come from the Army under Military Aid to the Civil Power (MACP). In the 1970s, for instance, police accompanied by Army units in armoured cars were sent to London Heathrow Airport during terrorist scares. But although the police 'sign over' the operation to the military under MACP, it is only for the duration of the operation; this means that the Army have control for conducting the operation but the ordinary accountability under criminal law still applies to the soldiers (Punch 2010).

ROUGH JUSTICE

There is all this talk about 'shoot to kill'. What do you think the IRA do ... shoot to tickle? (Army officer involved in covert operations). (Urban 1993:205)

The conflict-ridden context outlined in the previous chapter cannot but have had a significant impact on those within the security community. The RUC and UDR especially became prime targets for the terrorists. The Army, moreover, was trained to fight in regular combat with advanced weaponry against an identifiable enemy in a foreign country. Here, in contrast, soldiers might be shot on patrol in their own country by a fellow citizen making a swift escape with the help of ordinary people who might also visibly rejoice at the killing.[2] Many nationalists vocally celebrated the 'victory' when 18 British servicemen were killed at Warren Point.[3] But then a former paratrooper states that he is ashamed to admit there was cheering in his barracks in Britain when the television news announced the shootings by paras of demonstrators during Bloody Sunday (Asher 2004:65).

Yet the security community was meant to abide by the law. It was almost inevitable that feelings were generated seeking retaliation and exacting revenge along with considerable temptation to bend the rules. At times, for instance, terrorist suspects were released from court having remained silent for the stipulated number of days after which they could no longer be held. The police and military may have been convinced of their guilt but had to watch, for instance, alleged bombers walking free or, even more galling, to see one of the Brighton bombers go on to commit a grave offence (Ryder 2000:155). This may well have fostered feelings of 'setting the score right' and of exacting 'rough justice'.

For it is known that in warfare there is a tendency among frontline soldiers to abandon the formal rules of combat in the 'fog' of war. Many sources – official inquiries, memoirs and, nowadays, direct battlefield images through the internet – reveal that combat soldiers swiftly adopt informal, battlefield rules of 'rough justice' (Ellis 1982). According to this operational code of 'just deserts', an enemy unit that has put up prolonged and stiff resistance causing many casualties will be mown down when it eventually tries to surrender (McAlpine 2009). And in the Pacific theatre of operations in WWII it was standard that neither side took prisoners; if Japanese prisoners were taken, they were likely to be killed later in cold blood by their American captors (Dower 1986).

Furthermore, conflict situations which are effectively 'war' but without necessarily declaring war, create an environment, especially among those in the 'frontline', that invites the abandonment of the formal rules of conducting combat and of law enforcement. These deviant and often illegal practices may at times become routine, even when they are technically war crimes, due to processes of rationalisation, routinisation, neutralisation and of dehumanising the victims (Kelman 2009). This is evident in Browning's (2001) harrowing account of a German police reserve battalion mobilised for duty in Poland in WWII that routinely murdered large numbers of Jewish men, women and children by shooting them at close range. A few policemen could not bring themselves to participate and were allowed to avoid shooting without sanction; but the majority felt they could not let their colleagues down and had no option but to carry out this gruesome slaughter. This they began to do on a routine basis, killing an estimated 38,000 innocent civilians during a period of several months. As Browning (2001:189) comments; '... mass murder and routine had become one. Normality itself had become exceedingly abnormal ... Within virtually every social collective, the peer group exerts tremendous pressures on behaviour and sets moral norms. If the men of Reserve Battalion 101 could become killers under such circumstances, what group of men cannot?'

Furthermore, research on police deviance reveals that some officers maintain that 'if you play by the rules you lose' and disdain the law; they adopt alternative 'rules of the game' in fighting crime (Dixon 1999). This generates an operational, cop code of how 'things really get done here'. Of interest, then, is what 'rules of the game' or 'operational code' developed beneath the surface in Northern Ireland given that it was an exceptional situation with considerable provocation and an enemy that did not play by the conventional rules? This predicament was well expressed by 'Scott Graham', a former paratrooper who served with the SAS in Northern Ireland, saying that given free reign the SAS would have 'finished off' the IRA in no time. But it was handicapped by the 'stupid' rules of engagement that prevented SAS units from taking the initiative; 'the IRA could play as dirty as they wanted while we had to play by the bloody rules' (Asher 2008:445).

Of course the formal argument is that it is precisely those 'stupid', 'bloody' rules that distinguish the security forces in a democracy from the violent insurgents they are combating. But that response may not cut much ice with those watching an IRA ASU about to engage on a mission and collecting bombs and firearms; or following some gruesome incident in which fellow soldiers or police officers have been blown to bits or executed.[4] There must have been temptation to ignore the 'stupid' rules. For instance, several soldiers went out on a revenge mission related to some shootings of soldiers and stabbed two innocent farmers to death (Dillon 1991:124–60). And early on, the MRF proved trigger-happy in targeting Catholics with some of its operatives behaving like 'cowboys'; it was soon disbanded (Davies 1999:40–8). Indeed, throughout the Troubles there was a range of serious offences involving RUC officers and regular soldiers, but especially members of the UDR. And which units were especially involved in areas with the potential and opportunity for serious rule-bending? These were primarily CIUs in the RUC Special Branch (SB) and certain paramilitary units (SPG, HQMSU); for the Army, the FRU and 14th Int. involved in intelligence gathering, running informants, surveillance and covert operations. What emerges clearly is that other rules of the game operated in the Province than elsewhere in the UK and that parts of the security community reacted at times to the terrorist threat with its own counter campaign of dirty tricks (Dillon 1991). Encapsulated in the dirty tricks campaign are a number of elements that undoubtedly fed into the 'slide' towards the controversial shootings and collusion.

The key issue is whether or not there was a covert 'policy' on this in Northern Ireland. There can be little doubt that decisions were taken that led to controversial killings by CIUs. But where did the decision making leading to these incidents originate and could this be defined as official 'policy'? In response to the prolonged and bloody insurgent campaign was there an orchestrated element of 'shoot to kill' in Northern Ireland? Alongside dealing with the shoot to kill controversy, I shall focus on the other significant feature of institutionalised deviance in the Province, namely collusion between some members of the security community and loyalist paramilitaries leading to violence against nationalists and Catholics.

PRIMACY

Of importance regarding the relationships between these diverse and sometimes competing units outlined above is that early in the Troubles the Army had been granted 'primacy' on security in the Province. However, from the mid-1970s the RUC was reclaiming primacy to become again the lead organisation in the security situation with the military in a subordinate role. This followed the 1977 report 'The Way Ahead' which argued for 'Ulsterisation' and 'normalization' of the conflict (Mulcahy 2006:32). Normally in Britain the police are responsible for law enforcement and the use of force and only request the government to approve Army assistance within the MACP protocol. Here in the Province, in contrast, the Army had been dominant since arriving in 1969 and re-establishing police primacy was clearly a matter of institutional rivalry and fluctuating negotiations. For instance, I met by chance (Sir) Kenneth Newman at a conference in Britain in the late 1970s when he was the Chief Constable of the RUC. He was remarkably frank in telling me that his first task on arriving in Northern Ireland in 1976 was to try to get the Army off his back and in its place. In effect, he was saying that the Army had been the dominant player with the tendency to define situations as requiring a 'military' response. Newman was plainly a high-potential officer who later became the Commissioner of the Met in London. To appoint someone of his calibre from outside the Province can presumably only have been done with the assignment that he was to 'normalise' the security situation in Northern Ireland by re-asserting the role of the police.

In the early days, the Army could be heavy-handed with crude house-to-house searches accompanied by much verbal abuse, damage and even alleged looting. Its initial style was at first very much that of 'abrasive colonial policing' (Mulcahy 2006:69). On July 3rd 1970, for instance, some 1,500 rounds of ammunition were expended in exchanges with gunmen while 1,600 canisters of CS gas were used in Belfast during an Army incursion into the Falls Road area in a search for weapons; a curfew was imposed. This incursion sparked off mass rioting and some sniping in the area (Dillon 1991:232). In Operation Motorman in 1972, moreover, the Army entered the no-go areas of Belfast and Derry in a show of force with some 30,000 soldiers of the regular Army and UDR. This was to reassert control with the assumption that these areas were harbouring insurgents (Smith & Neumann 2005). But the reality was that in some areas in that period the RUC was so hated, intimidated and demoralised that it could not operate without heavy army protection, while the Army had taken over riot-control and other enforcement from the police. Given the continuing level of threat, two or three RUC officers might leave the station escorted by a squad of soldiers with a reserve unit as back-up and perhaps even a helicopter in attendance (Mulcahy 2006:42).

There was, then, an effort to achieve a gradual shift to the police achieving primacy and to putting the Army back 'in its place'. This eventually worked reasonably well, with regular forces on standard patrol and other duties together with the conventional RUC departments. But the Army never fully accepted primacy and tended to view itself as superior to the RUC, while it could argue that the military retains an independent responsibility under common law to restore order. Sometimes senior officers in their memoirs or interviews continued to be disparaging about the police with Lord Carver, Chief of the General Staff in the middle 1970s, being most uncomplimentary about the RUC's SB. He wrote of its inefficiency, loss of motivation and suspected links with loyalists as reasons for the expansion and increasing reliance on military intelligence units in the 1970s (Urban 1993:22).[5]

SPECIAL FORCES, SAS

In a counter-insurgency situation, the deployment of conventional troops has limitations and 'special forces' can play a key role in covert operations. Brigadier Frank Kitson, who served in the Province in the early 1970s, for example, has been credited with an influential role in stimulating counter-insurgency tactics. He was a published authority on both topics with experience during the emergencies in Kenya and Malaya. Although he was not in the Province for long, he had a considerable impact on redefining operations as 'low intensity conflict' (Kitson 1971). Proactive units such as the MRF stemmed from his ideas on tackling terrorists (Dillon 1999:27–9), and his previous operational strategy had been on 'turning' captured terrorists and using them in 'pseudo-gangs' within the suspect movement: and his method had been to first defeat terrorists and only then negotiating with them.

In the UK 'special forces' mean primarily the SAS; the Special Air Service Regiment, formally 22 SAS Regiment. There are also the SBS (Special Boat Squadron) and units of the Marine Commandos. In Northern Ireland the SAS was formally active from 1976, but actually from much earlier, while there were other special Army and paramilitary RUC units geared to surveillance, undercover operations and armed intervention. Initially the SAS as a CIU operated in 'bandit country' along the border, but in 1978 it began to operate throughout the Province. The SAS presence in Northern Ireland was strongly resented by the conventional Army; in turn, many SAS members felt that this was not the environment for them, preferring more challenging and unrestricted engagements in foreign locations where combat was mostly based on 'shoot-on-sight' (Asher 2008).

The subsequent accusations about 'shoot to kill' were not exclusively attributed to the SAS but included the RUC. Indeed, the original concern was not about the military but with three incidents involving the RUC. These led to a senior police officer from Manchester, Stalker, being asked to investigate the three cases. This was at the 'request' of the Chief Constable, Hermon, although there was apparently some arm-twisting from the Director of Public Prosecutions (DPP) in Northern Ireland and probably consultations with the Home Office and Her Majesty's Inspectorate of Constabulary (HMIC). There was at that time no external investigatory agency for policing in the UK and it was standard for a force with a problem, such as a corruption scandal or a dubious shooting, to be investigated by another force (Punch 2009). But unlike the mainland, the external investigating officer in Northern Ireland did not have a separate legal standing from the force under investigation and could only function with the consent and cooperation of the Chief Constable, the rigidly obstinate Sir John Hermon (Murphy 1992:27).

It is likely that the role of the RUC in these three 'Lurgan' incidents aroused so much controversy that it subsequently led to much closer cooperation between the military and the police in covert operations, with the SAS and 14th Int. taking the lead and with other Army units and the RUC providing back-up.

HQMSU, LURGAN AND STALKER

In November 1982 three RUC officers were blown up in their car by a land-mine at Kinnego near Lurgan. Then, within a few weeks, three shootings took place near Lurgan in which six suspected IRA activists died and one was seriously injured; five were unarmed while two were holding weapons without ammunition. The Deputy Chief Constable of the Greater Manchester Police, Stalker, was asked to investigate these shootings. He became convinced that these were revenge killings mounted by the RUC in response to the Lurgan bombing. In the first incident, RUC officers allegedly manning a roadblock opened fire on three unarmed IRA men without warning, killing all three (Toman, Burns and McKerr): 108 bullets were fired. In the second incident, two youths were shot in a hayshed: one (Tighe) died at the scene and the other (McCauley) was seriously injured; only McCauley was thought to be associated with the IRA; three antiquated rifles but no ammunition were recovered from the scene. In the third incident, two unarmed men (Grew and Carroll, both INLA members) were shot when they allegedly burst through a random road block manned by ordinary RUC officers after they had been flagged down, injuring a police officer. Both men died at the scene.

Later it emerged that the same special RUC unit, the undercover Headquarters Mobile Support Unit (HQMSU), was involved in all three incidents. A distressing aspect of this episode was that the explosives used in the Lurgan attack on the three officers had been taken from the hayshed of the second shooting. There was supposed to be constant surveillance with a 'bug' (listening device) planted to record any sounds in the shed. Normally the explosives could not have been moved without the security forces being alerted. Somehow, perhaps due to faulty equipment, the explosives were removed and the RUC patrol was cleared to enter a previously embargoed area to respond to what may have been a hoax call; the three officers were blown up in their car by the massive explosion. A grave operational blunder had seemingly contributed to their deaths.

Although Stalker never completed his investigation, he and his team did interview 300 witnesses and re-examined evidence in order to piece together what happened around the three shootings. He became convinced that an informant had passed on information to SB about the identities of several of the men who allegedly had connections to the Lurgan explosion. The informant may also have acted as *agent provocateur* by inducing some of the men to drive where RUC units would be waiting for them. After investigating two incidents, he futilely awaited the evidence from the hayshed 'bug' from the second incident, the inquiry team came to the conclusion that:

> Special Branch officers planned, directed and effectively controlled the official accounts given ... The Special Branch targeted the suspected terrorists, they briefed the officers, and after the shootings they removed the men, cars and guns for a private de-briefing before the CID officers were to be allowed to commence the official investigation of what had occurred. The Special Branch interpreted the information and decided what was and was not evidence; they attached the labels ... whether a man was 'wanted' for an offence, for instance, or whether he was an 'on-the-run terrorist'. *I had never experienced, nor had any of my team, such an influence over an entire police force by one small section.* (Stalker 1988:56, my emphasis)

Of course, Stalker had never been in a situation of intense civil strife in which counter-insurgency, and all the shenanigans that go with it, dominate the show. He was dropped into an environment where for some a 'war' was going on, in which deviation from the formal rules to achieve results was 'SOP' (Standard Operating Procedure). For example, officers involved in the three incidents were told to lie to protect an informant, that they were sworn to secrecy under the Official Secrets Act and were assured they would be protected by that Act. After each operation the group would meet with SB officers to rehearse the accounts to be presented (Stalker 1998:59). Yet a façade was maintained that all was legal and above board. Stalker was handed the poison chalice of conducting an investigation as if it was a standard British force on the mainland when this was effectively a war zone in a 'foreign' country where other rules of the game applied.

First Incident: The Shooting of Toman, Burns and McKerr

The RUC account of events given at the trial of three officers for the murder of Toman was that the IRA men were being shadowed (by E4A), were on a mission to kill a member of the security services and were suspected of involvement in the Lurgan bombing. The police defendants claimed that the vehicle carrying the three men broke through a roadblock, endangering the life of an officer causing officers to open fire; when a bullet flashed on hitting the car, they thought they were being shot at and returned fire. The prosecution held that Toman was still alive when the car came to a halt and that he was shot trying to get out of the car.

Second Incident: The Hayshed and the shootings of Tighe and McCauley

Then, rather strangely, the same hayshed where the explosives used to blow up the RUC patrol had been stashed also played a role in the second incident. This strongly suggests that several antiquated rifles without ammunition had been planted there to generate a cause for using violence if anyone handled them, even though the officers should have been aware that the weapons could not be activated and there was no danger. Their purpose presumably was to generate a spurious element of danger with a fake justification for firing, which is what Stalker suspected. Moreover MI5 had replaced the original bug with a more reliable device, presumably on the assumption that the IRA might use the location again.

The original police account was that the officers were ordinary officers on routine patrol; this 'front' was apparently standard procedure according to one source I talked to; and they suddenly saw a man with a weapon enter the hayshed. They heard voices and weapons being cocked and twice challenged the men to come out. An officer claimed he then saw both men aim the weapons; shots were fired at both men, who disappeared behind a haystack only to reappear once more with the rifles aimed; both were shot at again. Tighe died at the scene while McCauley was severely wounded. Tighe was 17 years old and had no security or criminal record; McCauley, 19, had been mentioned by an informant as being connected with the Lurgan explosion. In court a very different story unfolded. The officers began by admitting that they had not seen an armed man enter the shed; they were not on routine patrol but were part of a special unit, the HQMSU. They also said that they were told by senior officers to use fabricated stories to protect the life of an informant, and that they would be covered by the Official Secrets Act, which was incorrect. But the further sequence of events leading to the shooting remained unaltered in their evidence under oath.

McCauley had a quite different version of what had happened. He recounted that he and Tighe were checking an empty cottage for an acquaintance, saw a window open in the hayshed and climbed in to investigate.[6] Tighe saw a rifle and picked it up but then shots rang out and he was killed immediately; only then was a warning issued, but before McCauley could move he was hit and wounded. There was more gunfire and he was hit again and dragged outside; an officer held a gun to his head and talked about finishing him off. Judging which of the conflicting versions was correct would have been clarified by the recording from the electronic listening device. It appeared that the two young men 'walked into a sophisticated operation that had been camouflaged to look like a chance encounter' and that the officers had lied under oath in court (Stalker 1988:65). Indeed, the judge decided to exclude the police evidence; perversely, he found McCauley guilty of possession of a rifle and pronounced a suspended sentence.

Third Incident: The shootings of Grew and Carroll

The last of the three incidents led to the prosecution for the murder of Grew by a police officer, Constable 'Thompson'. In court again it emerged that 'Thompson' was not an ordinary officer as initially stated but was a member of the HQMSU. The 'random' roadblock was really part of an elaborate surveillance operation with RUC officers crossing into the Republic. Police Constable (PC) 'Thompson' divulged that he had been told to lie to protect the operation: 'It became clear that investigating CID officers, the DPP and, finally the courts themselves, all had been quite deliberately misled in order to protect police procedures and systems' (Stalker 1988:13). After the shooting 'Thompson' was taken from the scene with his firearm, uniform and car; CID officers were hence unable to interview him; at Gough Barracks, where an Assistant Chief Constable (ACC) was present, he was instructed to lie to protect an informant.

The operation was in fact geared around an important target, the highly-active INLA insurgent Dominic McGlinchey, and the two suspects were being trailed in order to reach McGlinchey (Cusack & McDonald 2008). Members of E4A were shadowing the two men in Ireland, infringing on its sovereignty, and possibly the two suspects picked up McGlinchey. The police plan, according to the most widely used account,[7] was that two unmarked police cars collided in the heavy rain and the blockade could not be mounted; the suspects' car sailed past. A bogus radio-call was then made to a second unit further up the road that the car had injured an officer when evading the roadblock. There, one of the pursuing E4A or SB officers picked up PC 'Thompson' and pursued the suspects' vehicle. They intercepted the car just before Armagh. McGlinchey was not in it so only two men were in the car. According to the prosecution, 'Thompson' got out of the police car and first shot Carroll, reloaded and fired again at Grew at near point-blank range; there were powder burns on Grew's body (McDonald & Holland 2010:264). The prosecution concluded that, 'It is inescapable that this was a deliberate shooting carried out in circumstances which must have made it clear that the deceased was not using a weapon' (Rolston 2006:15).

It also emerged at the trial that the E4A/SB officer with PC 'Thompson' then drove off after the shooting, and kept his evidence back from the authorities. The logs on undercover cars were falsified. Another officer rolled around in dirt to suggest he had been knocked down when the car allegedly crashed through the blockade. The identity of the informant was kept from Stalker on security grounds. Someone suspected by the IRA of being the informer was tortured and shot several months later, but another person was almost certainly the informant (McDonald & Holland 2010:267). None of the seven victims set out armed; two came to hold antiquated weapons they found in the hayshed, but these could not be fired; the police were apparently never in any real danger; no shots were fired at the police; the suspects were given no chance to surrender and were killed with multiple shots; and there was an elaborate cover-up involving senior police leadership.

Stalker admits that he faced a dilemma: should he accept that sometimes innocent civilians become victims in what was effectively a 'war' situation, or should he relentlessly pursue the truth? He felt, however, that he and his professional team could not walk away from this moral issue:

> As an individual, I also passionately believe that if a police force of the United Kingdom could, in cold blood, kill a seventeen-year-old youth with no terrorist or criminal convictions, and then plot to hide the evidence from a senior policeman deputed to investigate it, then the shame belonged to us all. *This is the act of a Central American assassination squad – truly of a police force out of control.* (Stalker 1998:67, my emphasis)

In his lengthy and highly-detailed interim report he concluded that senior RUC officers had fabricated lies and pressurised subordinates to repeat them in court. There was clear evidence of the RUC's efforts to pervert the course of justice; six unarmed men had seemingly been killed unlawfully and one seriously injured.

SPECIAL FORCES

There was a clear SAS hallmark on many of the controversial shootings, while all the special squads operating in Northern Ireland were given training by the SAS. The SAS is specialised in mounting deep surveillance operations behind enemy lines, in sabotage operations and in close combat fighting on special assignment in conventional wars or in counter-insurgency roles (Asher 2008). SAS soldiers also train to enter buildings or aircraft in hostage situations and 'take out' the hostage takers, while hopefully rescuing the hostages unharmed. Counter-insurgency operations employing Special Forces clearly have their own specific understanding of combat operations.

Moreover the 'war' situation was in constant flux as each side reacted to developments from the other side. For instance, the IRA went through a steep learning process from being somewhat amateur and mistake-prone to being equipped with increasingly sophisticated explosive devices and modern weaponry. They obtained versions of the renowned AK-47 Kalashnikov assault rifle; the light and compact Armalite rifle; heavy-machine guns; rocket-propelled grenades and SAM ground-to-air missiles (which they never managed to activate or decided not to use). They also manufactured a range of homemade mortars (Dillon 1991:418–42; Geraghty 2000:167–203).[8] There even developed a measure of grudging respect for the IRA, with an internal British Army document released in 2007 describing it as a 'professional, dedicated, highly skilled and resilient force' (*BBC News UK* 2007). In response, the security forces began in a rather reactive fashion but developed continually in a symbiotic relationship with the IRA. This constant action–reaction dynamic was reflected in technology, skills and specialisation; there was, for example, a continuous battle between the IRA bomb-makers and the Army's technical experts with regard to bugs and de-bugging, 'jarking' (bugging weapons or explosives or making then harmless) and intercepting the radio signals that detonated explosives. Furthermore, the RUC developed CIUs while the Army set up its own intelligence and informer handling units.

But the SAS soldiers considered themselves far superior to any of the RUC or army units. There were times when the security services went on the initiative and this was often in response to a rise in IRA activity or to IRA 'successes'. When the IRA leadership in the North became dominant over the movement, when it developed a more disciplined cell-structure, when it became more selective on targets and when its tactics and techniques improved, it became a far more threatening enemy. Politicians and the military responded to this. For instance, in 1976 after the murder of 10 Protestant workers the Labour Prime Minister, Harold Wilson, dispatched the SAS to Northern Ireland.[9] And after the killing of 18 soldiers at Warren Point, Prime Minister Thatcher responded immediately by travelling to the Province, demanding greater coordination between the Army and the RUC in combating the IRA and promising more resources.

If these responses meant employing Special Forces, then the SAS entered the fray with their own specific understanding of mounting combat operations. However, Urban (1993) argues that not all operations led to killing suspected terrorists and there were operations against the IRA leading to arrests. But after 1983 there was a definite change in tactics 'in favour of aggressive ambush operations' (Urban 1993:143). This was clearly related to the aftermath of the three Lurgan incidents involving RUC paramilitary units. The Army had deferred to these police units, according to a Stormont source; 'The SAS were reined back a bit to give the police a bigger role.' Among ministers and generals confidence in the RUC had improved and 'there was a feeling that it should have the ability to confront terrorists on the basis of its own intelligence, without Army help' (Urban 1993:147). That confidence evaporated with the three Lurgan shootings, which led to reverberations in the media, public opinion and politics and brought the RUC under external investigation. Another probable reason why the SAS went into more aggressive mode from 1984 onwards was in retaliation for the Brighton bombing. Almost killing the Prime Minister and her Cabinet had raised the stakes: almost certainly, Mrs Thatcher and others around her felt a 'robust' response was needed to counter this dramatic IRA success.

BIG BOYS' RULES

The SAS soldiers use the expression 'Big Boys' Rules' when they are put into action. They are at the sharpest end of the military spectrum and are used for the toughest, high-risk assignments. Their working philosophy conveys that when the going gets tough, the tough get tougher. It is also in the nature of such elite units that they can be disparaging about other units and maintain a measure of distance from them. They tend to adopt a highly assertive operational style; they train at length to bring intense firepower onto the target zone to eliminate an enemy taken by surprise in an ambush. These are tactics geared to small units operating behind enemy lines that need to avoid direct confrontations with the main enemy and, when necessary, to rely on stealth, surprise and aggression (Newsinger 1997).

And in Northern Ireland their perception was presumably that they were at war with an 'army' which spoke of 'Active Service Units', gave its fallen military-style funerals and vocally claimed it was conducting a war. Moreover, in the 'long war' mounted by the IRA from 1976 this meant a campaign of attrition aimed specifically against the security forces. The IRA was normally causing more casualties among the security forces than the other way around in that phase. Furthermore, the IRA attackers in an ASU did not usually try to take prisoners; they attacked when police and soldiers were most vulnerable, such as when they were off duty or in an ambush situation; they placed a second bomb or booby-trap to explode when the rescuers of casualties arrived at the scene of an explosion, such as at Warren Point; and they did not issue warnings before opening fire. They also often moved in to finish someone off with shots to the head during an assassination and killed people who would be deemed innocent by most standards, and whom the conventional military would normally respect as non-combatants. The IRA, like most insurgent terrorists, played very dirty indeed.

This must have fostered among the soldiers and their commanders the idea of playing firmly by Big Boys' Rules. For instance, the SAS conceptual vocabulary for an 'ambush' has an unambiguous definition which means that against an armed opponent, or even an unarmed terrorist who is clearly on an active service mission, the SAS unit takes the initiative at the slightest hint of danger or threat. But when the intention is to apprehend armed terrorists, the SAS soldiers are ordered a make a 'hard arrest.' Urban (1993:164) adds, 'There is no shoot-to-kill policy in the sense of a blanket order to shoot IRA terrorists on sight. Rather the knack is to get IRA terrorists, armed and carrying out an operation, to walk into a trap.' There then has to be an element of direct danger to the soldiers to justify fatal force within the plea of self-defence; and then to embellish the circumstances to make it a 'clean kill'. An SAS unit engaged on an ambush mission, or under the euphemism 'Observation Post/Reactive' used in Northern Ireland, was not primarily there to apprehend terrorists before, during or after the incident but to intervene at the moment the action takes place, or 'appears to be' about to take place, by attacking the ASU. The operational code for the troops on the ground was unambivalent: as one SAS member said, 'everyone knows what the mission is in an ambush ... when you do an ambush you kill people' (Urban 1993:164).

In short, the SAS went into the field with a different interpretation of an operation than that held by most ordinary RUC personnel and by regular Green Army units. The latter were more likely to be geared to the legal stance on the use of fatal force, which, I was informed, was conveyed to them with clarity in briefings. Let us then look at how the SAS operated in several incidents and at what their particular style was in taking on an ASU.

- In June 1978 a four-man ASU set out to blow up the post office in Ballysillan in Belfast. Three of them, unarmed, began to unload the explosives but there was a well-prepared, combined force of SAS and RUC officers who opened fire, killing the three men. The claim was subsequently made that warnings had been given. In a search for the fourth insurgent a local Protestant man, William Hanna, was shot dead in a field next to the mail depot and another man with him avoided injury by hiding. A total of 111 shots were fired. According to Urban (1993:62) there was 'jubilation' at Army Headquarters; but Chief Constable Hermon was dismayed and dissuaded the Army from mounting more undercover operations with shoot-outs in Belfast.
- In July 1978 John Boyle, 16 years of age, discovered an arms cache in a local graveyard; he told his father, a Catholic farmer,

who immediately informed the police; and a four-man SAS squad was sent to conduct surveillance on the graveyard. The farmer and his two sons went to work in the fields the next day, but John went back to look at the weapons and, while doing so, he was shot. When his father heard the shots he went to the graveyard where he and his other son encountered two soldiers in camouflage outfits. The Boyles were pushed to the ground and told that someone had been shot, with the words 'the other bastard is dead' (Urban 1993:63). Apparently the RUC had phoned the farm after the men had left for work to tell Mrs. Boyle that on no account was anyone to approach the graveyard. Somewhere there was a failure of communication and the RUC was 'furious' with the Army. For the SAS had shot an innocent teenager, whose curiosity had proved fatal; the Army claimed that a loaded gun had been aimed at soldiers, but this was simply untrue. Most unusually, two of that SAS unit went to trial.

In two years the SAS had shot dead ten people of whom three were bystanders. For a number of years after that the SAS was reined in by those in the security hierarchy who opposed ambushes and were aware of the powerful symbolic impact of IRA funerals following a shooting by the Army. The RUC also wanted the Army to back off so they could assert primacy and develop their own units for covert operations. For five years the SAS did not kill anyone in Northern Ireland.

- Then, in May 1987, an eight-member ASU and a passing motorist were shot dead by the SAS in Loughall, Armagh. The eight men were armed and conveying a bomb in a digger to blow up what they assumed was an unmanned police station as the RUC officers left it each evening for safety reasons, but SAS members were concealed inside. The IRA unit, in overalls and balaclavas, opened fire on the empty building; the digger then rammed the station's fence to place the bomb with an old-fashioned fuse. There was a large military and police presence in the area in anticipation of the raid about which there was accurate information. A heavily armed SAS unit was in the foreground, with several belt-fed 7.62 mm General Purpose machine guns, and the soldiers opened fire without warning. With the bomb detonating and bullets pouring in on the ASU, more than 1,200 rounds were probably fired and, with the ASU returning fire in a desperate effort to escape, there was considerable noise and confusion while the station was severely damaged. Some soldiers inside may have been injured although they would have been behind a blast wall. With the entire ASU wiped out this was the biggest defeat suffered by any IRA faction in decades and these were among its most experienced activists.

- A number of unsuspecting civilians driving into the area at Loughall also came under fire or were roughly treated, including two brothers who were shot in their car. Both were wearing work overalls and without warning the SAS opened fire, pouring bullets into the car. They killed one brother and seriously wounded the other who survived. The brothers had no connections with any IRA activities; the widow of the dead man received substantial compensation from the MoD in a settlement, but without an admission of liability (Urban 1993:235).

- In 1984 a four-man ASU set out to plant a bomb at a factory in Ardboe, Tyrone. A SAS unit was in place working on highly accurate information. Two members of the ASU were challenged; one ran off and another, Price, put his hands up; a SAS soldier said he shot at Price who, though injured, managed to escape. The two other members of the ASU ran off but were apprehended. A search located the wounded Price, but a soldier stated at an inquest that Price made 'a sudden movement of his hands towards me' and so he fired, blowing off the top off Price's head (Urban 1993:183). However, the SAS had on this occasion issued warnings and had taken prisoners.

- In 1985 a well-armed ASU set out to launch a night attack on an RUC vehicle near Strabane. When this proved fruitless, three of its members set out to hide the weapons in a field. They came into the view of a small SAS unit, probably on a surveillance mission, which opened fire without warning and continued to fire at close range. Some 117 rounds were fired and one IRA man, Michael Devine, was hit 28 times. Local people claimed to have heard cries of 'Don't shoot' from one of the wounded and this raised the possibility of the SAS unit administering the *coup de grace*. None of the IRA weapons had been fired and two still had their safety catches on when examined.

- Reliable information indicated that an IRA unit, comprising two armed men on a motorbike, intended to assassinate a UDR reservist at Gransha Hospital. When the motorbike drove into the hospital grounds, with the passenger allegedly brandishing a weapon (this was later disputed), it was rammed by an unmarked car driven by SAS personnel. This seriously injured the pillion passenger and the soldiers then opened fire, with one emptying his 30-round magazine as the driver of the motorbike tried to get away. In total 59 bullets were fired, the rider was hit 19 times and the badly injured passenger four times; both assailants died at the scene.

- In 1983, near Coalisland, an IRA arms cache was located after a tip-off. An SAS unit of six soldiers took up position around the spot. After two days of surveillance a car arrived, carrying three IRA men, two of whom, McGirr and Campbell, got out of the car; the third man stayed in the car. Campbell took a weapon and set off for the car while McGirr knelt by the cache. Soldier 'A' said he issued a challenge; McGirr 'pivoted round, pointing the shotgun in my direction' and the soldier opened fire; McGirr was hit by 13 bullets. Campbell was also said to have turned towards the soldiers as he tried to reach the car and was hit twice; other soldiers opened fire on the car, which was later found abandoned but covered in blood. This turn of events was disputed with the IRA, and a priest who attended the scene, maintaining that the bodies were near the fence and not near the cache, suggesting they had been shot on entering the field and before reaching the weapons.

- In Dunloy an Army Observation Post, manned by 14th Int. was spotted and attacked from the rear by a two-man IRA unit. The ASU killed one soldier and injured another but he was able to call for assistance. As the two IRA volunteers left the scene, two cars pulled up and firing broke out; both IRA activists were shot and local people said they heard one injured man calling for help, but then both were surrounded by 'SAS men' before they were shot. It seems they were shot while lying injured, as a soldier admitted in his statement to the inquest. As the soldier approached, the wounded IRA man had made 'a movement' which the soldier felt put him in danger. But here the IRA men had opened fire first and caused casualties including an army fatality (Urban 1993:179).

In short, the hallmark of so-called 'shoot to kill' operations by the SAS was primarily a set-piece ambush, based on prior information and/or long-term surveillance; often opening fire with no warning (although it was mostly claimed that a warning was given), intense firepower from automatic weapons and hitting the target many times, and sometimes with danger to ordinary people in the vicinity. Allegedly there was on occasion no mercy to the wounded and to unarmed ASU members wanting to surrender, with accusations of delivering the *coup de grace*. There was, for example, the highly dangerous IRA activist and Maze Prison escapee, Seamus McElwaine. In April 1986 he and another activist were about to set up an ambush when they were themselves ambushed; both were wounded but only McElwaine was apprehended by SAS soldiers. He was allegedly shot dead after his arrest following a brief interrogation; his companion, Sean Lynch, who was wounded and hiding in a ditch, claimed this took about 20 minutes (Urban 1993:219). He also asserted later that the wounded McElwaine had been physically and verbally abused and shot in the legs and stomach before the final bullets to the chest (Tóibín 1994:130). If this is true then the soldiers were not only refusing medical aid to a wounded suspect, which can also be a way of causing death, but had committed murder. Indeed, an inquest brought in a verdict of unlawful killing in that the soldiers had opened fire without attempting an arrest. But subsequently the DPP declined to prosecute the soldiers.

In purely military terms these were all doubtless seen as highly successful operations and prime examples of the much sought after 'clean kill' (Urban 1993). The clean kill was defined by catching an IRA ASU in the open when engaged on a terrorist mission. Under these circumstances the Army could hurt the IRA by inflicting casualties; eight highly experienced and armed terrorists caught planting a bomb had been 'taken out' at Loughall making this encounter the IRA equivalent of the Army's Warren Point, when 18 soldiers were killed. The diverse IRA movements had never lost more ASU members than this in a single incident in 60 years. Convincing justification could be found in one IRA weapon recovered at Loughall which had been used in 33 terrorist attacks (Ryder 2000:339). And the occasional loss of life to bystanders could be rationalised by the euphemism of 'collateral damage'. Urban (1993:237), furthermore, states that a senior security forces officer who played a key role in the operation told him:

'Loughall was a plum – it was an exceptionally heavy team of good operators. The temptation was there to remove them in one go. The terrorists played into our hands and everything went our way. Was it a decision to kill those people? I don't think it would have been phrased like that. Somebody would have said,

"How far do we go to remove this group of terrorists?" and the answer would have been "as far as necessary"'. Loughall was the apotheosis of the clean kill, a cleverly planned exploitation of intelligence resulting in a humiliation of the IRA.

THE FRONTLINE, PRACTITIONERS' PERSPECTIVE

Reading between the lines of diverse publications and drawing on a few informal interviews, I shall sketch the military 'practitioner's' view of the counter-terrorism (CT) campaign that is relevant to this chapter. That frontline perspective runs along these lines.

- There was no grand conspiracy. There is even scepticism as to whether the politicians were capable of mounting one or sustaining it. In any case the reality on the ground was not the way some people have described it; there was never any sense of it being driven by such a conspiracy. In practice, much of the CT soldiering was mundane, painstaking and time-consuming. For the most part, this dull, routine work has been ignored by commentators and writers in favour of a concentration on the few cases where things went wrong.
- The RUC's SB was always driving the CT campaign, but SB was relatively small and seriously under-resourced as well as sometimes being of mediocre quality. People seem unaware that the numbers in the intelligence agencies involved in the campaign were not large for such a major, around-the-clock CT effort. People think of the SAS contingent, for example, as large and ubiquitous when it was in fact puny, with the SAS having difficulty scraping enough soldiers together for their assignments. Also the intelligence from SB was never perfect; but then intelligence never is perfect. Units could be out on surveillance with an Observation Post for days and nights in all sorts of weather in anticipation of an incident, but they might not know exactly who was involved and when it was going to happen. It's a myth that all was known in advance; a unit could be in position working on ostensibly sound information, while the attack would take place at the right time but elsewhere.
- The CT effort was always geared to 'policing' incidents leading to an arrest, but almost no one focuses on the amount of routine effort put in and to the large number of arrests made. Often when incidents unfolded it could be a sudden surprise leading to confusion, misunderstanding and mistakes.

Sometimes soldiers only knew it was happening when the bomb went off or the firing started. The prime purpose was explicitly an arrest but when dealing with armed and highly violent terrorists, who do not heed warnings and who start shooting immediately, then the only choice is to return fire.

- The number of such incidents is relatively low. If there had been an explicit shoot to kill policy, then surely far more terrorists would have been killed. The same goes for collusion. Some collusion undoubtedly took place but if it had been as extensive and sophisticated as is alleged then surely far more targets would have been hit. Those who were hit were not particularly major IRA figures and were often wrong or random targets. The UDA/UVF efforts were often somewhat clumsy and lacked sophistication; so the accuracy one would expect if there had been extensive and effective collusion was missing.

- But above all there never was, according to this practitioner perspective, any notion that operations were being driven by a 'shoot to kill' *policy*.

In short, the practitioner's view is that much of the routine work leading to arrests has been ignored; working with SB intelligence the aim was always to 'police' the situation seeking arrests; in practice confrontations were often confused if not chaotic; sometimes it was not possible to police the situation and suspects were shot because there simply was no other choice. This is one specific view which is valid from the frontline perspective: perhaps operations are never as smooth as planned or as thought of by outsiders: in the 'fog of war' surrounding an intense encounter, operations can devolve into a 'Charlie Foxtrot' or 'cluster f***'. Interestingly, the IRA activist Hughes similarly describes IRA operations as replete with confusion, panic, poor intelligence, mistakes, premature explosions, hitting the wrong target, incompetence and common crime such as theft during actions (Moloney 2010). He adds that among the brave and competent activists he worked with there were also cowards and half-wits. But then almost none of the IRA members were trained military professionals with any combat experience; unless, ironically, they had served in the British Army.

Finally, the police and army practitioners' perspective is one of wrong intelligence, poor briefing, confusion and cumulative misperceptions leading to a deadly outcome that could probably have been avoided. This may well have been their ground-floor perspective but this is somewhat unconvincing given the reputation of, say, the SAS for being highly trained, well skilled and operationally ruthless. Furthermore, in the descriptions of umpteen planned encounters leading to deaths the soldiers seemed to be fully in control and quite conscious of what they were doing. It often seems that they were operating according to an understood code of rough justice and just deserts. Perhaps then they had no need, and consequently no perception, of a 'conspiracy' to do what they were trained to do and what they felt was richly 'justified' in those circumstances.

5
Dirty Tricks: Intelligence, Informants and Collusion

From many accounts we have learned that, especially in wars and emergencies, governments and their agencies tend to engage in a range of 'dirty tricks'. By their nature these covert and sometimes illegal practices are wrapped in secrecy. Later, with the opening of archives, the writing of memoirs and through investigative journalism, it is possible to learn a great deal about what happened in certain societies (as in the US: Prados 1996). On Northern Ireland much has been written about the Troubles, but there is as yet little solid material about the 'dirty tricks' aspect. Many of those involved are still alive, cannot publish their stories and might be in serious trouble if they did so. We do not know, for instance, if anyone from the British security community has given an in-depth interview to the Boston College Oral History Project. The two interviews published so far have been illuminating and it would be fascinating to hear similar detail from soldiers and intelligence agents. If they have been interviewed, then that material will only be available after their deaths. Hence we are missing a large chunk of what went on in this largely concealed area. This means there are only a few sources that, for various reasons, have to be approached with caution. Often the basic data that would give validity to their particular perspective is simply not available. Also, the writers and journalists among them have the freedom to make assertions that at times lack the scholarly distance required in academic work. What plagues them and this area, moreover, is that they are researching a secretive state that is loath to give up its secrets (Hillyard 2003).

This imbalance is especially acute as there are understandably so few insider accounts to counter the main publications. When 'Ingram', the pseudonym of a former military intelligence agent turned whistle-blower, provided one he was promptly discredited and prosecuted with the system employing its repertoire of dirty tricks to pursue him (Ingram & Harkin 2004). We know moreover that insider participant accounts will contain a limited perspective viewed through their institutional lenses and implicit or explicit vocabularies of motive replete with rationalisations and justifications (Sykes & Matza 1957). And as I pointed out earlier, given the divisiveness of the struggle and the numerous parties involved, there will be a diversity of discourses based on wildly discrepant versions of perceived reality. We have then to accept that the material in this area is limited and inherently difficult to verify.

DIRTY TRICKS

The security community's counter-insurgency campaign in the Province drew on two prime factors:

- Firstly, there was one clearly defined and overriding enemy, the (Provisional) IRA; and by association anyone with republican/ nationalist views, sympathies or connections who could be linked to it, however tenuously, was suspect.
- And secondly, there was deep bias within the security focus which favoured the loyalist paramilitary organisations, which like the IRA were patently illegal, criminal and extremely violent.

But then the latter almost never posed a direct threat to the security forces. Covert operations, for instance, were almost exclusively aimed at nationalists and hardly ever at loyalist paramilitaries. Indeed, of those killed by the state in the Troubles it is estimated that 86 per cent were Catholic, 37 per cent of whom were republican activists and only 4 per cent were loyalists (Rolston 2006). Internment was also at first focused exclusively on nationalists/ republicans and only later on loyalists. This was despite the fact that the latter carried out numerous murders and a number of explosions including the devastating car bombs in Dublin and Monaghan in 1974. This was a UVF operation but with persistent rumours of British intelligence services' involvement. This has been strenuously denied by UVF representatives and by the former insurgent David Ervine after his release from prison and taking up a career in politics (Moloney 2010).

Furthermore, in a four-year period, loyalists killed 185 people (Rolston 2006). In the later stage of the struggle they became well-armed, increasingly ruthless and were killing more people than the IRA; typically their targets were IRA activists, Sinn Fein politicians, republican sympathisers or ordinary Catholics. Loyalists also used the phrase 'terrorizing the terrorists' in focusing on

IRA activists and republican sympathisers (Cusack & McDonald 2008:171). This may be more rhetoric than reality as loyalists were not all that successful at reaching high-level IRA targets. There was also a tendency to be more sectarian than the IRA in that sometimes people were attacked simply because they were assumed to be Catholic. The UVF argued that as 'indiscriminate' IRA violence had led to the conference table it would in turn engage in even more violence for the same purpose; but their violence would be 'discriminate' by being 'directed at male Catholics' (Cusack & McDonald 2008:166).

This bias in favour of the loyalists within the security community went much further than not seriously focusing on loyalist violence in that these illicit organisations were actively used to eliminate people defined as the enemy or as associates of the enemy. It would be naïve to think that the security forces would not engage in techniques that enter the grey area between legality and illegality when involved in a prolonged CT campaign. The techniques open to security and intelligence services generally in combating terrorism will revolve around informants, surveillance, undercover work, subterfuge (front shops/scams), propaganda/disinformation, blackmail, infiltration, use of *agents provocateurs*, sexual entrapment, manipulation of the media, character assassination though leaks and black propaganda, interrogation including torture and, in some cases, fatal violence.

The key issue then is: how far did the enforcers of the law go in bending or breaking the law in order to achieve results? What was the underlying operational code? There have been extreme examples of a ruthless code as in Argentina during the regime of the military *junta* 1978–83 with extensive torture centres like the *Club Atletico* in Buenos Aires; or during the apartheid period in South Africa with horrific killings and torture. Many severe transgressions by the South African security forces were revealed by the Truth and Reconciliation Committee (Boraine 2000; Wilson 2001).

In Northern Ireland there were early accusations against the police and military of using violence during interrogations and of undue psychological pressure on prisoners (Amnesty International 1978; Bennett Report 1979). The ECHR ruled that the latter techniques amounted to 'inhuman and degrading treatment', but deemed it short of torture (*Ireland v UK*: ECHR 1978; Mulcahy 2006:60). Next to reports at the time there have recently been many complaints and claims for compensation from people maintaining they were seriously mistreated during interrogation at the RUC's Castlereagh complex. Indeed, some 200 former detainees have applied to the

Criminal Cases Review Commission for their cases to be reopened on the grounds their confessions were extracted through force. Their requests and accusations have gained credence from former RUC detectives who maintain that 'senior officers encouraged the systematic mistreatment of suspects at Castlereagh interrogation centre' (Cobain 2010a & 2010b). In practice, the three pivotal strategies in the murky bag of tricks were, firstly, using violence or threats of violence to extract confessions, as has been mentioned; secondly, the use of active informants; and, thirdly, collusion with the Protestant paramilitaries.

The significance of the informer system illustrates how far practice in Northern Ireland deviated from the formal procedures propagated on the mainland. The RUC did not abide by the Home Office guidelines on running informers, which hold that 'the police should not let a serious crime go ahead if an informer has told them about it, that they should not mislead a court to protect an informant and rules out the granting of blanket immunity to an informer' (Urban 1993:107). Urban states that those guidelines were often bypassed in Northern Ireland because the RUC felt this was essential in the battle against terrorism. Additionally, the intelligence agencies set out to infiltrate the IRA to get information on its personnel and operations and proved highly successful at recruiting informers (Barker 2004). This was a delicate, dangerous and often cynical game. They also increasingly located arms and explosives and 'jarked' them – rendering them harmless, dangerous to the user or placing tracking devices in them – and installed 'bugs' in houses, phones and under cars.

In combating terrorists the use of informers is crucial, and in Northern Ireland it does seem that many people were prepared to talk. The RUC also developed the techniques of intensive interviewing to a fine, and sometimes not so fine, art; the RUC interrogation centre at Castlereagh developed an intimidating reputation (Bishop & Mallie 1988:321). With jury-less Diplock courts it was valuable to provide the prosecution with a confession from a defendant. Often interrogators would work in relays and keep up the pressure on a suspect. There was 'no good cop, bad cop' routine according to one detainee but only 'bad cop and worse cop. It was sheer brutality' (English 2004:142). The Protection against Terrorism Act of 1974, brought in after the Birmingham bombings, also gave the police more powers for holding suspects for questioning.

Some informants were so-called 'walk-ins' who offered information for a particular reason, such as revenge for some incident or a paramilitary assault on a family member; many were recruited during detention and were swayed by the financial rewards. Others were effectively blackmailed by having possible prosecution for an offence, say some form of sexual excess, waved before them; this revelation might have proved embarrassing with spouses or family members. Although relationships of trust did develop between informants and handlers, the running of informants could be cynical and manipulative and in trying to 'milk' a good source undue risks might be taken. One informant who felt matters were getting too precarious and wanted to move to Australia found his migration application turned down. He was allegedly considered too precious to lose, so security agents intervened to keep him in the Province; subsequently he was killed by the IRA (Dillon 1991:318). There were also a number of spectacular cases involving 'super-grasses' who implicated many people and these cases hit both the IRA and loyalist paramilitaries hard. But, later, the use of supergrasses was discredited given their own involvement in crimes and alleged unreliability (Barker 2006).

FRU AND 'STAKEKNIFE'

Since the GFA in 1998, it has become clear that the intelligence agencies managed to penetrate the highest levels of the IRA. There were British agents within the IRA and *Sinn Fein*, including Kevin Fulton and Denis Donaldson as well as the driver for the *Sinn Fein* leadership (Simpson 2010:24). In particular, the agencies succeeded with an agent in a key position nicknamed 'Stakeknife' (there were various spellings: Ingram & Harkin 2004). He became deputy head of internal discipline, known colloquially as the 'Nutting Squad' for the executions it carried out on IRA members suspected of serious offences but especially of informing. Stakeknife has been identified, has given interviews but denies vehemently many of the accusations levelled at him.

The material in this area raises the issue of participating informants who take part in serious crimes. But as the former FRU agent 'Ingram' states (Ingram & Harkin 2004:59), 'no informant inside a paramilitary organisation could possibly get to the heart of the organisation without committing criminal offences, and this is where the agencies who employ such informants walk a fine line'. Ingram is a 'whistleblower' who reveals that the security agencies recruited killers, that innocent people died as a result and that nothing was done about this from 'above'. Clearly for him this crossed that 'fine line'.[1] In Northern Ireland the law, he maintains, allowed RUC informants to be given a 'participation status' meaning they could commit crimes in the interests of preventing more serious crimes. He admits accepting some of the 'seedier' sides of intelligence work during his career, but began to have serious doubts when 'sometime in the mid to late 1980s the "acceptable line" of operational ethics was crossed'. He gleaned that there was a 'mole' within the IRA producing high-grade intelligence; he was 'the jewel in the crown' (Ingram & Harkin 2004:59 & 64).

Speaking generally, it may well be that agents who have infiltrated insurgent groups will have to commit crimes to maintain their cover. In extreme cases this might even involve killing a fellow agent. For example, an IRA volunteer, Frank Hegarty, was found guilty of informing and was shot. Ingram and Harkin (2004:81) maintain that Frank Hegarty had revealed details of an important arms shipment; that he was an FRU informant; and that he was murdered by another FRU informant to help maintain that person's position. Hegarty had passed accurate information about a Libyan arms shipment to the FRU and its loss was a severe blow to the IRA. The intelligence services tracked the weapons and passed on information to the *Garda* in Ireland, allowing them to recover firearms and ammunition in the South. This was around the time of the Anglo–Irish Agreement, which was partly driven by a British conviction that enhanced cooperation with Ireland was vital to combating the IRA. Allowing the *Garda* the kudos for the find, rather than waiting for the arms to cross the border, sent out a fruitful signal about the benefits of cross-border cooperation.

Indeed, it was Thatcher herself who, according to Ingram and Harkin (2004:120), phoned the Head of MI5 to pass on information about Agent 3018 to the *Garda*. Hegarty's handler, fearing his informant would be compromised, decided to pull him out before the weapons were found and moved him to safe houses in the UK. But he slipped away and returned to the Province; he thought he would be safe as he had promised never to testify against the IRA in court. However, his body was found just inside the border; he had been extensively tortured, his limbs were bound and his eyes were taped meaning he was viewed as an informer. A British agent had apparently been murdered to protect one of the FRU's agents. Ingram argues that a number of people were 'executed' by the IRA, some of whom were innocent of any offence against the IRA; that the British state 'could have been aware of many of these killings';

and that this was done to protect agents in the field and 'throw the IRA off the scent' (Ingram & Harkin 2004:83).

These and other practices were investigated in Northern Ireland by the senior British police officer, (Sir) John Stevens, during a 14-year period related to three investigations, with a later focus on intelligence services' collusion with loyalist paramilitaries. Apparently his three reports convey that what happened was indisputably in conflict with the rule of law; but only a brief interim summary of the third 'collusion' investigation has been published. In it, Stevens (2003) states, 'My Enquiries have highlighted collusion, the wilful failure to keep records, the absence of accountability, the withholding of intelligence and evidence, and *the extreme of agents being involved in murder*' (my emphasis).

FRU AND LOYALIST PARAMILITARIES

What had developed was that elements of the intelligence agencies were leaking information to the loyalist paramilitaries about suspected IRA or Sinn Fein activists or sympathisers who were then murdered. Stevens (2003) reported that some of these victims were totally innocent of any illegal activity. It also emerged that the intelligence agencies even helped loyalist paramilitaries to try to arrange a shipment of weapons from South Africa. In effect, these agencies were responding to the dirty war by themselves opening a bag of dirty tricks that were clearly illegal and promoted further illegality in others. They were leaking information to illegal organisations that they allowed to continue functioning in violent crime, and they colluded in the assassination of blameless UK citizens on UK soil.

For example, when the solicitor Pat Finucane, who had mostly republican clients and who represented the families of deceased republican activists in coroners' courts, was murdered, the gunmen entered his house and shot him twelve times in front of his wife and children while they were at the dinner table. This was clearly a close quarter, shoot to eliminate style of assassination with shots to the head, neck and torso that suggests experienced gunmen (Simpson 2010:23–39). The 'hit-squad' from the UVF allegedly went on to celebrate their kill: a key FRU informer and two SB informers were 'among the guests at this macabre gathering'.[2] One of them claimed the murder had been instigated by his SB handler who said, 'Why don't you whack Finucane?' (Ingram & Harkin 2004:204). Finucane was innocent of any involvement in terrorist activity and had no involvement with the IRA or *Sinn Fein*, according to the RUC spokesperson at the inquest, and this was confirmed by Stevens. And, in addition, his murder could have been prevented and was not at first properly investigated. One of the killers apparently admitted the murder to an RUC officer who secretly taped the meeting; but before the tape reached Stevens, the confession had been erased. When Stevens realised this he was told the tape could 'no longer be found'. Someone in the RUC had, not for the first time, interfered with an external inquiry.

Some RUC officers even became embroiled in Protestant militancy. Members of the RUC's SPG were accused of involvement with the UVF and two were convicted of the murder of an innocent Catholic shopkeeper in 1977, both receiving life sentences (Barker 2006:49). The UVF allegedly received firearms from RUC sources and had RUC aid in the planning of raids (Dillon 1991:265). Intelligence and firearms from the UDR were also said to have reached paramilitary hands; some weapons were stolen in raids, and some were sold by individuals. One UDR member sold weapons and munitions primarily for profit; but these weapons were then used in many murders and other attacks (Cory Report 2004). The first Barron Report (2003) in Ireland into the Dublin and Monahagh bombings maintained that the RUC and UDR must have been aware of the activities of the UVF gang involved and that there were links between the Glenanne gang and the RUC and Army. But it ruled out direct British Army collusion in the bombings. The second Barron Report (2005) examined possible collusion by the security forces in several incidents, including the Miami Showband shooting, in which the 'Red Hand Commandos' were involved; this was a cover name used by the Glenanne gang. Furthermore, some 100 part-time UDR members were prosecuted for a range of crimes including murder, leaking classified documents and causing explosions (Dillon 1991:214 & 220). Four members of the UVF gang involved in the Miami Showband incident were UDR soldiers.[3] As a result of Stevens inquiry into collusion, some 30 of the 94 defendants prosecuted were UDR members; indeed, it was estimated that between 10 per cent and 15 per cent of the UDR had links with the UVF (Cusack & McDonald 2008).

FRU AND NELSON

If 'Stakeknife' was a key informer within the IRA, then Brian Nelson was his equivalent within the UDA. Nelson was born in Northern

Ireland and joined the British Army, but he was a poor soldier and constantly in trouble. He returned to Belfast and became involved with the UDA. His background as a soldier and familiarity with firearms was said to have been valued. Some of his comrades from that time say that he also became involved in killings (Ingram & Harkin 2004:165). After a spell in prison Nelson became an agent; and 'agent number 6137 was given a job that was paid for by British taxpayers: setting up Catholics for murder' (Ingram & Harkin 2004:173).

Initially Nelson's information was used to save lives by preventing murders, but later that changed; from late 1986, for three years 'he would not only be allowed to kill but actively encouraged to kill'. The game had changed. Nelson was now used for what one senior FRU officer called '"proper targeting" and his victims were largely innocent Catholics' (Ingram & Harkin 2004:181). In the Stevens Inquiry (2003), he was implicated in 15 murders, 14 attempted murders and 62 murder conspiracies: in detailing collusion, cover-up and lack of accountability in the security services Stevens went on to say:

> These serious acts and omissions have meant that people have been killed or seriously injured. The unlawful involvement of agents in murder implies that the security services sanctioned killings ... nationalists were known to be targeted but were not properly warned or protected. The coordination, dissemination and sharing of intelligence were poor. Informants and agents were allowed to operate without effective control and to participate in terrorist crimes. Crucial information was withheld from senior investigating officers. (Ingram & Harkin 2004:182)

Following the Stevens Inquiry, Nelson at first evaded arrest, having been tipped off by his FRU handlers, but later turned himself in to the authorities. At his trial in 1992, he pleaded guilty to five conspiracy to murder charges, 15 other charges and was jailed for ten years.

Increasingly, Ingram began to have qualms about these practices within the FRU. He felt it was wrong to try to help arm the Protestant paramilitaries. The IRA had received Libyan weapons and the FRU wanted to 'redress the balance' by using 'loyalists to take the fight to the republicans. The FRU was using loyalist paramilitaries as an extension of the British Army' (Ingram & Harkin 2004:191). Ingram claims, furthermore, that there was a definite shift in emphasis on the appointment to the unit of a new, ambitious senior officer determined to achieve results. Everyone in the 'business', moreover, was pressurised to bend the law because all agents were judged on results; and there was an 'insatiable appetite' for 'exploitable intelligence to aid their efforts to prevent loss of life and frustrate the enemy':

> There should have been safeguards in place, a series of checks and balances, which would have constrained individual officers ... but our legislators let everyone down by allowing the FRU to operate in Northern Ireland with no written guidelines other than Common Law. Obviously there is hierarchy above and beyond the FRU, but that did not, nor could it, impinge on the day-to-day operations of the Unit. I, for one, never received any advice or instructions from anyone or any organisation outside the FRU ... the FRU was a self-regulating body. (Ingram & Harkin 2004:211)

Ingram does not maintain that people high in the hierarchy would have known specific details of operations, but he does state that MI5 was fully aware of FRU activities and, 'it is certain that ministers were also kept informed by the security service of the on-going case files on agents' (Ingram & Harkin 2004:212). When the FRU was faced with the Stevens Inquiry, there were first denials that the Army had any such agents in the Province (there had been over 100 for more than 20 years), then prevarication on supplying files which when supplied had been doctored. Only after *eleven years*, were the 'registry books' finally handed over which indicated what was missing in the files.

Ingram became increasingly unhappy about the change in direction and about the crossing of moral boundaries and discussed this with others; 'There was a level of anxiety in the Unit regarding the direction in which Nelson was being steered, and, by implication, the way in which the FRU was being managed. Sadly, not one person, myself included, felt sufficiently outraged to take a stand' (Ingram & Harkin 2004:214). The turning point for him was when Nelson started to target an agent within the IRA in the late summer of 1987; the FRU faced losing an agent through the efforts of another agent. The FRU set up, according to Ingram, an alternative target, Francisco Notoratonio. He was a pensioner in poor health but was sold to Nelson as an IRA 'godfather' as he was an old-time republican who had been interned twice. An Army raid on his house was arranged to provide detailed maps of the premises.

After studying them the loyalist unit went in early in the morning and headed straight for Notoratonio's bedroom where he lay in bed with his wife; they shot him several times in the chest and back. On the day of the shooting there were no security forces in the vicinity whereas the day before they had been present in abundance; this was often a sign that something had been arranged for the hit-squad. Nelson was apparently gratified with the raid when he saw the full-scale republican funeral for Notoratonio with Gerry Adams carrying the coffin (Ingram & Harkin 2004:218).

Several years later, Ingram published a story with a journalist in the Irish edition of *The People* stating that a senior British intelligence officer, who was still in service in 2000, had 'set up the killing of 67-year-old Francisco Notoratonio' to protect agents within the IRA. Ingram quoted a Stevens Inquiry source as saying: 'There are no rules in this dirty war' (Ingram & Harkin 2004:219). The cynical substitution of Notoratonio for another target dismayed Ingram and led to heated exchanges with colleagues:

> I remember one of my senior officers said something like, 'Didn't Gerry Adams carry the coffin? It couldn't have gone better for us.' Another said, 'We must take the war to the enemy' ... I thought it was wrong then and I still believe it is wrong. It was state-sponsored murder. (Ingram & Harkin 2004:223)

Presumably the justification for the collusion was that in this dirty war of betrayal and deceit the ends are held to justify the means; or perhaps people had simply lost sight of the ends and had promoted the means to ends in themselves. On the attempt to supply South African arms to loyalists Ingram states some agents were convinced that this illegality was perfectly justified; the thinking was the 'end justifies the means' meaning 'rooting out of republicanism at its core'. Finance for the arms deal was organised through illegal activities such as bank robberies and extortion with the compliance of the FRU. After purchase, the 'imported weapons were tracked from source to distribution by the FRU and MI5 by electronic means' (Ingram & Harkin 2004:192). Ingram makes the assumption that this involvement of MI5 could not have happened without some senior politicians being informed. Nelson, who was used for the deal, met South African and MI5 representatives in London before flying to South Africa where he was given 'safe passage' through customs; 'And so, with the indirect help of South African agents and the complicity of the FRU and MI5, the UDA and UVF were able to intensify their violence up until the 1994 cease-fire' (Ingram & Harkin 2004:193). Ingram maintains the arms were actually delivered but the Cory Report (2004) disputes this.

Ingram provides a convincing 'insider' account of a military security agent turned whistle-blower after he became troubled by his conscience when he felt the FRU had stepped over a moral boundary. There are three other sources on collusion, one referring to the FRU and two others with regard to the RUC, which I shall draw from to amplify his first-hand account. The first is a book written about the FRU and Nelson by a former Army officer, journalist and writer, Nicholas Davies. He initially heard the FRU story from an agent and then spent five years investigating and verifying it; he was aided by three confidential interviews with security agents. Although it is impossible to check the authenticity of this material it does convey much detail, which could only have come from people intimately associated with security matters in Northern Ireland (Davies 1999). Indeed, much of what he claims was echoed by the much more reliable second source which is the Cory Report (2004) into the murder of Finucane and three other victims of loyalist violence and the possibility of collusion between the security forces and loyalist paramilitaries. The third source is the so-called 'Ballast' Report from OPONI (2007) on collusion between loyalist paramilitaries and the RUC. It is based on a thorough judicial investigation into police collusion with loyalist informants. The OPONI investigators had the advantage that they were working several years after the GFA and with a relatively compliant PSNI; this compliance was not necessarily true of all former or serving officers.

On the basis of confidential interviews, and written in the 'fly-on-the-wall' style of reconstructed events and conversations, Davies (1999) makes a strong case about the deep involvement of the FRU in systemic deviance. In particular, he strongly asserts that senior government members must have been fully aware of what was taking place. In essence, Davies (1999:239) maintains the following position about the FRU handling of double agent '1033'.[4] Namely, that it raised 'serious issues relating to policing, covert intelligence and the administration of justice in Northern Ireland ... the facts have revealed that senior government ministers, MI5 and Military Intelligence came to the conclusion that it was justifiable to violate the rule of law in fighting a dirty war'. Nelson himself approached the Army and voluntarily offered information on the UDA. Although he was recruited ostensibly to provide intelligence on the UDA – army intelligence was sorely deficient on the loyalist paramilitaries given the overriding attention paid to the IRA and the long-standing contacts between the loyalists and the RUC's SB – he began to be used as a conduit for information that could be used to target people suspected of IRA or *Sinn Fein* activities. The Army was 'desperate for good contacts with the loyalist paramilitaries' and agents felt the RUC was holding back intelligence from them. The military suspected that the RUC's SB was getting intelligence direct from the loyalists as cooperation in the 'Protestant Cause' to stay within the UK at all costs (Davies 1999:34). Also, the Home Office and MI5 felt that after the MRF disbandment the Army should be more active in gathering intelligence and running informants.

An enticing opportunity opened because Nelson became Intelligence Officer for the UDA (legal until 1992). With an FRU computer and technical assistance he built an impressive data base of potential targets. Although he was not always well-disciplined, he impressed his handlers with his attention to detail and dedication in maintaining a meticulous, up-to-date list of some 400 names. FRU agents could see that some data came direct from the RUC and UDR, including photocopies of 'P cards'. A P card was opened on any suspect attracting the interest of the intelligence community, and it contained personal data and information on habits and acquaintances; it was continually updated. Incredibly, Nelson also had direct access to level-5 intelligence data; there were eight levels and most standard Army and RUC units could only access level 2; presumably this could only have been approved at a senior level (Davies 1999:107). He was also paid for his services and helped with setting up as a taxi-driver, buying a house and with a cover-story to satisfy the curious about his means of income.

Nelson was not an easy agent to handle: he drank too much, bragged openly, lacked discipline and was unreliable. Also some UDA operations were conducted in an amateurish way, even to the extent of selecting the wrong target due to carelessness or mistaken identity. Nelson could be frustratingly laconic and dismissive on such occasions. Above all, the agents began to feel that he was lying to them. Yet at the same time there developed a strong dependence on him. At one stage, for instance, Nelson went off to Germany and there emerged a tug-of-war between MI5 and FRU over ownership of him. The FRU feared losing him and a FRU 'delegation' flew to Germany, which was strictly forbidden, and persuaded him to remain loyal to them (Davies 1999:61).

The reservations about Nelson arose because he continually claimed he only passed on information and was not personally informed of any action taken; but suspicion grew that he took an active part not only in selecting the targets but also in the actual attacks. Indeed, the FRU, according to Davies (1999), passed this concern up the hierarchy through an 'MISR' (Military Intelligence Source Report):

> ... over the next few days, however, nothing came back from Downing Street or the JIS to the Force Research Unit officers; no advice, no instructions and no orders. There was no suggestion from any political, military or security service source suggesting that anything must be done to stop such attacks taking place. With no advice, guidance, instructions or orders the Force Research officers also decided to take no action. (Davies 1999:17)

The trouble with a 'crown jewel' informant for any intelligence agency is that their dominant position can disturb the balance of power in handler-informant relations. To protect a rich source of intelligence flowing from a participating informant the handlers have to decide how far to let the informant go in taking part in criminal activities; and how far they will go in providing cover. Ingram makes plain that the FRU went too far with agents within the IRA and Davies argues the same with Nelson within the UDA. Who was running whom? Was Nelson a genuine 'walk-in' or was he a double agent milking the FRU for intelligence of value to the UDA?

With Nelson, the concern arose not only when it appeared he was taking part in killings but also when the UDA started to target people who were simply assumed to be Catholics by location. In the ghettoised geography of Northern Ireland cities, to be walking in a particular direction late at night or to hail a taxi going in the 'wrong' direction could sign someone's death-warrant. There was a rash of purely sectarian killings, on the principle 'any Taig will do' (as loyalist graffiti proclaimed) with 'Taig' being slang for a Catholic, which could only unleash retaliatory, 'tit-for-tat' killings by the IRA. Other victims were only associated with the republican movements by hearsay or association. The human rights lawyer Rosemary Nelson, for instance, was killed by a bomb under her car with the loyalist 'Red Hand Commandos' claiming responsibility. She had assisted republicans in a number of high-profile cases, and had received death threats but had not been offered adequate police protection. There was no evidence of her involvement in any nationalist/republican movement. Davies comments that the UVF gunmen were carrying out killings that forced the IRA to retaliate, hence bringing about the 'fear and anarchy' they sought. But they were not the 'only people responsible for bringing about this dreadful state of affairs; the Force Research Unit, a secret arm of the Army, could also be held responsible for the rapidly deteriorating situation between the two communities' (Davies 1999:99). In the decade after 1985 following the signing of the All Irish Agreement, the loyalists were killing more people than the IRA.

Davies portrays FRU handlers who were increasingly frustrated by Nelson's conduct; he seemed more and more to be beyond control.[5] Indeed, on occasion they ordered the saturation of areas by security forces to forestall an attack. But of course the FRU was engaged in a dangerous game. For it encouraged hits by loyalists against 'hard' republican targets – and would provide them with intelligence, addresses, photos and safe passage – but tried to halt the indiscriminate attacks against targets not of their choice. On one occasion Davies claims they even suggested that a security conscious IRA target be approached with a hit-squad wearing RUC uniforms to get him to open his front-door; this happened and he was killed. On another occasion the UDA had identified someone they suspected of being an active Provo; the FRU provided information, the UDA conducted surveillance and a hit squad was sent in to murder him when he slipped back from a hide-out to visit his family.

> This had been a totally successful operation between British Intelligence and the gunmen of the UDA, with Nelson as the go-between. British Intelligence had provided the photographs [of the suspect] and his home address; the UDA intelligence had correctly traced and targeted a man they believed to be a Provo activist. The UDA gunmen had provided the killers and the weapons. And only a handful of people had any idea that Britain's Army Intelligence, working on orders from above to act aggressively, had been responsible for providing the information that led to the killing. (Davies 1999:126)

The real difficulty arose when the FRU tried to halt the attacks, which targeted popular, solid members of the community. For instance, UDA gunmen shot and wounded Alex Maskey who was a 'well-respected, well-trusted, well-known Belfast city councillor who represented the ordinary Catholics of West Belfast' (Davies 1999:105). Moreover, the RUC's SB noticed this sudden assertiveness in UDA operations and picked up rumours about Nelson and Army involvement. It raised its concerns in the JIS and in the TCGs of

SB. This did not lead to any action. That the FRU continued for so long with Nelson is due, according to Davies, to FRU operatives receiving no firm guidance from above and interpreted this non-intervention as tacit approval. He argues that all covert operations were cleared with the JIS, which then sought a political decision from London in the JIC:

> On no occasion were instructions received by the FRU in Belfast telling them to halt the sectarian targeting and killings. And yet ... MI5 officers, senior security advisers and all members of the Joint Intelligence Committee, who usually met once a week in London, were aware that a man named Brian Nelson, the intelligence officer of the UDA, was involved in many of the murders and dozens of the conspiracies to murder during that period. It was further known that officers of the Force Research Unit were 'handling' Nelson at that time. And yet nothing was done to stop the killings. The battle against the Provisional IRA had entered a new phase about which [senior government members] appeared fully aware. (Davies 1999:22)

In essence, he firmly maintains that the top level of government was fully informed on what was going on: but there is, of course, no way of confirming this. Yet Mrs Thatcher was the assertive Prime Minister who went to war with Argentina over the distant Falklands and authorised the sinking of the Argentine warship, the General Belgrano. Davies (1999:69) further argues that she was 'incandescent with rage' after the Brighton bombing and the incompetence of the intelligence services and forcefully demanded 'improved performance'. This may well have been perfectly legitimate but what Davies is suggesting is that senior government members wanted to take the fight to the IRA but the controversy surrounding the three RUC shootings persuaded them to turn to the Army. As a result of this pressure from above the SAS and FRU took up the initiative in what Davies refers to as a 'brilliant strategy':

> To the FRU ... the ruthless killings also showed the aggressive methods now being taken by the government in its bid to defeat the IRA. The government had not been slow to learn the lessons from the Stalker affair which had aroused heavy, critical media investigations. That singular experience had shown the politicians that when the RUC took tough, hard-line action against the Provos, the political fall-out was more difficult to contain than

when the army became involved in such tactics. Although the Provos had undoubtedly been armed during their attack on the Loughall police station, no attempt had been made by the SAS to arrest them. The soldiers had simply laid an ambush and mowed down the gunmen and bombers with heavy and sustained fire. (Davies 1999:153)

However, given Nelson's uncontrolled behaviour, his all too revealing bragging and the 'village' character of Belfast, it was only a matter of time before his role between the UDA and FRU started to unravel. According to Davies, an FRU member was approached by a colleague from SB to say it was now crystal clear within the intelligence community that Nelson was working hand-in-glove with the FRU. The noticeable rise in UDA activity and its new assertiveness had clearly indicated that something had helped change the UDA's style; and repeatedly Nelson's name came up as the linchpin. Another important factor was that around that time the investigating team of John Stevens from the mainland was examining police collusion and its brief had been extended to the Army. The FRU had hoped to stay out of sight until this scrutiny blew over but now the cover of their key operative was about to be blown, while they faced an unprecedented investigation for an agency that was not supposed to exist. The FRU was eventually forced to cooperate due to pressure by Stevens on the Army hierarchy to order the handing over of documents and recordings or face legal action.

According to Davies, some SB members were prepared to lend their military colleagues a hand, as SB had earlier experienced the intrusiveness of the Stalker investigation. Davies refers to a fire that started in offices used by Stevens. The RUC official investigation concluded it was an accident caused by a cigarette end, but Stevens spoke of 'arson'. And an attempt had been made years earlier to start a fire in the offices of the Stalker Inquiry. Whichever version is correct, accident or conspiracy, the Stevens team certainly felt it was being obstructed. Indeed, the Criminal Investigation Department (CID) officer who investigated the fire wrote that Stevens admitted, 'his team was under extreme stress during most of their stay, almost to the point of paranoia ... To them, Northern Ireland was an evil, treacherous and hostile environment in which they felt they could trust practically no one' (Simpson 2010:49).

With external pressure mounting, Nelson was called in and told firmly by his handlers to say nothing to Stevens about his relationship with the FRU. He was not a registered agent as was often the case with MI5 operatives, which would have given him protection; he was informed that if he confessed to anything he would have to face the consequences of any criminal conduct in court. If he kept silent then he would be safe. When interviewed by the Stevens' team, however, he ignored the FRU advice and immediately started to 'sing' about his activities with the FRU. Initially Stevens had concluded that collusion had not been 'widespread or institutionalised' but he had not considered the Army; he became more forceful by his third report. Fortunately for the FRU personnel, no prosecutions of agents took place in order to keep information about the workings of military intelligence out of the public arena.

Following Nelson's exposure there was a protracted form of plea bargaining whereby he would plead guilty to several offences and receive only a modest prison sentence. Many meetings were held between 'Military Intelligence, the Director of Public Prosecutions, Chief Constable John Stevens and a host of lawyers, including the all-important Army lawyers in a battle over the charges Nelson would face' (Davies 1999:236). The trial was, then, one of those charades in Northern Ireland when deals had been struck and 'national security' was at stake; for there was much praise for the incorrigible and violent Nelson. An unnamed officer in military intelligence, 'Colonel J.', the then CO (Commanding Officer) of the FRU, spoke of Nelson being motivated, 'by team spirit and loyalty to the army... I have no doubt it was to make up for past misdemeanours, to save lives and eventually to bring down the terrorist organisation'. He tried to exonerate Nelson by claiming he was, 'an important agent of some standing whose product was passed through the intelligence community of Northern Ireland at the highest level'; and that this information had saved *217* lives (Davies 1999:237, my emphasis). Nelson's defence counsel went on to reinforce this by claiming that Nelson had been of 'great service to the community', saving many lives. In sentencing him to ten years' imprisonment, the judge added that Nelson had 'with the greatest courage submitted himself to constant danger and intense strain for three years' and repeated that he had 'passed on possibly life-saving information in respect of 217 threatened individuals' (Davies 1999:238). He was out of jail within four years, relocated abroad by the authorities and said by his family to have died of cancer in 2003 (Ingram & Harkin 2004:188). The Cory Report (2004) maintains that the FRU's CO misled the court, that he was following a prepared script and the claims for Nelson saving 217 lives by the CO and the judge were widely at odds with reality.

Finally, if both Ingram and Davies are to be believed, ministers and officials in the government were aware of attacks on republicans by the RUC, the SAS and by loyalists 'run' by the RUC or FRU. In such matters there are generally no direct 'orders' but there may well have been 'signals' that could have been seen by others as tacit approval. This was reinforced by the almost unrestricted autonomy granted to the RUC's SB and the Army's FRU and by the lack of guidelines and instructions:

> In the last three years of the 1980s, however, it was the conspiracy between Military Intelligence and the Ulster Defence Association which carried the battle on the streets to the very heart of the republican movement. And the campaign of intimidation and killing of Sinn Fein/IRA politicians, gunmen, bombers, supporters and sympathisers by the UDA, aided and abetted by British Military Intelligence, was known about by MI5 – and a few senior government ministers and civil servants. (Davies 1999:199)

Again, this is speculation that simply cannot be verified. It can be viewed, moreover, as a form of special pleading with a whiff of censoriousness that is often found in hierarchical organisations of pushing blame back to those at the top, which may or may not be justified.

The extent of collusion between the agencies and loyalist paramilitaries does, however, sound conceivable given the supporting material from other sources, including the Cory Report (2004) and the Stevens Inquiry (2003). There is, moreover, what we know generally about intelligence agencies, covert operations, informant handling and the repertoire of 'dirty tricks' employed during serious security situations (Marx 1988). The Cory Report (2004) illuminated the intimate links between SB and loyalist paramilitaries in the late 1980s and there was also a report from OPONI in 2007 that portrayed a similar pattern but then almost a decade after the GFA and cessation of hostilities and I shall deal with these next.

Putting the material of Ingram and Davies together leads to the conclusion that the Army's FRU and the RUC's SB had been complicit in murders and assassinations by proxy. Within the ranks of loyalist paramilitaries it found people happy to serve the interests of the British state by becoming its willing executioners.

SB AND COLLUSION: CORY AND OPONI

Cory Report

With persistent rumours of security forces collusion with loyalist paramilitaries in the deaths of people associated with nationalism/republicanism in some way (however tenuous or unfounded the link), the government set up an inquiry into the evidence. This was not a full-blown public inquiry, with witnesses under oath and with possible judicial consequences, but a review of the documentary evidence to ascertain if there were grounds for further action. The former Canadian Supreme Court Judge, Peter Cory, reported in 2004 and he and his team examined the material into the deaths of Patrick Finucane, Robert Hamill, Rosemary Nelson and Billy Wright.[6]

The Report clearly indicates that the RUC's SB was receiving intelligence from the FRU based on strong inside information, which had originated from participating informers within the loyalist paramilitaries (including Brian Nelson), that indicated possible attacks against a number of people. The pattern that emerged from Cory's review was that the SB continually downplayed the significance of that intelligence from the FRU (viewing it often as 'rubbish'); persistently failed to warn those seen to have nationalist sympathies or links to the republican cause about the serious threats to their lives; was in contrast far more likely to warn those loyalists subject to threats from the republican paramilitaries (mostly PIRA and INLA); and repeatedly failed to conduct forceful investigations into certain deaths. In effect, the Inquiry revealed a pattern that both FRU and SB were primarily geared to agent security more than the safety of proposed targets of paramilitary violence; that they did not cooperate well and misled other parts of the enforcement community including the courts but particularly the RUC's CID; and that this pattern was motivated by protecting the 'national interest'.

Concretely, regarding the solicitor Finucane there was solid and repeated intelligence of threats against his life which were not passed on to him. After his killing, there was convincing intelligence about the possible killers and the firearms used which was not followed up with any vigour by SB; and there was poor cooperation between SB and the CID investigators into the murder (which led to 'angry exchanges'). Indeed, the SIO (Senior Investigating Officer) on the Finucane case was surprised to receive a highly unusual visit from the ACC responsible for the CID in the Province who advised him; 'Alan, if I were you I would not get too deeply involved in this case' (Simpson 2010:31).[7] Finucane was a law-abiding citizen of the UK and deserved to be warned of the imminent danger to his life and to be protected; he was not.

Underlying that reprehensible bias was a dominating tendency to assume guilt by association regarding anyone who worked with nationalist suspects during trials, for assisting families at inquests related to the deaths of alleged IRA members, who had family members in nationalist/republican circles or who were simply rumoured to be involved in such circles. This corrosive partiality was not only prevalent within the SB but also at the highest levels of the RUC. For example, the then Chief Constable, Hermon, was involved in darkening Finucane's name prior to his killing, both in a conversation with Douglas Hogg MP – who subsequently spoke in the House of Commons about lawyers 'unduly sympathetic' to the IRA – and later in an interview for the *Sunday Times* in 1999. This reveals something of the animosity generated by anyone who simply associated professionally with republicans. Indeed, Hogg later said that he had been briefed in a meeting attended by the Chief Constable and Deputy Chief Constable of the RUC and SB officers about Finucane and others (Cory Report 2004). By all accounts Finucane was a dedicated professional who stood for the protection of the civil and human rights of the people he represented, who also included some Protestants, but he did have family members in republican circles and this led SB consistently to refer to him as if he was an active nationalist/republican or 'republican sympathizer' although there was no evidence for this. It is reprehensible that this bias was not only present among the members of SB but also within the highest echelons of the RUC; and that an MP took part in darkening the reputation of several people who were subsequently killed. This indicates that there were dubious practices within the UK and that these were not unlike those in contemporary Russia where those who fight for peoples' rights are intimidated or meet an untimely end (Rawlinson 2009).

The Cory Report (2004:63) remarked on these specific cases and the wider pattern of bias that led to avoidable fatalities with what some might view as overly mild language:

An unbiased observer reviewing the work of the RUC around the time of the Finucane murder [1989] might decide that, although the Royal Ulster Constabulary always displayed great courage in its work, it failed on occasion to meet the very high standards of impartiality and fairness required of any police force, but particularly of a Northern Ireland police force.

It is disturbing, then, that the deficiencies within SB that Cory had laid out with great clarity in reference to a murder in 1989 were still present well over a decade later. And if the motive earlier had been 'national interest' at a time of turbulent conflict, then that could hardly be offered as a rationalisation long after the GFA ended that conflict.

OPONI and the 'Ballast' Report

OPONI, the Office of the Police Ombudsman for Northern Ireland, was established as part of the peace process and became operational in 2000. This independent and impartial oversight agency enjoys extensive powers and resources and it investigates all complaints against the police. It has established itself as a solid and thorough investigatory body that has attracted respect internationally for its professionalism and for its willingness to tackle tough assignments, as in its critical report on the RUC regarding the Omagh bombing (OPONI 2005). Although it faced some predictable opposition from certain loyalist politicians, including personal attacks on the first Ombudsman (Baroness) Nuala O'Loan,[8] and from some in the RUC who were reeling from the Patten Report, it has gained credibility and also profited from new leadership of the PSNI. This is far more compliant than the prickly, if not obstructionist, predecessors at the top of the RUC. The PSNI's first Chief Constable, Sir Hugh Orde, was in fact Senior Investigating Officer (SIO) to Stevens during his inquiries in the Province and hence familiar with some of the skulduggery that had taken place in police and Army circles. Cooperation by the PSNI with OPONI has, then, improved considerably since 2001.

In the Ballast report (OPONI 2007), the Ombudsman ostensibly examines the circumstances surrounding the death of one person, Raymond McCord Junior; but, effectively, this report amounts to a penetrating spotlight not only into collusion between SB and a loyalist informer but also conveys a portrait of SB's working-style, particularly with regard to informant handling. The report is based on interviews with former and serving police officers, intelligence reports and 'many thousands' of documents. Of interest is that some former officers, invited to cooperate on terms of strict anonymity and in a location of their choosing, refused to talk to the investigators and these included 'two retired Assistant Chief Constables, seven Detective Chief Superintendents and two Detective Superintendents' (OPONI 2007:5). Some of those who did reply, along with some serving officers, gave 'evasive, contradictory and on occasion farcical answers to questions. On occasion these answers indicated either a significant failure to understand the law, or contempt for the law' or were later found to be 'completely untrue' (OPONI 2007:6). Three retired officers were arrested for not attending an interview under criminal caution. A number of officers who did talk portrayed themselves as 'victims' of the situation in the period under scrutiny.

The investigation focused on a number of violent incidents but also the blocking of a CID operation by SB; in particular attention was paid to the relationship between SB and 'Informant I' who was suspected of involvement in ten murders, including that of Raymond McCord Junior, and in a number of other criminal activities. The identity of Informant I has since become public (Simpson 2010:37). His offences included armed robbery, assault and grievous bodily harm, punishment shootings and attacks, possession of ammunition, criminal damage, drug dealing, extortion, hijacking and conspiracy to murder. The report concludes that little or no police action was taken with regard to these offences.

This led the Ombudsman to conclude that there were grave concerns about certain police practices. These included the failure to arrest informants for crimes they had allegedly confessed to or to treat them as suspects; concealing intelligence about informants' involvement in murder and other crimes; arresting murder suspects, holding sham interviews and releasing them without charge; deliberately producing misleading interview notes; and failing to record and retain original interview notes. There was, further, the failure to record notes of meetings with informants; no recording that an informant was suspected of a crime although he had been arrested and interviewed for that crime; not informing the DPP that an informant was a suspect in a crime about which a file had been submitted to the DPP; and withholding intelligence, including the names of suspects, that could have been used to detect or prevent crimes. The inventory continues with blocking searches of an informant's home and of an alleged UVF arms cache; providing misleading and inaccurate information for possible consideration by the Court with the effect of protecting an informant; finding ammunition at an informer's residence but taking no action; and withholding information about an alleged hide-out of murder suspects. On occasion, junior staff members were instructed not to complete records of incidents. There were efforts to ensure that there was no formal link between an informant and the possession of explosives which, according to informal notes, might have been used in a crime; and cancelling the 'wanted' status of murder suspects because of 'lack of resources' and not following up on those suspects. There was a pattern of destroying or losing forensic exhibits; continuing to use informants suspected of crimes without a risk assessment as to their suitability as informants; and not complying with Home Office guidelines on informant handling nor with the Regulation of Investigatory Powers Act of 2000 (known as 'RIPA').

Having listed these serious shortcomings in standards of professional policing, the report concludes:

> The cumulative effect of these activities, as described by police officers and as demonstrated in documentation recovered, was to protect Informant 1 and other informants from investigation. In the absence of explanation as to why these events occurred, the Police Ombudsman has concluded that *this was collusion by certain police officers with identified UVF informants.* (OPONI 2007:13; my emphasis)

It also states that intelligence indicates that a member of a specific UVF unit killed Raymond McCord Junior. Furthermore, from the analysis that emerges from the investigation, one can discern that rules and procedures on informant handling as used in part by the CID were not employed by SB. When new rules were introduced in 1997 they were not applied in SB following a decision at chief officer level.

The information on Informant 1 indicates that he was a member of the UVF and became an informant through close friendship with a police officer; he worked for both CID and SB, became an SB informant in 1991 and worked only for SB from 1995–2003. Yet he was never registered as a CID informant and was never given participating 'informant status' by the RUC/PSNI. He provided over more than 400 pieces of intelligence during twelve years and was himself the subject of some 500 pieces of intelligence. He was paid around £80,000 between 1991 and 2003. He had a long career of involvement in crime including murder and attempted murder and intelligence linked him to 72 different crimes including punishment attacks, bombings and drug dealing between 1989 and 2002 (OPONI 2007).

This relationship with Informant 1 was replicated with other informants who were members of the UVF and who were associated with Informant 1. From this material, the investigators concluded that there was a 'major failure to ensure the proper management of

Informant I and other informants' (OPONI 2007:36). A major factor in trying to conduct the OPONI investigation was the 'generally poor standard of record-keeping', which made retrieval difficult for the investigators (OPONI 2007:38). The TCGs, the most senior groups involved in SB decisions, routinely destroyed their documents, and the financial management of funds to informants 'lacked any clear structure, was totally inadequate, lacked transparency and had no audit processes' (OPONI 2007:39). Many important documents were missing, including some on the most serious of crimes, and some had been destroyed by SB.

With regard to the murder of Mr McCord Junior, as a result of a vicious beating, it emerged that initially he was arrested for possession of drugs that he was trying to bring into the Province at the request of Informant I. The loss of the drugs by police confiscation was most disadvantageous to Informant I:

> Police documentation, received over the hours and days following Mr. McCord's murder, indicates that Mr. McCord died following instructions issued by Informant I, following a dispute over the drugs for which Mr. McCord was previously arrested, and that Informant I's creditors threatened to inform the UVF senior hierarchy of his involvement in drugs. (OPONI 2007:43)

Suspicion fell on 'Man D', who was being held in the Maze Prison; but a police request for a search of his cell and examination of his clothing was refused by the prison authorities on the grounds that the paramilitaries controlled the various wings of the prison and a search would cause a riot. In liaison with the 'Commanding Officer' of the UVF wing, Man D was arrested but his cell was not searched. A number of other people were arrested, including Informant I, who was released after questioning.

In relation to the specific complaints about the murder of Raymond McCord Junior the Ombudsman concluded that a police informant was a suspect. Furthermore, there were failures in the investigation that may 'have significantly reduced the possibility of anyone being prosecuted for the murder'. The Ombudsman could not confirm that a police informant had ordered the murder but she could substantiate the complaint that an individual and 'those working for him had been protected from arrest and prosecution for years'. She goes on to say intelligence was ignored by the police, that they went on utilising Informant I, 'despite his criminal record and the extensive intelligence they held in respect of alleged serious criminality because he had value to them as an informant. This was wrong' (OPONI 2007:50).

Following that part of the report there follows an examination of informant involvement in a number of murders and the police response. I will summarise some of the main points made by the Ombudsman in the detailed investigation of this matter. Informant I was arrested and questioned in relation to a murder. Generally the interview team comprised his own CID and SB handlers. The official interview notes did not always reflect the content of the interview. CID prepared a file for the DPP on a murder and an attempted murder; CID then requested that SB check its files under the requirement to inform the DPP of any informant involvement. The Deputy ACC responsible for SB replied that 'no such disclosure was required, despite the fact that there was a clear obligation to do so' (OPONI 2007:53). Informant I admitted involvement in an attempted murder to his CID and SB handlers but the CID record of the conversation does not mention this. The records 'implicating Informant I in murder and the four attempted murders have been destroyed, thus protecting Informant I from potential prosecution ... The police interview process was seriously flawed and contrary to any model of ethical policing' (OPONI 2007:57).

In addition, Informant I admitted to a murder to his SB handlers, but they did not respond. A senior CID officer is alleged to have said, at the prospect of Informant I being arrested and confessing to the murder, that SB 'could not afford to lose Informant I, as he was probably the most important intelligence asset in that UVF grouping' (OPONI 2007:64). When Informant I was arrested for a murder he was released without charge. A Detective Sergeant officer stated that this was 'just going through the motions' as it was common practice to arrest 'a source who had provided information about an incident, so as to provide cover for them'; he went on to say that he 'felt like a gooseberry' during an interview by Detective Constable A of Informant I was because the informant was the officer's source and the interview was a 'sham' (OPONI 2007:73). Detective Sergeant M stated that Informant I admitted to involvement in a murder in 1993; he did not arrest him because SB was in 'total control of the RUC' and that RUC Force Orders 'restricted the activities of police officers dealing with informants' (OPONI 2007:68). With regard to another murder there were failings in the investigation and the destruction of and loss of exhibits with the Ombudsman concluding that SB 'did not deal properly with information about the wrongful acts of its agents, and that Special Branch colluded with the murderers of Mr Harbinson, by concealing information received following the murder, and by continuing to employ the two informants after the murder' (OPONI 2007:91).

In 1997 the CID received information about the location of UVF arms and explosives as well as a list of intended murder targets. CID applied to SB for clearance to search a number of premises but this was denied for four locations (including two locations used by Informant I and the supposed site of the UVF cache). Because this was assumed to be on grounds of National Security, CID could not challenge this. Quite amazingly, two detectives took munitions from a location and transported them in an ACC's car, without his or the driver's knowledge, and placed them in a hide on the M2 motorway; one of them then directed search teams to the site as if the UVF had hidden them there. Then, in 1997 a device exploded near the *Sinn Fein* offices in Monaghan in the Republic; only the detonator exploded and there was a suggestion that the explosives had been 'jarked' and returned to the UVF. A confidential report to the DPP mentions that Informant I 'thwarted a bomb attack in Monaghan' but does not mention that Informant I took part in the attack, that 'the explosives had been returned to him by the police' and that he subsequently claimed a reward (OPONI 2007:102). An officer tasked to collect the explosives and return them to Informant I stated that he was under instructions to make no written records. On this incident the Ombudsman again concludes that there was collusion. There is detailed intelligence from CID and the Drugs Squad that Informant I was involved in drug dealing. He sometimes supplied SB with information about other drug-dealers 'including some of his own associates. In analysing this intelligence, it appears that his motivation in supplying this information was to incriminate rival drug-dealers, in order to protect his own interests and maintain control over the drugs trade in his area' (OPONI 2007:111). A punishment shooting by Informant I persuaded another informant to deal for him. The North Belfast UVF had moved into drug dealing but used local dealers to work on their behalf:

> Police documentation records that monies from drug operations formed a major part of the revenues of loyalist paramilitaries during this period. The failure by police to deal with this aspect of criminality meant that this source of funding continued ... The Police Ombudsman considers that Special Branch deliberately disregarded most of Informant I's involvement in drug dealing from 1994 onwards. (OPONI 2007:114)

A central feature of the inquiry is the attention paid to failings in the supervision and management of informants. There were Home Office Guidelines for the handling of informants but these were geared to ordinary criminals and conventional crimes and were not compiled with terrorists in mind. The report maintains that the guidelines could have provided a structure for 'regular assessment of informants, clearly defined and auditable processes for intelligence handling, annual reviews of their contribution and situation, and control over any notified future occasions on which an informant was permitted to engage in a crime' (OPONI 2007:123). Encapsulated in the guidelines was the element of 'participating informants' who could be authorised to commit crimes within certain limitations. The rules were not applied to SB and some officers perceived them to be 'unworkable' as they had not been designed to accommodate terrorism. The investigators could find no documentation that any of the informants examined in the report had been given participating informant status. A system for doing this was established in 2001. In practice, SB decided what information was to be a passed on to the CID or Uniform Branch; on terrorist murders SB was supposed to liaise with the CID investigating teams but the OPONI investigators found intelligence which should have been passed on to CID that was marked as 'No Downward Dissemination' (OPONI 2007:126). Then, in 1997 the RUC adopted new rules on informant management taken from ACPO guidelines drawn up in 1995. A decision at chief officer level was taken, however, that these would not apply to SB. In 2000 RIPA came into effect (the Regulation of Investigatory Powers Act); in the act informants are referred to as 'Covert Human Intelligence Sources' or 'CHIS' and this was followed in 2002 with a code of practice. RIPA also established the Office of the Surveillance Commissioner to review and oversee practices and procedures.

The Ombudsman reports that there was evidence of non-compliance with RIPA by SB and referred this to the Surveillance Commissioner who concluded that there were multiple failures within SB to comply with RIPA in relation to the handling of Informant I. This non-compliance also applied to CID where the handling of informants was sometimes 'quite bizarre' (OPONI 2007:129). Behind this was also a lack of training and of intrusive supervision by chief officers responsible for SB.

In brief, this OPONI Report maintains that there was RUC collusion in the cases it examined. It quotes (Lord) Stevens definition of collusion in his third report: 'The wilful failure to keep records, the absence of accountability, the withholding of intelligence and evidence, the extreme of agents being involved in murder'. And Judge Cory, in his report on collusion with regards to several murders (including that of Pat Finucane) states:

> The definition of collusion must be reasonably broad ... That is to say that army and police forces must not act collusively by ignoring or turning a blind eye to the wrongful acts of their servants or agents, or supplying information to assist them in their wrongful acts. Any lesser definition would have the effect of condoning or even encouraging state involvement in crimes, thereby shattering confidence in these important agencies. (OPONI 2007:132)

The Ombudsman, working with these definitions, concludes that collusion did take place in the cases it examined and she summarises the collusive practices (OPONI 2007:133–7); she adds that the conduct with regard to handling Informant I indicates 'systemic' failures.

For example, the report states that there was a culture of 'subservience' to SB within the RUC but traces this to chief officer level. The conduct of officers of lower rank was related to 'knowledge and support at the highest levels' of the organisation:

> Chief Officers should have been aware of the processes used. The most serious failings are at Chief Officer level, particularly those officers who were responsible for Special Branch, since they are responsible for ensuring that training and systems are put in place to meet legal and policy requirements.

She adds significantly a comment on the dominant role of SB and how that distorted other areas of policing:

> *A culture of subservience to Special Branch developed within the RUC.* Officers in the rest of the RUC have articulated quite clearly that Special Branch maintained control over those normal ethical policing activities which affect either Special Branch informants or Special Branch operations. The consequence of this was that, in the absence of effective Chief Officer management of Special Branch, *it acquired domination over the rest of the organization which inhibited some normal policing activities.* (OPONI 2007:143; my emphasis)

Reflecting on this, the Ombudsman sums up with the vitally important observation, 'This investigation demonstrates graphically the dangers of a separated and effectively unaccountable specialist intelligence department with extensive and uncontrolled powers' (OPONI 2007:145).

In brief, the OPONI Ballast Report on collusion reveals the following. There was systemic deviance from rules, policies and procedures by SB, but also CID, in informant handling; informants were involved in the most serious of crimes and were effectively protected from investigation and prosecution by police officers who also richly rewarded those informants; on occasion officers actively assisted in planting evidence to deflect suspicion from informants. This collusion was effectively routine and systemic and persisted through changes of RUC leadership and through changes in policy, procedure and legislation; it persisted after the official end of terrorist activity, during the peace process and during concerted efforts to reform the RUC/PSNI. It also continued when it was clear that some of the informant activities were related to involvement in ordinary crimes rather than offences related to the security situation. There existed a resilient and persistent culture of collusion that fostered poor record keeping, interference with evidence, destroying documents and evidence, conducting sham interviews with suspects, pressurising officers not to take notes or to falsify notes and carrying out arrests on informants which were not designed to further investigations into crimes allegedly committed by them but to provide them with a cover story within their paramilitary organisation and criminal environment. The evidence indicates that one part of the RUC, Special Branch, had a disproportionate influence on the rest of the organisation; that its culture and practice of giving primacy to intelligence from active informants made the organisation dependent on those informants. The organisation ended up allowing them to be involved in crimes related to terrorist organisations but also ordinary crimes; this overwhelming emphasis on the special status of active informants carried with it the 'capture' of the organisation by the informants. Informants were at times virtually handling the handlers while there was mutual manipulation and abuse of the financial reward system. The final responsibility and accountability for this long and systemic deviance must rest with the force leadership.

There are, finally, two more observations to be made arising from the Ballast Report. The first is that there patently was still at the time of the inquiry a defensive if not dismissive culture among some former and serving officers of non-compliance with external oversight. Perhaps one can understand this, given the turbulent and stressful times the RUC has been through and the amount of hostile scrutiny to which it has been exposed; but it is disappointing that former chief officers did not respond to a request from OPONI for an interview. If officers of this level treat oversight with disdain then this must surely give off a powerful message that condones non-compliance in the lower ranks. This is especially the case in that non-compliance, and even obstruction by chief officers, was a feature of the Stalker Inquiry some 20 years earlier. Someone said that the GFA was Sunningdale for slow learners, meaning it had taken over 20 years to achieve what had been proposed much earlier. The OPONI Ballast Report can, then, perhaps be seen as Stalker for very slow learners. The second concluding point is more encouraging in that the report contains evidence of a positive paradigm shift within the RUC/PSNI since 2003 to strong and active compliance with external oversight (Orde 2003).

6
Investigations, Courts, Inquiries and Whistle-blowing

In this chapter I shall turn to those key institutional arrangements that normally in a democratic society serve as the guarantors of legitimacy and legality in the search for justice and truth in relation to probable misconduct or crime. These are criminal investigations, the inquest, the courts and external inquiries. But throughout the Troubles there was often a discrepancy between the promise of reliability, impartiality and integrity within these institutions and the reality of poor functioning, serious malfunctioning, illicit manipulation and systemic bias. For example, Mulcahy (2006:71) asserts that in the Province over half of those killed by the security services, 357 individuals, were 'unarmed at the time of their death; many of the killings involved suspicious circumstances; and in many cases civilian eyewitnesses and/or forensic evidence directly contradicted the official account of events'. Yet often these cases were not seriously investigated, were not prosecuted and rarely ended in a conviction. In the light of the material presented earlier and taking into account the special circumstances in Northern Ireland, I shall examine the impact this skewing had on the functioning of the institutions of enforcement, justice and oversight.

CRIME SCENES: INVESTIGATIONS AND INQUIRIES: COURTS

One element in greasing the 'slide' into biased functioning and dubious non-functioning was a sense among many law enforcers that the law, and the criminal justice system, was simply not effective or, worse, biased towards the insurgents. One former SB officer writes of the frustration on confronting suspects of terrorism in interrogation who remained silent, enabling them to be released under the rules then in force:

> It is hard for the general public to understand how frustrated and helpless those interviewing officers throughout Northern Ireland felt as these PIRA, INLA, UDA and UVF murderers sat in front

of them, guilty yet fully protected under the Queen's law. The system was a joke and the joke was on us. (Barker 2004:110)

Suspects could be held for three or seven days depending on the offence and legislation under which it fell but, if they could hold out and remain silent, then they had to be released. There was also the case of Collins (1998); he was a dedicated IRA member who worked for H. M. Customs but used this as cover to take part in operations. When he was arrested he 'coughed' and told in detail everything he knew about IRA activities and personnel; in the dock, however, he recanted and complained of undue pressure to confess. The judge accepted this and ordered him to be released. It must have been difficult for his interrogators and prosecutors – and for the families of the victims killed in operations he was involved in, including the murder of a fellow colleague in Customs – to watch a self-confessed terrorist walk out of court a free man.[1]

Another feature was the collapse of umpteen cases involving 'super-grasses'. There were about 30 of them from both sides of the paramilitary divide and their information led to some 600 arrests, with half of these being charged, and to sentences of collectively almost 4,000 years (McDonald & Holland 2010:254). Yet many convictions were later overturned on appeal. This also happened with criminal cases in Britain that were based on evidence from super-grasses. The difficulty of using them in court in Northern Ireland was illustrated by the SB officer Barker (2004) who had a long and close relationship with a super-grass, known as 'Raymond'. On the basis of Raymond's testimony, which took six weeks to present to the court, 39 defendants appeared before Justice Lowry:

On 18 December, however, Lowry suddenly stopped the trial and threw all the cases out of court ... The reason given by Lowry was that Raymond's evidence was uncorroborated and he described him as 'a selfish and self-regarding man to whose lips a lie comes as easily as the truth.' It is almost impossible to describe the shock that the investigating team and I felt at this turn of events. If the court had wished, I could easily have given evidence to corroborate Raymond's testimony from documentation I had in my possession, evidence that detailed the activities of those defendants ... I was never given the chance. We were left dumbfounded and could only sit and watch in total disbelief as the jubilant defendants and their families left the court. (Barker 2004:218)

Subsequent super-grass trials also collapsed. Barker's view as an SB officer is that this was a travesty of justice and claims that the judiciary succumbed to political pressure. That evening on the television news he saw 'murderers' walking free and felt 'the whole thing was a total farce'.

Indeed, disrespect for the workings of the law, the judicial process and sanctioning is often reported as a crucial factor in police officers turning to rule-bending to affect arrests and achieve results (Dixon 1999). One feature of that disdain for the law in this context was that the 'border didn't mean anything' to some units and they operated across it into Ireland, even to the extent of abducting suspects from over the border. The FRU, for example, operated 'without reference to any border as such. What we were doing was clearly a breach of international law, but as far as the FRU was concerned, our need for information was more important than observing the law' (Ingram & Harkin 2004:54).

Furthermore, it is standard when attending a sudden death as a result of police activity in Britain that the police will thoroughly investigate the scene and any officer involved will be interviewed. Nowadays the officers involved in firearms cases will also routinely be tested for the presence of alcohol or drugs. Clearly the techniques of forensic examination have advanced dramatically in recent decades, but at any stage of policing it has always been the expectation that the scene of a violent crime will be professionally and thoroughly searched and examined. It was SOP, however, for SAS members operating in Northern Ireland to be taken from the scene of a shooting almost immediately after the incident and to be debriefed and coached by the Army's Legal Service in making and giving their statements.[2] Their statements, then, were often closely geared to one another's and were usually repetitively formulaic. They tended to be somewhat staccato, to try to make the events look spontaneous rather than planned, to proffer excuses for certain choices taken (the rifle had jammed, so a pistol was used), to play down the role of the individual who was simply reacting to events and to include always a sudden moment of danger causing an instant response. Some of the loyalists' statements were also crafted to convey lack of information in advance as to what was to happen, the lowly role of the individual concerned, confusion leading to blind reactions, and fear that refusal would mean punishment within the movement. In other words, they were not sure what was going on, their reaction was not premeditated and they had no alternative but to do it.

This side-stepping of common procedure elsewhere also happened with the RUC special units, which would be swiftly removed from the scene to be debriefed by SB officers and kept away from questioning by CID. This clearly made a standard investigation difficult. Sometimes, moreover, access to the scene of crime was blocked for forensic investigation for 'security reasons'; this meant that ballistic evidence – shell cases, angles of fire, and so on – could not be obtained *in situ*. Pathologists were often unable to visit the scene but had to work from photos. Later, when there eventually was access to the scene, it had often been contaminated and evidence (such as shell cases) had disappeared or been destroyed (such as clothing).

This happened with regard to the Lurgan shootings and Stalker is particularly damning about the quality of investigations on the three cases. There was no 'coordinated investigation' by a senior officer into the three Lurgan shootings and the incidents were seemingly not examined as possible crimes or murders; the files were of a poor quality; the pathology work was weak; the rules of evidence were 'blatantly ignored'; there were 'low standards of the basic techniques' and his team encountered a 'lamentable standard of professionalism in investigations' (Stalker 1988:51). One explanation is that a rather insular force locked into counter-terrorism mode is simply not up-to-scratch on techniques and standards in leading forces elsewhere. Another, of course, was that there was a 'fudge factor' at work that saw to it that devious operations escaped thorough scrutiny. It might also be that cutting corners, ostensibly on security grounds, encourages sloppy police work and an easy-going culture of laxity of not having to comply with formal rules, regulations and administrative procedures.

There has, furthermore, been a whole range of public and other inquiries into various aspects of security and law enforcement in Northern Ireland since the beginning of the Troubles. Two of the most well known are those by senior police officers from the mainland, Stalker and Stevens. Stevens became Commissioner of the Met in London having previously held senior positions in several forces, including Chief Constable in one force, before moving to London. Until fairly recently it was standard in the UK for one police force to be investigated by another at the request of the Home Secretary. Even if such an inquiry was done professionally and thoroughly, there remained a sense of unease about the police agency investigating itself (Punch 2009). There has, then, in response to that unease and to criticism of weak oversight systems, been a move in the last decade towards independent oversight agencies with OPONI, the Independent Police Complaints Commission in England and Wales and the Police Complaints Commissioner in Scotland, which started work in 2000, 2004 and 2007, respectively. OPONI had a special significance because it was part of the raft of reforms following the GFA, which were designed to restore confidence and legitimacy in the battered police force. OPONI has examined many cases, including the Omagh bombing of 1998, and in relation to collusion it published the 'Ballast Report' in 2007, which was dealt with in the previous chapter.

One element in the conduct of external investigations is the issue of the level of compliance with the investigating team and the degree of any obstruction displayed towards it. And it is the case that large and powerful institutions – governments, corporations, the military, even universities – may employ a battery of techniques when their interests or reputations are threatened by a journalist, whistle-blower, researcher or outside investigator. These may include various forms of surveillance, telephone tapping, counter-accusations, leaks to the press, entrapment, black propaganda, delays, dodging appointments, doctoring documents or shredding them, interfering with evidence, moving personnel to make it difficult to interview them, mounting a battery of intimidating legal moves and physical sabotage. Some of these defensive counter-measures were not unknown in Northern Ireland. Indeed, several leading political figures in the Province, as well as some senior Labour politicians in London who were unpopular with the security establishment, had their reputations blackened by leaks and smears in attempts to discredit them. This allegedly originated from within the intelligence agencies and especially the Security Service according to the former Army information officer, Colin Wallace (Urban 1993:77).

STEVENS INQUIRY

Stevens (2003:13) states baldly that, 'Throughout my three Enquiries I recognised that I was being obstructed'. At one stage, as mentioned earlier, there was a fire in his Incident Room that he initially claimed was arson but others state was an accident. The CID investigating officer argued that because the team had back-ups of their files at a secure location a fire would have had little effect. This misses the harassment element, if the fire was deliberate, of simply disrupting the team's work along with a crude signal that the team was not welcome (Simpson 2010:46–58). Stevens was, moreover, denied documents and videotapes that later were shown to be available at the time of asking; some eventually did surface but had on occasion been tampered with, while others had simply 'disappeared'. Stevens' long involvement in Northern Ireland, conducting three investigations during a period of 14 years, was doubtless helped in the later stages by the advent of the peace process and by having a colleague from the Met, and former SIO during part of his inquiries in Northern Ireland, appointed as Chief Constable of the PSNI (Hugh, later Sir Hugh, Orde). Unlike Stalker, furthermore, Stevens was able to move by agreement to the executive stage of arresting suspects. This required the cooperation of the RUC and DPP as he and his team had no powers of arrest in the Province; subsequently there were many arrests and a substantial number of convictions with sizeable sentences as a result of his team's work (Ryder 2000:385).

STALKER INQUIRY

Stalker arrived in 1984 in a period of prickly defensiveness when the RUC was under hostile scrutiny. Indeed there is often antagonism generally in the Province to 'experts' from the mainland who want to 'teach Paddy how to sing' (Simpson 2010:46). Stalker was asked by the Chief Constable of the RUC to investigate allegations against RUC officers arising from the three Lurgan shootings (dealt with in Chapter 3). In a crucial phase, he was removed from the inquiry and also controversially suspended from his post as Deputy Chief Constable of the Greater Manchester Police (GMP). He found himself facing an inquiry into alleged misconduct; this was conducted by Colin Sampson, a senior officer from another force. Although nothing of substance emerged from this and he was reinstated, he resigned from the police soon after (Stalker 1988). He is convinced that an RUC lobby fostered the allegations, which were timed to coincide with his highly critical Interim Report and his return to the Province to pursue the investigation. The report was some 3,600 pages long in 20 volumes. He had further let it be known that he was prepared to resign from the inquiry and go public on his provisional findings if he faced more obstruction. The source of the accusations against him apparently included an RUC informant of poor repute and the 'lobby' was mobilised at a meeting in Scarborough that included the RUC's Chief Constable Hermon, Anderton (Stalker's Chief Constable in GMP), the head of the HMIC and the regional inspector for the North-West and

Northern Ireland (Hainsworth 1987:206). The inquiry launched against him successfully prevented his return to the Province to complete his own investigation where he intended to interview the Chief Constable, his Deputy and at least one ACC in relation to possible criminal charges arising from the two shoot-to-kill cases that he and his team had fully investigated; the third investigation was never completed.

Strangely and most unusually the officer who investigated the 'allegations' against him, Sampson, also completed the RUC investigation. The assumption from several sources is that Sampson came to similar conclusions to Stalker, but the report has not been published (Taylor 1987). In 1988 the Attorney General, who is a member of the government and of the Cabinet, decided that there would be no prosecutions arising from the two Lurgan cases, which Stalker had investigated, on grounds of national security and public interest. The Secretary of State for Northern Ireland then ordered two further inquiries. One looked at possible disciplinary charges against RUC officers below the rank of chief officer and recommended that 20 officers be disciplined; of these one officer was cautioned, 18 were reprimanded and in the remaining case charges were dropped. The other inquiry examined the possibility of disciplinary charges against the top echelon of the RUC, at chief officer level. The Police Authority for Northern Ireland (PANI) then deliberated on whether or not to follow up Sampson's report by investigating the conduct of the Chief Constable, his Deputy and an ACC. PANI decided by one vote not to pursue the matter.

Perhaps Stalker was somewhat naïve about what he would encounter or maybe he had not been properly briefed. In retrospect, Stalker appears to be the 'squeaky clean' representative of the myth system, based on the dedicated and fearless pursuit of truth, arriving from the outside world to a 'jungle' (the welcoming words of Hermon). There the game was precisely to work with a concealed operational code and the expectation was that others would show some allowance for it by turning in a sympathetically bland report that would elicit a ritual wrist-slapping. There was in this bracing encounter with Stalker a mixture of provincial defensiveness, local chauvinism, institutional pride and personal egos, but in a context of a Protestant and unionist community that had developed a siege mentality as it fought for its existence and with a police force under attack where some felt that corners had to be cut to achieve results.

In this context it was informally argued that the neat, formal, legal rules no longer always applied. In such a dichotomous world of inclusion and exclusion there was only a single overriding choice – 'which side are you on?' – and loyalty to one's side was paramount. The RUC seemed to feel that Stalker, although an outsider, would as a fellow police officer at least display loyalty to his police 'clan'. They had not reckoned on a motivated crusader prepared to lift sensitive stones and challenge taboos. For example, he and his team went unarmed and unprotected into republican areas to talk to the families of the victims of the shootings; this was unprecedented and definitely not appreciated by the RUC. The RUC leadership responded by slotting into defensive mode towards him and his team. Also, Stalker was roundly scolded in a Belfast court by a young RUC officer for conversing with a lawyer for an IRA suspect. Effectively the RUC man was saying that those who represented suspects accused of terrorist activity were tainted by association and that he and his colleagues were embarrassed by a senior police officer openly consorting with the 'other side'.

By professional standards of conduct in public life, the way in which Stalker and his team were treated by Hermon and others in the RUC was disgraceful. There was outright obstruction and personal hostility, especially from SB officers, calculated insults and blatant failures by Hermon to keep appointments. This occurred when Stalker had travelled especially to the Province for an agreed meeting with Hermon. Hermon even returned some of Stalker's letters unopened (Ryder 2000:347). There were also point-blank refusals to hand over evidence or to take action against personnel arising from the team's inquiries. Stalker was warned anonymously that his offices were bugged and his telephone was being tapped; he felt he could trust no one. Also the two men did not hit it off personally. Hermon was a proud, rigid and defensive autocrat; he was almost paranoid about the media and leaks and openly contemptuous of PANI; it was as if he engaged on a mission to protect and shield his force to 'save' it in order to professionalise it. This was simply not viable in the long run. He clearly disliked the assertive outsider who saw himself as a first-rate investigator faced by recalcitrant and intransigent provincials with much to hide. The two men would both complain loudly and sourly about one another to others.

Yet this abrasive defensiveness from the top and from the SB segment was far less evident when around 300 officers were interviewed. Only a handful ('no more than half a dozen') were cool if not hostile while the vast majority, Stalker states, were cooperative and conducted themselves in a professional manner.

He writes interestingly of the officers directly involved in the three shooting incidents; he was familiar with the style of the SAS and had visited their headquarters in Hereford. Stalker (1988:60) anticipated that these officers would be similar to the SAS men:

> But they differed from the soldiers in the way they talked to us. The military SAS troops are, by and large, taciturn and anonymous. These policemen ... were prepared to talk about their work and did not see themselves as soldiers at all, although many of them had come to the police from the Army. It was clear that their confidence had taken a serious bruising. They impressed me and my team with their honesty and openness. They were glad to talk to us, and obviously felt badly let down by their senior officers, who they believed had left them carrying the responsibility for operations that had gone seriously wrong. They had risked their lives, obeyed instructions and looked in vain for the expected support. Four of their number had been charged with murder, had been kept in custody for up to eighteen months in solitary confinement awaiting trial, and eventually acquitted. They hoped for some legal support – but it never came. A private fund contributed to by lower-ranking policemen paid for a barrister on a private basis. They seemed to me to have been abandoned and isolated by a police force that had identified a need for them, selected them, trained them, used them and then cut them adrift.

They responded positively and helpfully, but above all, honestly he said while Stalker adds that he saw a 'great deal more to admire in that small group of constables and sergeants than I did in many of their more senior colleagues'.

This statement is rather strange in that elsewhere Stalker refers to the three incidents as orchestrated revenge killings where the officers must have known what they were doing; he refers to the hayshed shooting as a pre-planned operation made to look like a chance encounter and that the antiquated firearms must have been planted. What, then, went 'wrong'? It may well be that they felt misled when they realised that they could not seek protection under the Official Secrets Act as they had been assured, and that they felt abandoned by a force that had used them but would not provide legal support. But these were officers who opened fire on three occasions without warning, killing six unarmed people in highly dubious circumstances. Perhaps the explanation was that the initial intention was to apprehend the suspects and only to open fire if there was danger, but that due to circumstances the incidents developed differently than planned and some officers perceived danger and opened fire. This is again a rather unconvincing 'chaos' theory and would amount to a 'vocabulary of motive' on the lines of 'it wasn't supposed to happen like that'. But where was the danger in the hayshed incident with old weapons that could not be fired? Or had some other unit (MI5 perhaps) planted the weapons without disclosing to them that there was no ammunition? If this was such a well-trained unit then, surely its members did not panic amid confusion but were in control. Also is it not a coincidence that two cars managed to get through two separate checkpoints only to be attacked by a second unit? Is it not plausible that the two ineffective roadblocks were part of the scenario to generate an element of danger? Perhaps there were no roadblocks at all or any serious attempts to stop the vehicles, and the officer rolling around in the dirt to simulate jumping aside to avoid being run down was part of the pre-arranged script.

The explanations, moreover, sound very similar to some of the SAS accounts – that they lay in wait for suspects, there was a sudden perception of danger, the soldiers were taking no risks and shot to eliminate the danger. There are also echoes of the 'encounters' in India where after police shoot-outs with criminals the police provide near identical justifications for shooting the criminals. So, it is rather confusing that Stalker suggests that there was a conspiracy to kill yet finds something 'admirable' in these officers who took part in deadly and retaliatory ambushes and gave false statements to the courts.

In other contexts, furthermore, openness and honesty were not forthcoming during his inquiries. Stalker assumed, for instance, that there had to be an SB file on the Lurgan explosion in which three officers died but was repeatedly told that none existed; his team then spent several months carefully piecing together the events of that night:

In March 1985 I interviewed a very senior RUC officer under caution as a criminal suspect. He was upset, angry and defensive, and by way of explanation and justification for certain of his actions he asked me to consider a file of papers. He reached into his briefcase and handed me the bulky folder whose existence he and his colleagues had denied nine months earlier. Three month's extra work by six of my colleagues could have been avoided if this file had been provided then. (Stalker 1988:35)

Perhaps the most telling feature in this campaign of obstruction was that of the missing 'bug'. At the barn of the second shooting a new listening device had been installed by MI5. Stalker wanted this and the transcript as evidence; Hermon refused access but diverted him to MI5; MI5 promised Stalker cooperation on getting it. But Hermon turned down a further request for the tape, and for information about the informant involved, on grounds of security. Stalker then asked the ACC heading SB about the tape but he replied, 'you will never be able to hear it' and added 'I doubt if it exists'. A constable who had listened to the tape refused to cooperate by saying what he had heard or by producing the transcript unless instructed by his senior officers:

> The situation was bizarre. Here was a constable telling a Detective Chief Superintendent that he would not cooperate with a murder enquiry unless he was instructed to do so. He was told, equally politely, that he was very close to obstructing us. He responded by saying that if that were the case then he was only acting on instructions. (Stalker 1988:69)

But the team had no legal authority in Northern Ireland and could take no steps against the non-compliant constable. Stalked never did get to hear the tape or see the transcript.

The Stalker affair forms one of the most illuminating examples in recent decades of the hypocrisy of the British state. Cynics may find all of this somewhat ironic if not amusing, that the police establishment had apparently 'stitched up' one of its own with the flimsy accusations and weak investigation against Stalker in Manchester (Hainsworth 1987). That Stalker's own chief constable did nothing to aid his own Deputy is also far from savoury. And, of course, Stalker was obstructed in Northern Ireland precisely because he was 'not one of us' and the conduct of the RUC and its hierarchy, in terms of accountability and transparency within the criminal justice system, was indefensible. A police organisation that refuses to accept accountability and obstructs an investigation is either not under control or is under the wrong sort of control. But an unaccountable police force that is permitted to remain so by the state is proof of that state's deviancy.

However, it is clear that the stakes were very high and Stalker threatened to unmask the real nature of the conflict in Northern Ireland with the RUC locked into counter-terrorism, SB ruling the roost and members of the security community frequently and illicitly crossing the border into Ireland. To have pursued his investigation, which was reaching the highest echelons of the RUC, would have threatened the legitimacy of the RUC and by extension its central role in some form of devolved government and even the very future of a reconstructed Northern Ireland 'state'. It would further have threatened the legitimacy of the British state which was formally responsible for security in the Province and which could have been seen as condoning if not encouraging dirty tricks while running roughshod over Ireland's sovereignty at a moment of rapprochement with the Republic. The whole edifice inherited since Partition, and which the British state had been bolstering since the 1920s, threatened to collapse. Hence Stalker, his investigation and the notion of 'justice' being done, and being seen to be done, were considered expendable.

INQUESTS AND COURTS

> One in ten of those killed during the last thirty years of conflict over Northern Ireland was killed by the state. Yet very few British army, RUC or Intelligence personnel were ever charged with murder, punished or disciplined for what they did ... The state had the power to carry out these killings with impunity, to block, legally and otherwise, any investigation, and to vilify and harass those who opposed its actions. (Rolston 2006:2 & 12)

Under the exceptional circumstances in Northern Ireland, it was plainly difficult to operate coroners' courts and to adjudicate in criminal courts according to the standards of the mainland and of established international practice. From the technical point of a fair and sound trial there were frequently difficulties with the quality of evidence, forensics and pathological reports and of obtaining witnesses. Giving a statement as an eye witness to be used as evidence in court was not a particularly healthy pastime during the Troubles, while at some incidents literally hundreds of potential eyewitnesses, who must have seen or heard something, would refuse to come forward and cooperate with the police. Some of these features also hampered the work of coroners. For example, in 1980 the rules on inquests were changed for Northern Ireland. Inquests could no longer bring in an open verdict when coroners believed someone other than the deceased had caused his or her own death, but could only register 'findings' on time, place and manner of the death. Furthermore, the police selected coroners' juries in Northern Ireland (Urban 1993:73). The rules also meant that soldiers involved in fatal shootings were no longer obliged to attend the sitting in person but could make a sworn statement for the court instead.

The difficulties of operating under these guidelines were evident, for instance, when the Armagh coroner resigned in 1984 in the face of 'grave irregularities' in an RUC file related to shootings; and frustration caused one solicitor to walk out of proceedings saying the inquest was a waste of time for, 'The police and the Army got together shortly after the incident and worked out the version they were going to tell the world' (Urban 1993:203). On many occasions, families of victims were not informed about the date of an inquest or were told that they did not need to attend, while some inquests were dealt with within a mere three hours.

The problems this brought can also be illustrated when, in October 1983, the coroner opened proceedings into the deaths of the six men during the three Lurgan incidents. He then suspended the inquest on the grounds that the trials of four RUC officers and the one survivor of the shootings were pending. Another coroner reopened the inquest in 1988 but decided that the written statements of the RUC officers were sufficient and that they did not have to appear in person; by then this was standard. The victims' families and their representatives objected to this, withdrew from the proceedings and applied for a judicial review. A High Court judge ruled that the coroner's decision on the statements was valid; this was appealed successfully meaning the officers would have to appear in person, but the government in turn appealed to the House of Lords and the judgement was reversed. When the inquest reopened yet again the coroner had read the Stalker and Sampson reports. These were versions vetted under a Public Interest Immunity Certificate (PIIC); twice during this long trajectory the British government intervened with PIICs to restrict considerably the documentation that could be made available. This time, another judicial review was demanded by the victims' families in relation to jury selection.

The court began once more in 1994 with the coroner calling on the Stalker team as witnesses. The members of the team asked for access to the dossier with their original papers and report, which was lodged with the RUC; but access was denied by the Chief Constable. The coroner thereby served a writ on the Chief Constable to produce the documents, but he refused to comply; then, a judge ruled that the RUC did not have to comply with the writ. The *fifth* coroner on the case, who had hoped to bring fresh light on the circumstances of the deaths, could not proceed further and hence, twelve years after the shootings, decided merely to issue statements of death. In the Ballysillan case, moreover, where an innocent bystander (Hanna) was shot dead by the SAS, it was originally said that the IRA had opened fire first and that Hanna had been killed in cross-fire. But when no weapons were found at the scene, this was altered to stating that the fourth IRA man who had evaded capture had fired first. At the inquest no evidence was presented to support this contention, but the two SAS soldiers maintained that they saw flashes and heard what they thought were gunshots (Urban 1993:61).

In the criminal courts there were a number of prosecutions for serious offences by members of the security services (RUC, Army and UDR). But, as Rolston intimates above, it often proved difficult to obtain a conviction. Following the graveyard shooting of young John Boyle, for example, the RUC pursued an investigation for murder and the DPP, for the one and only time in Northern Ireland, approved that SAS soldiers should go to trial. One of the soldiers stated that the 'suspected terrorist' had pointed a weapon directly at him. There was a discussion as to the entry of the three bullets with regard to whether or not Boyle had his back to the soldier when shot. The judge then accepted that a bullet had entered the front of the boy's head, which indicated that he was facing the soldier. He also questioned the soldier as to why the squad had not first inspected the weapon which would have shown it was unloaded, why did he allow the 'terrorist' to pick up the firearm in the first place and why was the young man not arrested? The judge, Lord Lowry, who was the Province's Chief Justice, considered the soldier who spoke for both SAS men involved in the incident an 'untrustworthy' witness; he remarked also that it should have been possible to 'capture the deceased alive'. Yet he could not find that the prosecution had proven beyond reasonable doubt that the two soldiers had deliberately intended to kill anyone who entered the graveyard. They could, therefore, not be convicted of murder.

In a number of the cases there were patent weaknesses and glaring discrepancies in evidence from the security forces, with judges lambasting them for unreliability and lack of credibility as witnesses or even setting aside their statements (as in the trial of RUC officers for murder in regard to the third Lurgan 'shoot-to-kill' incident in 1984). But when the tests of 'clear intent' and 'beyond reasonable doubt' were applied, they were nevertheless given the benefit of the doubt. Soldiers, for example, did not enjoy the legal immunity of the battlefield for use of force and were subject to the criminal law; but the way it was framed left the judge little choice but to convict for murder rather than manslaughter (Geraghty 2000:102). This may have swayed judges towards leniency and to mitigating sentences. The leniency pattern continued within the Army, which effectively softened some sentences. For instance, the first soldier to be prosecuted and convicted in Northern Ireland for murder was Private Ian Thain, but he was released from a life sentence after only 26 months and went on serving in the Army (Dillon 1991:xxxi). Private Clegg, who fired at teenagers in a hijacked car who drove through a roadblock in Belfast in 1990, was also convicted of murder. The soldiers at the roadblock continued firing at the rapidly disappearing vehicle which no longer presented a danger to them; 19 rounds were fired killing two of the car's occupants. Clegg hit one of them, Karen Reilly (18 years old), killing her with his fourth bullet. Here, the court was clearly applying a judgement related to the diminishing danger to the soldiers as the car drove away, while there was no indication of weapons or shooting from the vehicle, and to the application of minimal force. Clegg's original conviction was later appealed and quashed in the Lords leading to a retrial and a conviction for a lesser offence, which was also overturned in 2000; but he had already been released in 1995 under licence by the then Northern Ireland Secretary. He continued his career in the Army and went on to serve in Afghanistan. When this release was made known in Northern Ireland, it sparked off severe rioting in nationalist areas.

There were, too, a number of cases involving shootings by members of the security forces, which viewed from now seem to have led to remarkably lenient sentences. In one case, a Sergeant Williams of the MRF was acquitted of attempted murder; he was in civilian clothes in an unmarked car when he opened fire on two men near a bus terminus in Belfast in 1972. He had stated that the two men were armed, that they opened fire on him and hit the rear window of the car. The Crown claimed that the men were unarmed and that the car window had been deliberately knocked out. Sergeant Williams stated that there was a report about a gunman at the location; he confirmed this, seeing a pistol and a M1 carbine, and then he was fired on by the two gunmen before returning fire with a burst of automatic fire from a Thompson sub-machine gun. The Thompson is not standard issue in the British Army and just happened to be in his car. The jury returned a not guilty verdict by eleven to one (Dillon 1991:46–52).

Then three members of the RUC SPG were involved in an attack that led to a murder charge, but were given only suspended sentences by Justice Lowry (Dillon 1991:226). Another three RUC officers were brought to trial on charges of murder in relation to the third Lurgan incident, involving the shooting of Toman and two other men. The forensic evidence seemed to support the prosecution's case that Toman was still alive and trying to get out of the car while he had been shot in the back. The policemen argued it was self-defence on the assumption they were being fired at and they continued firing until all three were dead. Furthermore, they argued that these were dangerous men on a mission to kill. This was reinforced by Deputy Chief Constable McAtamney who, in testimony, stated that this was a special squad, based on aggression and firepower, and that it worked according to the rule, 'if you decide to fire, you shoot to take out your assailant … permanently' (Rolston 2006:16). Hesitation was excluded because others who had hesitated had suffered. The Judge, Lord Justice Gibson, did comment on the unreliable evidence presented by the police at a preliminary hearing, but he went on to acquit the three officers; he held that they had acted in self-defence against violent people about to commit a murder. In pronouncing his judgement, he stated:

> I wish to make it clear that, having heard the entire Crown case, I regard each of the accused as absolutely blameless in this matter. That finding should be put on record along with my recommendation as to their courage and determination for bringing the three deceased men to justice, in this case, to the final court of justice. (Stalker 1988:38)

This judge seemed to be condoning the shootings and the judgement seemed also to convey that shoot to kill, which was virtually admitted and justified by the Deputy Chief of the RUC, would go unpunished. The IRA did not forget this statement: later Justice Gibson and his wife were blown up in their car on returning from the South. The Attorney General subsequently advised the DPP not to pursue further prosecutions arising from these incidents; this advice was followed, although disciplinary cases were mounted.

Then, Constable 'Thompson', a former British soldier serving with the RUC, was brought to trial on the murder of Seamus Grew. Grew and his companion were under surveillance on the assumption that they were about to bring the INLA chief McGlinchey to the North. The INLA men's car was said to have crashed through a roadblock injuring an officer. 'Thompson' claims he followed the suspect's car, identified himself as a police officer and approached the vehicle. The passenger door then opened, there was a loud bang and he shouted a warning. But the car started to reverse and he opened fire: 'I fired to kill because I believed they were trying to kill me'. PC 'Thompson' was cleared of murder and was allowed to return to duty with the RUC.

In general there was, then, a clear and persistent attempt to shape the accounts for the courts to fit the plea of self-defence under Common Law. The prevailing rules in the Province on armed engagement, known as the 'Yellow Card', instructed soldiers to use firearms as a last resort, to issue a warning if possible and only to open fire if there was imminent danger to life and no other way to avert the danger. This was a guideline with no legal force according to Geraghty (2000:105). An officer who had taken part in ambush-style operations told Urban (1993:72), '"I always told my soldiers that nothing would happen to them so long as they could justify their actions by the Yellow Card" ... The implication is that the justification for opening fire can be pieced together afterwards'. Another SAS officer illustrated rule-bending regarding the card's guidelines in relation to the Loughall shoot-out: 'The Yellow Card rules are officially seen to cover Loughall, but of course they don't. You put your men in the [police] station. That way they [IRA] are threatening you without even knowing it. That's how you get around the Yellow Card' (Urban 1993:230).

The Army Legal Service, furthermore, would routinely meet with soldiers shortly after an incident involving firearms had taken place and before they were confronted by the CID, and instruct them on making statements containing a clear perception of danger for use in court:

> The need to satisfy the court that the amount of force had been reasonable and necessary, resulted during the 1980s in statements which sounded remarkably similar from one incident to another, despite the obvious confusion that surrounded some of the deaths. (Urban 1993:75)

Court depositions consistently attempted, then, to convey that the SAS and other soldiers only ever employed lethal force when they perceived themselves to be in immediate danger. William Hanna, the unarmed bystander at Ballysillan who was shot, had reached for what the soldiers thought was a gun; 'suddenly he moved in a twisting motion and we thought he was going for a gun so we both opened fire'. William Fleming at Gransha was knocked off a motorbike by being rammed with a car and, although this shattered his leg and bits of his flesh were later found on the car, he was said to have been raising himself and pointing a weapon; it was also claimed that he was brandishing a weapon when entering the hospital grounds but this was disputed. The unarmed IRA man shot in an incident in Derry in 1978 was said to have '"spun around" and brought his right hand up'. Urban sees an apparent desire among IRA members to reach, pivot, point or swing towards SAS soldiers with 'real or imagined weapons'. He caustically remarks that on a number of occasions people seemed 'to have the urge to reach for weapons which they were not carrying' (Urban 1993:75–6 & 204).

Plainly, it proved difficult to achieve a conviction for murder against RUC or Army members in Northern Ireland. To a degree certain court hearings in the Province were a charade in relation to independent, impartial adjudication because the 'weasel words' – of national security and protecting informants' lives – meant the 'whole truth' often never emerged. In the Miami Showband case, for instance, the two survivors gave statements that they firmly believed a British Army officer, in a different uniform to the others and with a crisp English accent, was present and seemingly in charge of the operation. In fact, an English accent within the security services was not unusual in the Province, although unlikely among the Portadown UVF. However, in court the survivors were informed that this material was to be discarded; one of them wondered if 'a cap, or ceiling, was being put on the investigation' (Travers & Fetherstonhaugh 2007:180).

Furthermore, if reliable intelligence indicated an attack or activity by an ASU then a court under normal circumstances would surely want to know the following: when was this known; how long had the suspects been under observation; was their reliable information on the target; were they tailed to the site; why were they not arrested en route; why were they not apprehended at the scene before the firing commenced; could weapons at the scene have been rendered harmless in advance, and so on. Generally these questions were not raised, and if they were then they were parried on grounds of security. At times the prosecution almost seemed to be taking the role of the defence and some court performances appear rather weird, if not cynical, in the cold light of day:

> Post-mortem evidence [in relation to the Strabane shooting of three IRA members] showed that each of the IRA men had at least one shot to the head. Yet their balaclavas contained no bullet holes, leading to suggestions that the soldiers had approached them, lifted off the masks to identify the men and then shot them. The soldiers' statements admitted that they had taken the balaclavas off the men, but said it was after the firing stopped. The Crown suggested by way of explanation that the bullets might have entered through the balaclavas' eye holes. (Urban 1993:201)

It is hard to believe this last sentence but the explanation, from the prosecution, could only be offered because the evidence to prove or disprove it was not available. The terrorists' clothes had been destroyed and a proper forensic investigation of the site had been obstructed for security reasons.

These are not mere technicalities that can be easily waved away: there were indications that wounded insurgents had been 'finished off' as in the Strabane incident:

> SAS men carried on pouring fire into the prostrate IRA men, who were only 5–6 metres away, reloading their weapons with fresh magazines as they did so. In all they fired 117 rounds, 28 of which hit Michael Devine. A pathologist later said his wounds had almost defied interpretation ... Local people were to claim that they heard cries of 'don't shoot', 'don't shoot' from one of the injured. (Urban 1993:201)

Urban argues that there are indications that the SAS men used their 9 mm pistols to administer the *coup de grace* to the wounded men; both soldiers claimed their rifles had jammed, but Urban considers it most unlikely that two well-cared for rifles in an elite unit would just happen to jam simultaneously. He offers that they may not have wanted to use their rifles for a headshot because of the extensive damage that this would cause and opted instead for their side-arms. Urban, himself a former soldier, is here reading between the lines of their testimony and setting this interpretation alongside other accounts he collected from soldiers. Obviously this does not amount to evidence but is informed speculation; however, such speculation grows in credence when there has not been a fair trial.

Urban also had the advantage of access to good sources in the security forces. He tries to give a 'soldier's eye' view of SAS involvement in the Troubles and gives a fair and balanced account.

He gleans from his interviews, for example, that there were deliberate efforts to mislead the media and not to tell the courts the full story. To the military the courts were part of the 'battlefield' and they did not want the niceties of law to make them reveal information of value to the enemy that might, above all, endanger the soldiers' lives or reveal sources of information. For in their eyes there was a 'war' going on during which it was unfair to judge soldiers by peacetime standards. Indeed, a judge sitting on the case of a soldier who shot a farmer whom he assumed to be a terrorist when the farmer ran away from him, but who later proved not to be a terrorist, accepted that the soldier had reasonably believed he was dealing with a terrorist. He added that Northern Ireland counted as a 'war or semi-war situation' that gave the soldier the right to shoot if he believed someone might be a terrorist; this judgement was upheld by the Lords (Urban 1993:69). It is almost as if at times the exceptional context led to a wilful suspension of legality and due process in adjudicating cases in Northern Ireland.

In practice, the DPP in Northern Ireland proved itself on occasion prepared to pursue cases that took RUC officers, UDR soldiers and SAS members to court on murder and other charges. However, many shooting incidents were never investigated as potential crimes and were only cursorily dealt with at inquests.[3] Rolston (2006, 2010), for instance, convincingly documents the large number of violent deaths attributed to the security forces that did not result in the prosecution of a soldier or police officer. The military attitude to this legal threat relating to 'executive actions' was, moreover, that officers resented coroners' courts prying into covert operations when it is impossible to answer many questions because 'there is a war going on'. Enoch Powell, the controversial Conservative politician who had become the Unionist MP for South Down in Northern Ireland, regarded this as a dangerous argument implying equivalence between the two sides as declaring 'war' on insurgents grants them recognition; 'The IRA isn't a thing against which war can be declared ... then you would in fact have installed the IRA in the very position which it seeks to attain by means of terror' (Urban 1993:205).

WHISTLEBLOWING AND MUZZLING THE MEDIA

Both 'Ingram' (Ingram & Harkin 2004) and Davies (1999) indicate that writing about the intelligence operations mounted during the conflict in Northern Ireland could prove to be a troublesome if not hazardous enterprise. Ingram was a whistleblower and it is predictable that in general establishment figures, institutional leaders and frontline practitioners will look with disdain on whistleblowers and endeavour to discredit them in some way. This will especially be the case where a sustained conflict is taking place and the establishment is engaged in propaganda, disinformation and dirty tricks while trying to maintain a front of probity and rectitude. In what for some is a war situation it is most damaging if highly negative revelations emerge from a clearly knowledgeable source inside the security community. Typically the authorities will portray the whistleblower as someone who is unstable or who is ventilating a grievance; but, importantly, he or she is dismissively deemed unreliable. That may well be true in some instances but we would need to know more about the individual cases in order to make a judgement. In practice, some whistleblowers are near ideal employees who, with the best motives, bring serious problems in the workplace to the attention of superiors with the assumption that these will be rectified. It is when their message is ignored, but especially when they experience informal or formal sanctioning for being a messenger with ill tidings, that they 'become' a whistleblower by taking their message outside. Not infrequently this takes them on a 'career' of sustained resistance to the system in the face of persistent reprisals and defamation from it; sometimes they win but more often they lose such battles at great personal cost (Gobert & Punch 2000).

Davies, however, relied heavily on three interviews with security agents familiar with the Northern Ireland situation that were conducted on grounds of strict confidentiality. Yet he claims that two of them were threatened with 'executive action', which implies that they were identified but he does not say how and by whom. Furthermore, the government pursued Davies with a High Court action when it was heard he was working on a book about the FRU; but after some ten months of legal argument he was able to continue with the project (Davies 1999:7). In a number of other cases, the authorities pursued members of the police or intelligence agencies who wished to tell their inside story as well as investigative journalists who were getting too close to inflammatory material. Urban (1993:xxi), who had excellent credentials including service in the military, had checked his sources carefully and relied on non-attributable briefings. Nevertheless, he was contacted prior to publication by the Secretary to the D-Notice Committee, by which the MoD restricts the media in reporting matters the government wishes to keep confidential. There was concern from the security and military forces about its contents and, having scrutinised it, the Secretary asked for a number of amendments. When Urban questioned some of these he was told that 'these points constituted a real threat to life'; he acquiesced with the excisions. Barker (2004) presents himself as a loyal member of the RUC of 30 years service. Yet when he planned to publish his experiences in the SB he was confronted early in the morning with three RUC Land Rovers before his home; then his former colleagues searched his house thoroughly and arrested him. After two and a half years he appeared in court charged under the Official Secrets Act, but the Crown offered no evidence and the jury returned a 'not guilty' verdict.

When the former member of the Army's FRU turned journalist, 'Ingram', was unravelling the Stakeknife affair he was prosecuted in the High Court action under the Official Secrets Act, with the proceedings held in camera. When he had published several newspaper articles under the pseudonym Martin Ingram, the MoD applied through the State's Treasury Solicitor for an *ex parte* injunction against him under his real name. He states that this conduct, which endangered his life, made him determined to continue with his revelations and confirmed him as a whistleblower (Ingram & Harkin 2004:10). When he started to write about the murder of Notoratonio, which was designed to protect a 'mole', the editor of the *People* newspaper was visited in London by two representatives of the Treasury Solicitor (UK State Solicitor) and the MoD with two injunctions (Ingram & Harkin 2004:218). One injunction banned the newspaper from publishing the articles and the other banned the paper from reporting that it had received an injunction! The *Sunday Times* also received an injunction in 2001 and its Northern Ireland Editor was threatened with the Official Secrets Act. When Ingram was to testify to the Saville Inquiry (on Bloody Sunday), moreover, he was forbidden to quote from security files by a PIIC from the MoD.

Ingram also became the subject of harassment when e-mails started to circulate about his and his family's identity, signed by 'Friends of the FRU'. The Stevens Inquiry traced these to the computer of a former FRU colleague who apparently had been in contact with serving and former members of the FRU. Ingram was expecting action to be taken against this person, on the grounds that he had the right to protection and had been intimidated as a witness, but was dismayed to hear that the CPS had decided not to proceed with the case. He withdrew cooperation from the Stevens Inquiry:

Here we had direct evidence of an individual breaching the same Official Secrets Act that was being used against me but, for whatever reason, the British State decided that both myself and my family did not warrant their protection ... Personal details were leaked to certain journalists, details of which could only have come from the Ministry of Defence ... Society is not yet ready to protect whistleblowers, and your life is definitely in danger if you are a whistleblower who worked for the security services in Northern Ireland. (Ingram & Harkin 2004:262)

In short, the intelligence community and the government set out to protect their interests with a range of intimidating practices. Most institutions, but particularly authoritarian ones, close ranks against whistleblowers and 'trouble-makers' and mobilise their legal muscle as well as resorting to darkening reputations (Gobert & Punch 2000). A retired British army Major, Fred Holroyd, was a whistleblower who revealed that he had recruited loyalist informants in the 1970s, which suggested that the military had been involved in condoning if not promoting loyalist violence (Cusack & McDonald 2008:133). He was removed from the Army on 'psychiatric grounds'. Colin Wallace who worked in 'PSY OPS' at the Army's Information Policy Unit, which generated and spread black propaganda, made allegations about the smearing of politicians by the Army and MI5 and fought his subsequent dismissal. An independent inquiry upheld his claim, recommended compensation and revealed that his appeal to the civil service had been turned down following an intervention by the MoD. (Urban 1993:77)

Of course, the IRA and other paramilitary groups also did not welcome revelations of their inner workings. Collins (1998) gives an intriguing insider account of his time as a terrorist. He was highly committed to the movement, but was not himself a gun-man; however, he took part in many operations and was involved in planning, logistics, transporting and hiding weapons, criss-crossing the border and concealing ASU members. As a Customs' officer he had an excellent knowledge of the border area while his uniform and official duties provided a perfect cover for his activities. In describing his time with the IRA he writes of incompetence, sexual escapades, petty power struggles, operational 'cock-ups' and of IRA members misusing their terrorist role for ordinary crime (cf. Dillon 1991). By the time of his release from prison after two years on remand he had become disenchanted with the movement and with the violence, and distanced himself from it; he also made some denigrating remarks about the leadership and particularly about Gerry Adams. Normally, the IRA accepted that its members would be likely to break under interrogation and, following debriefing after release from custody, no sanctions would be taken against them, especially if they recanted in the dock. This was initially the case with Collins but restrictions were placed on him as if he was still subject to IRA discipline: and for not abiding by these he was banished to the Republic. After a while he returned to Northern Ireland and was at first left in peace. But Collins went on to abandon the movement and to write an authentic but sometimes disparaging account of its dark side. When he was out walking his dogs on a day in 1999, he was shot dead; the night before, graffiti appeared on a wall near his home, 'Eamon Collins: British agent: 1985–99'.

It was, then, generally not healthy to reveal anything about the inner workings of the IRA or to question the movement and its leadership. Moreover, those suspected of being a 'tout' (informer) were sometimes extensively tortured including a version of 'waterboarding' (Moloney 2010). This use of gross violence was also powerfully conveyed by the inhumane manner in which Mrs McConville and her children were treated before she was shot in the head as an alleged informer. This widowed mother of ten children was denied the very rights that the IRA and its members vocally demanded when they were arrested, interrogated, prosecuted, tried and sanctioned. These standards and procedures associated with the common principles of justice were denied to her and others. It would have added some moral authority to the legitimate accusations about serious misconduct by the security community if the IRA itself had abided by the principles and practices of humane, legal and proportionate justice within their own movement. Insurgents who often promise a more equitable and just society can be ruthless, uncompromising, unforgiving and gravely unjust on their path to that new society.[4] They can construct regimes as venal, mendacious and repressive as the ones they have dislodged.

7

End Game: State Deviance: Learning from the Past

The Troubles lasted some 30 years and cast a dark shadow over life in Northern Ireland, and to a degree also in Britain and Ireland. They presented the British state with a testing and painful predicament, for it faced forceful and resilient insurgent terrorism. And at times it almost seemed as if the Province might slide into the abyss of all-out civil war: 'Groups within the Protestant community began to prepare for the overthrow of the executive and others toyed with the possibility of establishing an independent Northern Ireland through a unilateral declaration of independence' (Dillon 1991:69). The dilemma was that just the whiff of a possible agreement with the nationalists was likely to foster insurgency in what were ostensibly Britain's most 'loyal' citizens. The Protestant, unionist majority operated with a duality in that if their loyalty was not respected then they felt justified in mounting dissent, if necessary by force (Moloney 2010:325). Indeed, unionists had been playing this card since the founding of the first UVF in 1913; successive British governments had caved in to this threat. By the 1970s and certainly the 1980s the signs were beginning to show that this ploy would not work indefinitely. But early on, Britain faced the doom scenario of possibly having to intervene between two warring groups of insurgents, with perhaps elements of the RUC and UDR choosing the loyalist side, who both opposed the British administration while having to cope with some kind of Irish military presence on the border.

The international community, but particularly the Irish lobby in American politics, would have looked askance at the sort of sectarian strife that became familiar in the volatile Balkans with 'ethnic cleansing'. Fortunately, the situation did not fully slip over the abyss into full civil war and the insurgents did eventually abandon violence. But the complexity and difficulties of this unstable context within the UK, and the grim scenarios that it raised, have to be taken into account in explaining how the British state and its agents came to stray from the rule of law and engaged in widespread deviance including illegally shooting some of its own citizens.

Peace did come to Northern Ireland, and the insurgents did lay down their weapons, but it was a long and perilous haul. The diverse stakeholders had to shift positions significantly, learn to change and in some cases accept major reform. The IRA went through a long and vacillating process of development. It endeavoured to be a centrally-led and disciplined organisation but leading personalities and individual units sometimes determined what happened. Furthermore, the baffling number of splits, feuds, denunciations, vendettas and fratricide within and between the republican organisations, and to a lesser extent among the loyalists, was almost unfathomable (McDonald & Holland 2010). Nevertheless, the IRA as an insurgent terrorist organisation became more sophisticated and increasingly more focused and hence more dangerous. The Provo activists did achieve a range of 'successes', according to their standards:

- Bugging Army Headquarters in Northern Ireland and later bombing it.
- Breaking out *en masse* from the Maze prison (with 38 absconders, this was the largest escape in British prison history) and daringly mounting an escape by helicopter from Mountjoy Jail in Dublin.
- In hitting ostensibly secure targets on the mainland (No. 10 Downing Street, army barracks and within the Houses of Parliament).
- The Brighton bombing, in particular, which nearly took out the Conservative Cabinet and Prime Minister and which might have changed the course of history.

If war is causing enough physical or psychological damage to your enemy that they desist, then the IRA/*Sinn Fein* leadership realised at a fairly early stage that it simply could not defeat the British Army and could not persuade the British government to abandon the Province. The show of strength by the British Army in Operation Motorman, allied to the effects of internment and the miscalculation of the mid-1970s cease-fire, weakened the IRA's position and its resolve (Smith & Neumann 2005). The high point of IRA violence was 1972 and after that it was killing less, taking casualties not only from the security forces but increasingly from the loyalists and was having to put considerable effort into remaining effective. It was still a force to be reckoned with, but politics and compromise became more prominent on the agenda. Indeed Brock (2008:9) argues that: 'Adams may well have been inclined towards politics; but he had no choice. There was no fallback to force if politics failed; force was over. The IRA still had guns and semtex, but betrayal and mistrust trapped its members in what a poetic spycatcher once called a "wilderness of mirrors".' To IRA hardliners and others the question even became, 'Why did the IRA settle for so little?' (Brock 2008:8).

It was clear that the British government remained committed to the wishes of the majority in Northern Ireland while the government in Dublin had de facto long abandoned the claim of sovereignty over the six counties (Boyle & Hadden 1985). Margaret Thatcher was obdurate and repeatedly stated that she would never negotiate with terrorists; but there was a subtle thaw when John Major succeeded her as Prime Minister in 1990. And when Northern Ireland Secretary Brooke conveyed in 1990 that Britain had 'no selfish strategic or economic interest' in the union with Northern Ireland, it was an unmistakeable signal that Britain was seeking a way out and a political solution. Brooke could seek this exit in the knowledge from 'moles' inside the IRA that the IRA had for some time dropped the demand for British withdrawal (Brock 2008). The IRA did learn, and had to learn, to pursue a political campaign alongside the armed struggle (English 2004:225). But the IRA continued to 'negotiate' through violence by again taking the struggle to the mainland with an increasing focus on massive physical and economic damage with attacks on the Baltic Exchange and in Bishopsgate while, after the collapse of the 1994 cease fire, there was a devastating explosion at Canary Wharf. The latter caused almost one billion pounds of damage, while a bomb in central Manchester destroyed much of the shopping area.

In short, during the Troubles the IRA became a dedicated and technically sophisticated insurgent terrorist organisation with increasing self-confidence at the negotiating table. And particularly since the GFA and up to the time of writing, it has become plain that throughout the Troubles there was a series of meetings with British representatives at different levels and locations, and through various intermediaries, including some with the Catholic hierarchy in Northern Ireland and also with John Hume. Apparently some hardliners in the Security Service were for continuing the struggle to weaken the IRA before negotiations, the Kitson doctrine, while other officials kept up informal contact with leading republicans.

The British Army concluded early on that it could not 'defeat' the IRA. From the time that both the IRA and the British government realised that a clear-cut victory was not feasible, both parties became locked in an embrace of calculated punch and counter-punch. The IRA began to use carefully calculated attacks as bargaining chips not only to concentrate British minds but also to maintain the confidence of its hardliners (Moloney 2007). In response, the security community gave the IRA an occasional bloody nose to remind them it still meant business. In retrospect, this raises the uncomfortable reality that by the late 1970s the 'war' was effectively over and from then on there was 'haggling' or 'skirmishing', in a 'two decade period of stalemate' (Smith & Neumann 2005:427), designed to bring the warring parties to the bargaining table. Subsequently, most commentators acknowledge that the *Sinn Fein* leadership displayed acumen in this prolonged and painful process and went on to dominate the peace talks, but it was a long and precarious process for all involved that might easily have gone awry (Cusack & McDonald 2008).

No one, however, seems to be very complimentary about the loyalist paramilitaries. They come across as more sectarian and crude and primarily reactive to IRA violence or external political developments, with little evidence of a carefully thought through strategy. When the UDA/UVF engaged in sectarian killings it was often indiscriminate:

> It should never be forgotten that, while the UVF leadership protested that they did not see the general Catholic population as their enemy, many of the rank and file, especially in areas like Portadown, simply hated Catholics. A few of them would have no problem 'stiffing a taig' [killing a Catholic]. There is ample evidence to show that in many UVF attacks if their units failed to find a republican target then the nearest Catholic would be killed to satisfy their bloodlust. (Cusack & McDonald 2008:271)

In addition, the armed wing never fully developed a sophisticated political equivalent to compare with *Sinn Fein*.

It could be, however, that they have received a largely negative press and have never attracted the amount of attention paid to the IRA and republicanism (Cusack & McDonald 2008; Taylor 2000). It is now apparent, for instance, that when nationalists and loyalists became incarcerated together in the Maze Prison, some insurgents from both sides began to engage in a dialogue about the future of the struggle and of the Province. From around the mid-1970s, a number of the more enlightened loyalists were surprisingly ready to compromise on reaching the cessation of violence and on the sharing of power in post-conflict Northern Ireland. This is evident in the detailed account given by the former UVF activist, David Ervine, who later became a prominent unionist politician dedicated to peace (Moloney 2010). But outside of the Maze Prison there was the intransigence both of the loyalist insurgents' rank-and-file and of political unionism (Cusack & McDonald 2008:143, 150).

Moreover, the general unionist movement was dourly defensive and locked into reactionary mode based on the primal fear of abandonment. The unionist rhetoric was replete with bitterness, resentment, hatred and defiance with 'treason', 'traitor', 'no surrender' and 'betrayal' running through speeches. The mindset was dead set against changes to the status quo making it weak at the negotiating table. The loyalists and unionists had difficulty grasping that the tide of history had turned against them. Also the politics of unionism was hopelessly split in factions based on the hard-soft dimension. Any mildly forward looking unionist leader willing to compromise was likely to face a damaging lack of support from the hardliners. And importantly, throughout the Troubles the obdurate Paisley positioned himself outside the centre of power but, with his barking rhetoric and unremitting energy, he effectively held the veto over unionist politics and loyalist sympathies. For many he was the dominating figure in Northern Ireland politics (Moloney 2008).

The RUC was institutionally a biased organisation that was recruited largely from Protestant stock and had discriminated against Catholics leading to it being associated with the loyalist cause. This was even more the case with the B Specials and the later UDR (Mulcahy 2006). This bias became graphically evident at the beginning of the Troubles from which the RUC emerged damaged, demoralised and exhausted; and the Army had to be called in to restore order. Especially from the time of Kenneth Newman as Chief Constable (1976–80) onwards, one can see a constant struggle to reform the institution from a biased agency with an inbred paramilitary, colonial style into a professional, impartial and accountable police force based on the traditional British notion of 'policing by consent'. But the proposals were being transferred from Britain, where the consent paradigm reflected a more integrated society. Northern Ireland was simply quite different and was a segmented if not sectarian society which continually raised the questions 'whose consent?' and from 'which community'? These dualities were clearly reflected in the person and functioning of Hermon as Chief Constable (1980–9). He was a proud, inflexible, aloof autocrat who was not keen on receiving criticism. He tried to turn the organisation around while also trying to preserve the autonomy and morale of his institution. Unfortunately there were the controversial shootings of 1982 that attracted outside scrutiny. But it was almost as if Hermon's response was, 'we want to be accountable but this is not the right time to criticize us'. This was impossible as there was mounting pressure to change the RUC which could not constantly be shielded from criticism. Hermon, however, was contemptuous of PANI (the police authority), hostile to the media and behaved unprofessionally towards Stalker and his investigation. When the two locked horns, the government had to choose between Stalker, his investigation and the RUC.

It was still not unthinkable that a full-scale civil war might break out and in whatever scenario was envisaged the authorities doubtless accepted that the continued functioning of the RUC, at least in the short term, was essential. For 'reasons of state', then, Stalker was expendable and he was sidelined in a shameful manner. But he understood the stakes at hand: 'I respect, if not admire, the way in which Sir John took the fight to me. He protected the force and himself from intrusion by me into its anti-terrorist efforts, and he succeeded. I was expendable and he was not' (Urban 1993:157). Yet this defeat for external scrutiny by circling the wagons only reinforced the conviction that the RUC remained partial and unaccountable and was running out of time to reform itself.

Mulcahy (2006), furthermore, portrays the official discourse of the RUC as based on the themes of sacrifice and bravery. The sacrifice and bravery is without dispute, but the reputation of the RUC is indelibly tainted by its record of systemic deviance during the Troubles. The evidence is overwhelming that segments of the organisation were deeply deviant. It took new leadership from outside the Province in the wake of the peace process to take the new PSNI into a period of genuine reform with a fundamental paradigm shift (Doyle 2010). This was a major challenge, as the RUC always wrestled with the resilience of the paramilitary, colonial model of policing and its politically mandated role as a biased enforcer of law and order within an essentially Protestant state (Mulcahy 2006). It enjoyed no real operational independence, 'responding directly to directions from ministers, with senior police officers sometimes attending cabinet meetings. The political, legal and policing worlds were thus inextricably mixed: one community governed, judged and policed the other' (McKittrick & McVea 2001:11). Furthermore, several police leaders had endeavoured to reform the RUC. It took them collectively 30 years; but then it took 30 years to implement political reform in Northern Ireland and reach a settlement that ended hostilities.

That political side of the Troubles is an intricate one of many interested parties, fluctuating circumstances and shifting alliances. As with much of Irish history there were opportunities that were not perceived or not grasped. And there never emerged one dominating figure, a Hibernian Mandela, with masterly statesmanship to navigate a long-term solution and to lubricate reconciliation. Or a de Gaulle who first strongly supported French Algeria but who realised it was necessary to withdraw; using all his personal authority he completed a *volte face* and extracted France in a most painful operation (Horne 1979). And there has been no TRC in Northern Ireland as in South Africa.

In Northern Ireland there were continuous shifts within the diverse movements that were deeply divided between appeasers and hardliners, by personality clashes and by leadership struggles. Personalities were also important and Margaret Thatcher could be particularly abrasive;[1] John Major was clearly more accommodating and built a sound relationship with the Irish *Taisoaech*, Albert Reynolds. There was tendency, moreover, for the British establishment to view Ireland as a political graveyard, a daunting and malignant quagmire that could only damage reputations, and some allegedly cursed the island for its intransigent people and its intractable problems. When Reginald Maudling, the Conservative Home Secretary, returned from visiting Northern Ireland in 1969 he apparently ordered a large whisky on the plane remarking, 'what a bloody awful country!' (English 2004:135). Margaret Thatcher was doubtless incredibly frustrated that a few hundred Irish rebels could tie down a substantial part of her professional Army, could kill several of her closest friends and political allies, could nearly destroy her and her Cabinet and yet could remain at bay. It was surely difficult for the 'Iron Lady' to explain to her European counterparts that she was incapable of pacifying Northern Ireland. For Northern Ireland remained an open wound, became a serious drain on resources (Ryder 2000:315) and formed a permanent embarrassment on the international political circuit. This was particularly the case when controversial incidents occurred like Bloody Sunday, the shootings on Gibraltar or the deaths of the hunger strikers that attracted worldwide attention (Williams 1989).

Throughout the conflict, then, there were fluctuating relationships between Dublin and London, between Dublin and Stormont, between London and Belfast and between US politicians and the major players. Slowly positions started to change and the old animosities began to wither. And after nearly 20 years of Conservative rule there was the advent of Tony Blair and New Labour in 1997, bringing fresh hope of a settlement. Behind this was also the realisation that the strategic significance of Northern Ireland had diminished considerably, with new geopolitical realities and the Gulf War against Iraq of 1991 absorbing British resources. There were new enemies on the horizon in the Middle East with different ideologies and methods, posing a more severe threat than the IRA. The first attack on the Twin Towers in New York by jihadists was, for instance, in 1993. The latter brought home to Americans what terrorism looked like on their doorstep; and the US public was dismayed when it emerged that IRA members had instructed the Colombian FARC in bomb making (English 2004:331). US Noraid funds dropped dramatically. Meanwhile the Republic of Ireland had become a more diverse and even secular society and was a far less threatening presence than in the past.

Furthermore, *Sinn Fein* had returned to campaigning for elections and won several seats at Westminster (including ones for Gerry Adams and Martin McGuinness); they also had some success in the *Dáil* but *Sinn Fein* never made much of a showing nationally in the Republic.[2] In Northern Ireland the party eventually came out ahead of the moderate SDLP in elections for Westminster and began to claim many council seats in local elections. There were negotiations, with John Hume of the SDLP playing a key role in the background, and contacts between *Sinn Fein* and the British government. There was the ceasefire of 1994, but then the disappointment of the abrupt return to hostilities. There was, however, a discernible momentum for a peace settlement from the early 1990s. American politicians, aware of the huge Irish Diaspora in the US, often paid a close interest in the Irish Question and President Clinton proved crucial in promoting a settlement. He had granted a visa to Gerry Adams and invited him to the White House, where Hillary Clinton publicly kissed Adams, during Adams' widely publicised visit to the US. It was partly due to Clinton's intervention, and Tony Blair's determination and acumen, that a settlement was reached on the symbolic day of Good Friday 1998. The paramilitaries of both sides then called permanent ceasefires. There followed the return of self-government, tortuous discussions over the composition of the

Northern Ireland Assembly that were dogged by the issue of IRA disarmament, again direct rule from London and, finally, a new devolved government for Northern Ireland. The once archenemies, Ian Paisley and Martin McGuinness, amicably shared power after frosty relations during the negotiations. But Paisley's Democratic Unionist Party (DUP) had become the largest party and he grasped the chance of taking power as First Minister; in a remarkable U-turn the man who always barked 'never', now said 'yes' and agreed to govern with *Sinn Fein* and with McGuinness as his Deputy.

However, in pulling Northern Ireland away from the abyss there were many politicians, officials and citizens, of different persuasions and from several countries, who played important roles publicly or in the background. Two of them, John Hume and Martin Trimble, were awarded the Nobel Peace Prize. Hume, in particular, worked tirelessly for a peace agreement, kept a line open to Adams and framed many of the documents that became the cornerstones for the political solution. McKittrick and McVea (2000) see Hume, Adams and Paisley as the three giants of Northern Ireland politics, and of these Hume had probably the most impact in setting the path to peace. Then there were the republican and loyalist leaders who finally and fortunately saw the need for compromise, the futility of endless bloodshed and that there was an opportunity to be grasped to share in government. And there was the turn around in the RUC which shed the symbols which divided it from the nationalist minority and which moved strongly towards becoming the impartial, professional, accountable 'service' for all, which many officers from Newman onwards had striven for and had cumulatively helped to implement. This process was vital because the republicans refused to accept the continuance of the existing RUC following the peace process and it was only when *Sinn Fein* announced its confidence in the new PSNI, and promised cooperation with it, that the unionists returned to talks on shaping a coalition. A somewhat fragile peace had finally been reached in Northern Ireland.

SLIDE INTO STATE DEVIANCE

The British State organised and participated in state-sponsored murder ... The State was not just an arbitrator, a peacekeeper, it became a participant on the loyalist side. (Ingram & Harkin 2004:12)

During the Troubles, segments of the security community adopted highly deviant practices that were clearly violations of the rule of law.

Such trying circumstances form a test of the integrity and resilience of governance and criminal justice in a democratic society; in Northern Ireland parts of the security community, and by association the government, failed that test (Campbell & Connolly 2006). In a democratic society security and law enforcement are above all a matter of legitimacy. Society relies on trust that those responsible for safety and security will abide by the law with impartiality and professionalism; will respect standards of due process; will be transparent in allowing review of decisions; will respect the rights of citizens and of suspects; and, will be accountable to oversight and, crucially, to the law (Bayley 2006; Braithwaite & Levi 1998).

Of course, these are the components of the myth system or explicit paradigm of democratic, accountable policing and law enforcement while there is much empirical evidence to suggest that in practice police and security agents deviate from that ideal in terms of an operational code. The evidence from police research, for example, indicates that forms of 'corruption' can be found in virtually all police forces at some time (Newburn 1999; Punch 2009). Politically motivated excesses in the form of torture or extra-judicial executions are most often reported in special units close to government direction. Typically, but not exclusively, such extreme scenarios are found in totalitarian, repressive or rogue states where law enforcement is an extension of arbitrary power that is not accountable. In Argentina under the military junta or with the 'Third Force' in apartheid South Africa, dealt with in Chapter 2, the repression was harsh and ruthless, the law was irrelevant and there was no respect for human rights (Wilkinson 2010).

The democratic state in contrast affirms that it is legitimate, not arbitrary and is genuinely accountable. When deviance from that formal paradigm is found, the state can appeal to extenuating circumstances but it cannot push aside fundamental principles to accommodate particular circumstances. Some of the key actors in Northern Ireland appeared to be conveying the message, 'the situation here was exceptional, so you can't judge us on outside standards, you *have* to make allowances'. Effectively they are claiming that the circumstances were *crime facilitative* in pushing them towards rule-bending. But at trying moments the state cannot compromise when it comes to fundamental rights – to freedom under the law, to a fair trail, to life and the right not to be exposed to violence, discrimination and abuse of authority.

The evidence is crystal clear. In Northern Ireland segments of the security community indisputably breached the rule of law, displayed contempt for due process and ran roughshod over the rights of citizens. Those exceptional circumstances bred a *criminogenic* environment. Indeed, for some the working environment may well have been *crime coercive*. In this context control agents feel 'forced' to break the law and even come to see it as SOP. It may have been 'good people and dirty work' but some of the work was very dirty; and few desisted from doing it (Hughes 1963). Ingram and Harkin (2004:255) remark that almost no one within the 'Intelligence Corps' raised concerns about the limits to the deviance and dirty tricks despite the fact that the 'vast majority' were 'decent people with solid moral values'. But it is mostly the case that actors who chose deviant options view themselves individually as 'decent people' with 'solid moral values'. It is what they are prepared to do *collectively* in a specific context that counts (Jackall 1998). This reflects the prime sociological and social-psychological insight that people are social animals who are powerfully influenced by group norms and pressures.

This is also the persistent theme throughout Zimbardo (2009) in which he maintains that 'systems' create 'contexts' in which 'individuals' take on roles and identities that cause them to behave in ways they would almost certainly not do as 'moral' individuals outside of that context. Zimbardo's analysis is based on the renowned Stanford Prison Experiment of the late 1960s, which he led: students took on the roles of prisoners and guards in a mock prison on the university campus. Within a few days, the prisoners were displaying sullen submissiveness and the guards were behaving with near sadistic aggression. The regression in both groups, who were randomly chosen for their roles, was so rapid and disturbing that the experiment was prematurely ended (Zimbardo 2009). Zimbardo, moreover, views the way once 'normal' individuals behaved within the Abu Ghraib Prison in Iraq, humiliating and abusing prisoners, and photographing themselves next to corpses, as a grim replication of his experiment. And, as Zimbardo predicts, the system having created the context blamed the individuals as scapegoats. This echoes much of my work and the field of 'organizational deviance' (Ermann & Lundman 1982), that it is not the individually weak or devious – the 'bad apples' – who are to blame for what goes wrong. It is more often bad barrels if not bad orchards or even a polluted fruit industry. Which raises the questions: who designed the orchards, who owns the industry, and who is to be held liable for the rotten fruit?

Following on from Zimbardo, I view the prime cause of the Northern Ireland 'experiment' becoming so prolonged and generating so much deviance, was the system effectively defining the context as a state of 'war'. That brought with it the justification that normal law enforcement did not apply and alternative if not extreme solutions were required. There was an initial goal of 'winning' the war against the IRA, but with a lengthy campaign and the inability to defeat the IRA there emerged a covert, subsidiary goal that drove the operational code; this can be defined as hurting the IRA by deviant means. And when people are put under pressure to achieve goals they may see the ends as justifying the means or the means becoming ends in themselves; as Gross (1980:72) remarks, 'whatever the goals may be, it is the emphasis on them that creates the trouble'. And Shover (1978:15), reflecting on the stress to reach organisational goals, noted that:

> Many times organizations become so preoccupied with the achievement of goals that they virtually give their employees – or demand – *carte blanche* powers to use 'innovative' methods to assure those goals are attained.

That overriding covert goal in Northern Ireland dramatically distorted security operations. The perception of exceptional circumstances requiring non-standard solutions clearly generated creative rule-bending and systemic deviance. This was enhanced by organisational structure in that there was a shifting bevy of agencies that not only competed more than they cooperated but were also granted considerable operational freedom. This is graphically illustrated by the functioning of the RUC's SB and the Army's SAS and FRU. These became near autonomous units dictating the counter-terrorism response and exercising a profound influence over other agencies. They went their own way largely undisturbed and were able to evade accountability.

SB, for example, was seen as an 'exclusive and secretive sect' (Ryder 2000:150); and by the Patten Report (1999) as a 'force within a force'. With the mantras of 'national security' and 'protect informants' SB became a law unto itself; a self-regulating, high-handed and impenetrable island:

- SB derived its power from the redefinition of policing as emergency, 'CT' policing with a low priority for conventional policing. The CT response revolved largely around intelligence, informants and specialist units for covert tasks. The pivotal role attributed to these meant that SB was effectively running the show; in 1988, Stalker wrote, 'I had never experienced, nor had any of my team, such an influence over an entire police force by one small section' (1988:56).

- Almost 20 years later an OPONI Report (2007:143) similarly commented on the dominant role of SB and how a 'culture of subservience' had developed toward it; 'The consequence of this was that, in the absence of effective Chief Officer management of Special Branch, it acquired domination over the rest of the organisation which inhibited some normal policing activities.'

- Reflecting on this, the Ombudsman sums up the absolutely crucial message: 'This investigation demonstrates graphically the dangers of a separated and effectively unaccountable specialist intelligence department with extensive and uncontrolled powers'[3] (OPONI 2007:145).

- The unusual policing situation was magnified by the powerful presence of the military, but armies have largely proven to be a crude instrument in public order and law enforcement (Elmsley 1996). The military mind tends to define situations in military terms of war, battles, victories and defeats (Campbell & Connolly 2003). The Army did learn and adapted pragmatically, leading some to laud its performance, but the prolonged British military presence was experienced as highly negative by the minority community.

- SAS 'executive operations', for example, were interpreted by some in the military as combat against an armed and dangerous enemy that had to be eliminated. This style is geared to close-quarter warfare but is not appropriate legally, politically or morally in a society that believes in the rights of suspects and in the minimal use of force. Formally martial law had not been declared, the law of the land was not in abeyance and armed terrorists clearly engaged on a mission have the right to life and the right to be treated as suspects under the law.

- But it is plain from diverse accounts that for some segments of the security community the law was de facto in abeyance, they were in a combat zone and it was 'legitimate' to take out insurgents engaged on a mission or presumed to be on active service.

- This military operational mode of proactive, 'shoot to eliminate' combat generated, in turn, institutional efforts aided by the Army's Legal Department to construct accounts of the encounters as posing direct danger.
- Another factor was the proliferation of agencies engaged in intelligence, surveillance, informants and covert operations. The secretive and murky world of 'spooks' can readily lead to devious practices that blur and exceed legal boundaries (Hoogenboom 2010a). The two key agencies involved, SB and the FRU (with MI5 in the background) apparently engaged in serious criminal offences. They both recruited 'crown jewel' informants who were encouraged to take part in criminal activities including the murder of innocent citizens and even of other British agents.
- These most serious offences, however, including accusations of murder and conspiracy to murder, generated secondary deviance as the original offences had to be covered up. Around covert actions, informants and executive operations there was a web of deceit and dissimulation. Crime scenes were not investigated properly; statements were fabricated; bugs went missing; recordings were doctored; evidence was interfered with or destroyed; senior officers lied in court; and external inquiries were obstructed. Nothing was what it seemed in the game and the 'truth' was reinvented to accord with institutional and political exigencies. And those who tried to tell the truth were sanctioned.
- A feature of serving the overriding goal was the reversal of the edict that a suspect is innocent until proven guilty. There was guilt by association in that any interaction in republican circles, or merely rumour and gossip about involvement, could taint a person. This bias extended to the families of insurgents – perhaps the insurgent had been killed, was in prison or on the run – who might be continually and aggressively harassed. Family members of deceased insurgents or suspected insurgents were often not informed about the circumstances of the death or the inquest; and personal possessions were not returned.
- From the functioning of SB and the FRU, it is plain that some of their targets were only linked to the republican movement by friendship, through relatives or drinking circles rather than by any solid intelligence or direct involvement in current terrorist or republican political activity.

- In the shoot to kill operations mounted by the RUC and SAS, some suspects had a record of violent activity. But this was used to impute danger and to assume they were engaged on an active service mission; this gave the green light to 'execute' them even when unarmed.

In short, my conclusion is that this represents systemic, *organisational deviance*. Ermann and Lundman (1982:91) state, 'The deviant behaviors are not produced by dramatic or aberrant actions of a few isolated individuals, but instead are an integral part of the organisation. Deviance thus exists alongside legitimate organisational activities and frequently serves to advance important organisational goals.' The 'slippery slope' had led members of the security community to serious deviance involving criminal offences. From other cases of organisational deviance we know that individuals are capable of adapting to deviance though processes of routinisation, rationalisation, depersonalising, and demonising the victims; and by the strong wish to conform to group and institutional norms (Browning 2001). In the military, police and business organisations, people are socialised to abide by orders from the hierarchy that can elicit willing compliance or compliance from fear of negative consequences. Furthermore, collectives can powerfully demand conformity to group norms, to developing an un-inquiring mind, to suppressing individuality and even to adopting a new identity. That collective behaviour may further lead to distortions in decision making through processes such as groupthink, cognitive dissonance and 'tunnel vision' which are not uncommon in policing and the military and can lead to disastrous decisions (Dixon 1979).

Certainly in the circumstances of Northern Ireland, where the emergency situation lasted some 30 years, there was ample time to become used to routine deviance. Newcomers to certain units would have encountered deviant practices that were inbred and would have been expected to fit in without question. The deviance was not individual but collective and *systemic* and could become a way of life. And in specialist units of the RUC and Army with a strong sense of mission one can hardly expect dissident voices. In general, people in organisations do what they are told to do and follow orders, even if those orders are illegal and/or initially troubling to their conscience. Indeed, behaviour within organisations can be seen as replications of Milgram's (1974) experiments on obedience or Zimbardo's (2009) experiment on incarceration.

My analysis leads to the conclusion that the grave and persistent illicit practices in Northern Ireland represent a case of system failure. This occurs when a system or significant part of a system undermines or side-steps the checks and balances designed to enable that system to achieve legitimate goals in a responsible and accountable manner. In Northern Ireland a legitimate goal – 'combat the IRA' – became reinvented as an illegitimate goal, namely 'hurt the IRA in any way you can' which invited illegitimate means. Allied to this is groupthink, which is a psychological mechanism that can seriously distort decision making (Janis 1985). When a collective gets locked into group think it tends to neglect critical external information, to be overly positive about its own potential, to stereotype those who do not fit in, to suppress dissent and diversity and to intimidate doubters. This is likely to be true of police and military circles with a strongly authoritarian ethos and a culture of solidarity that allows little space for individual autonomy and discretion in decision making and coping with informal deviance. The context created was, for some, 'crime coercive'; participants felt they had no option but to break the law. The consequence was that segments of the security community were routinely and persistently bending the rules and breaking the law. The context facilitated their crimes as it was a resource, a facilitator, the camouflage and an excuse; the context provided motive, opportunity and means. In Northern Ireland the deviancy uncovered within segments of the security community was indisputably organisational and systemic.

ALL BUT A POLICY?

A key factor in unravelling this material is, how far in the hierarchy did decision making go and was there a formal or informal 'policy'? To a degree, senior officials and leading politicians typically manoeuvre to create distance from decisions that might rebound and damage them. But there is enough data to show that during the Troubles many leading actors were well-informed and intimately involved in hands-on decision making. There has, for instance, been a dramatic glimpse of ministerial involvement in decision making illustrating opportunism and a willingness to turn a blind eye to terrorist murder.

In Claudy in 1972, IRA activists planted three car bombs that killed nine people including several children; attempts to phone a warning had failed (OPONI 2010). Information indicated the involvement of a Catholic priest, Father Chesney, who had become

OC (Officer Commanding) of an IRA unit. Fearing mass disorder among Catholics if the priest was convicted, the Secretary of State for Northern Ireland (Willie Whitelaw) reached an agreement with Cardinal Conway, Primate of All Ireland, that the priest be moved to a parish across the border in Donegal. The criminal investigation was not pursued with the full knowledge of the RUC's Chief Constable. The priest lived across the border in Ireland until his death in 1980 during which time he apparently confessed to the murder; this has been denied by the Catholic Church. This clandestine deal can only be interpreted as high-level collusion in perverting the course of justice and a serious criminal offence (OPONI 2010); but the main players are now all deceased. One assumes that Whitelaw would have informed key security officials in the Province while he was the closest political colleague and confidante of Margaret Thatcher. The conclusion can only be that some members of the British government were so obsessed with not stirring a hornets' nest in Northern Ireland that they colluded in a cover-up and effectively condoned murder.

However, it is most unlikely that any minister or government official gave direct, clear and traceable permission for illicit operations. But ministers would certainly have faced pressure 'to do something' when the IRA was especially active. One can imagine that Prime Minister Thatcher and her Cabinet sought some kind of retaliatory action on the day that 18 British soldiers died at Warren Point and Lord Mountbatten was killed on vacation in Ireland. Indeed, Mrs. Thatcher visited the Province immediately, demanded assertive action and promised immediate reinforcements (Ryder 2000:159). This certainly brought enhanced coordination and cooperation between the various agencies and led to a more concerted effort. But alongside these legitimate steps it is obvious that there was an increase in proactive, covert operations leading to controversial killings. There was clearly strong pressure from the Prime Minister for results and for a time she took a strong personal interest in the Northern Ireland question, cementing the process personally with frequent phone calls and meetings with the Chief Constable and GOC.

With regard to a more assertive use of force, it is conceivable that a signal was given from above that 'tough action' needed to be taken without specifically spelling out what that meant. Urban (1993:170), however, maintains that the initiative for firm action could also originate at the operational level, travel up the hierarchy to the JIS before transfer to the JIC in London. If the JIC was told there was an opportunity 'to deal a significant blow to the IRA' the response was likely to be, 'do what you think is right'. This would avoid clear, traceable instructions and officials would be kept 'fully uninformed' (Cohen 2001:68). Ingram and Harkin (2004:212) do maintain that ministers would have been informed by the JIS of the 'on-going case files on agents' but add, 'great care would have been taken to ensure that there was no paper trail, or indeed smoking gun, in the hands of any minister'. Urban (1993:168) adds to this that, 'The result was one of those compromises, typical of British government, in which real power is exercised by those who are not responsible to Parliament or the electorate who, in return, shield those who *are* responsible from painful decisions.'

In this world of implicit understandings and unspoken agreements, some sort of 'nod' from above was an influential factor. But a nod is not a 'policy' and following his prematurely terminated inquiry into the Lurgan shootings Stalker stated, 'I never did find evidence of a shoot to kill policy as such. There was no written instruction, nothing pinned up on the notice-board. But there was a clear understanding on the part of the men whose job it was to pull the trigger that that was what was expected of them' (Davenport 1988). A further significant argument against some coordinated effort is conveyed by the extensive fragmentation of security agencies and the often extensive rivalry and mistrust between them, while some were not 'tightly controlled' (Dillon 1991:56). There was, in fact, a bewildering array of parties at work in the police, security and intelligence agencies and, by all accounts, relations were not always smooth and cordial. There was fundamental disagreement about who should take 'overall control of the security effort, and how an integrated structure for the sharing of intelligence should be created' which plagued the counter-insurgency campaign (Urban 1993:13). Ingram and Harkin (2004:31) observe, moreover, that people may believe there was 'well-oiled' central coordination but this was 'totally overlooked' largely because of 'intense distrust between the various agencies'. The murky activities of the state can then be attributed particularly to specialised units outside of the mainstream law enforcement apparatus with a great deal of institutional rivalry, lack of coordination, distrust, failures of communication and competition. These units covered among them diverse functions such as surveillance, intelligence gathering, undercover operations, running informants, 'PSY OPS' and covert 'executive actions'.

This segmentation of deviance within and between particular units can be seen as the sort of 'natural' institutional fragmentation of bureaucratic systems with often dysfunctional consequences. But this may have unintended positive elements for government. Politicians often operate on the basis of 'divide and rule' so that no one agency becomes all powerful; grant autonomy because it pushes responsibility down and muddies the audit trail to higher echelons; encourage rivalry, engendering competition to enhance performance; and because, with several agencies they can keep options open, abandoning one if it gets into rough water while still being able to rely on another. It is probable, for example, that initiatives for assertive operations came primarily from the middle ranks of the Army and RUC. These would have been contingent, incidental and focused on specific individuals or small groups viewed as 'due', or 'overdue', for attention. Urban (1993:69) reports a source at Stormont as stating that ambushes 'give the IRA an occasional rap across the knuckles, something which may deter them from carrying out more attacks'; but he adds that this derived not from 'ministers who might have more qualms about the political repercussion of such "raps" but from "within the security edifice itself".' And an army officer admitted, 'there comes a time when we say "We need a kill – such and such a person is a thorn in our side and we have got to do something about him".' Then the decision on pulling the trigger was left to small units in a 'corporals' war' (Ryder 2000:156). In contemporary 'command and control' terms this is leaving matters to the implementation level without a supervisory, monitoring hierarchy of senior officers that builds in operational and institutional accountability (Markham & Punch 2007a & 2007b).

There were, then, fluctuations in the security response throughout the Troubles with four main periods, drawing on the first three outlined by Ni Aoláin (2000):

- The early years of 1969–74 were largely based on 'militarisation' with set-piece confrontations between the Army and demonstrators or in urban shoot-outs with insurgent gunmen. And for almost eight years the police did 'what the Army told them to do' (Ryder 2000:114).
- There was a period of so-called 'normalisation' from 1975–80 in which the number of killings dropped considerably and more agencies were involved in the fatalities (Green Army, SAS, 14th Int. and RUC).
- From 1981–94 there was another shift, partly in response to the IRA's 'Long War' of attrition and partly due to the

controversy surrounding the RUC's three shoot-to-kill cases at Lurgan. There was a move toward intelligence-led, set-piece operations aimed at active insurgents by specialised military units, especially the SAS and 14th Int.

- In the decade 1985–95, as the latter trend in turn came under critical scrutiny, there was a fourth phase of 'outsourcing' killing to the loyalist paramilitaries (Jamieson & McEvoy 2005).

It is most unlikely that some grand political strategist could have directed the security response through these successive phases over such a long period. But there is more than a whiff of cynical opportunism where some developments cannot just be coincidental; as in the final stage, after the SAS had come under increasing criticism for its ruthlessness, leading to the adoption of 'murder by proxy' using loyalists. But given the length of time, changes in personnel and fluctuations in the situation, it is difficult to conceive that a long-term, coherent, consistent and explicit conspiracy could have been sustained. The most intriguing question is, of course, how high did decision making go; how much did those at the top 'know'; and how often did they give off strong signals that they wanted vigorous action? Given what has been said earlier we are unlikely to get clarity on this for some time. But there are indications that the top was well informed and that it encouraged tough action if only by negative confirmation: not saying what should not be done thus seemingly approving mutely what was being done or going to be done.

This is the position taken by Davies (1999). That the FRU continued for so long with Nelson and the loyalists in that fourth phase is due, according to him, to the fact that the FRU received no firm guidance from above and interpreted this non-intervention as tacit approval. Davies (1999:22) argues, moreover, that all covert operations by the FRU were cleared with the JIS in Northern Ireland which then sought a political decision or sign from the JIC in Whitehall. He maintains that never 'were instructions received by the FRU in Belfast telling them to halt the sectarian targeting and killings'; and that senior government members, MI5 officers, senior security advisers and members of the JIC, who met almost weekly in London, must have been aware that an informant within the UDA 'was involved in many of the murders and dozens of the conspiracies to murder during that period'. Yet no moves were made to prevent the killings and the 'battle against the Provisional IRA had entered a new phase'. In essence, he firmly maintains that the top levels of government were fully informed on what was going on within the security community in Northern Ireland.

Davies (1999:153) intimates that senior members of the government wanted to take the fight to the IRA and took the leash off the FRU; 'the ruthless killings also showed the aggressive methods now being taken by the government in its bid to defeat the IRA'. If Davies and also Ingram are to be believed, these leading ministers and officials were aware of the illegal attacks on republicans by the RUC, the SAS and by loyalists 'run' by the RUC or FRU. They both assert that from the late 1980s there was a conspiracy between the intelligence agencies and the UDA/UVF to attack the republican movement. And this campaign of 'intimidation and killing of *Sinn Fein*/IRA politicians, gunmen, bombers, supporters and sympathisers by the UDA, aided and abetted by British Military Intelligence, was known about by MI5, ... and a few senior government ministers and civil servants' (Davies 1999:199).

There is no way of knowing if these assertions are valid and they remain speculation. But in political practice generally there are often norms and procedures of *deniability* that avoid operational decisions being tied by any footprints in the sand to specific politicians. That is a taken-for-granted way of life when risky, devious or potentially inflammatory decisions are taken. This leaves the central issue: was this an example of a deliberate conspiracy or was it more semi-conscious *reinforcing collusion*? This remains a matter of interpretation and conjecture, but my sense from the swelling evidence is that there was a degree of pressure with expectations from above which fostered decision making, and implicitly the blame, lower down the institutional hierarchy. There does also seem to be a pattern of testing the limits of state activity, of moving to new options if the negative reactions were too powerful and of concealing the decision making trail.

Just about every source, however, concedes that there never was an explicit, acknowledged 'policy' on shoot to kill and collusion. But perhaps there did not need to be one if there was an implicit conspiratorial web of understandings and implicit signals. As Human Rights Watch (2005) expressed it on Abu Ghraib,

> [T]his pattern of abuse did not result from the acts of individual soldiers who broke the rules. It resulted from decisions made by the Bush administration to bend, ignore or cast rules aside. Administration policies *created the climate* for Abu Ghraib and

for abuse against detainees worldwide in a number of ways. (my emphasis)

Stalker uses the phrase, *all but a policy*. Perhaps we can conclude that 'all but a policy' was effectively creating a 'climate' that fostered 'taking the gloves off' – the favourite phrase in relation to Abu Ghraib – among some and that became a form of shadow policy making. Following Zimbardo (2009), the system creates the context and the individuals take their cue and slot into their deviant roles without explicit orders from the system's leaders who by rhetoric, metaphor and innuendo convey what they would like to see done. In a way, the explicit conspiracy is not necessary because if one sets up a structure, a culture and set of expectations then the rest will follow, rather like Zimbardo's Stanford Prison Experiment but then for real. This dynamic led parts of the British security community in Northern Ireland to 'take off the gloves' whereby the state responded to terrorist insurgency by creating a context in which tacit 'reinforcing collusion' stimulated its own counter-campaign of state-sponsored violence.

STATES: INSURGENT TERRORISM: LEARNING FROM THE PAST

The democratic state is an abstraction that is expressed in a set of principles and values that articulate the high-ground within which society should function and the politics of government is to be conducted. It sets out parameters, the ground-rules for those who act within the 'ring', and conveys a comforting message. This is that the democratic state will stay out of the ring, will adjudicate impartially in the 'game' played by diverse stakeholders within the ring, and will hold itself to account for its judgements and actions. Above all it conveys that the state is fundamentally benign and will operate in the interests of its citizens.

In practice, however, some of the worst crimes ever committed have been when individuals or groups capture and misuse the state in their own personal, ethnic, religious or ideological interests (as outlined in Chapter 2). Power in this context is to manipulate the state in order to operate beyond public scrutiny and evade accountability for one's crimes (Tombs & Whyte 2003). In ostensibly solidly democratic states, however, there are challenging and demanding situations where representatives of the state face the 'dirty hands' dilemma of Sartre. Weber in his 'Politics as a Vocation'

(Gerth & Wright Mills 1948:123) recognised this dilemma for those exercising power:

> He who lets himself in for politics, that is, for power and force as means, contracts with diabolical powers and for his action it is *not* true that good can follow only from good and evil only from evil, but that often the opposite is true. Anyone who fails to see this is, indeed, a political infant.

Clearly having to face the gravest situations, such as war, can give rise to engaging with 'diabolical powers' and being forced to make 'rotten comprises' (Margalit 2010). States tend to anticipate this dilemma by passing emergency provisions that can be mobilised and, in trying times, with resort to elastic concepts such as 'national security' and 'public interest'. These can be utilised to invoke special powers, suspend habeus corpus, restrict privacy and the press, round up suspects, ban organisations and give the security forces extra powers (Parker 2007:169). Wilkinson (2005:23) argues that this conduct produces the paradox of 'suspending democracy in order to defend it'; and it raises the risk that 'by using heavy repression to crush the terrorist campaign the authorities will alienate the innocent majority of citizens caught up in the procedures of house-to-house searches and interrogations'.

Especially sustained insurgent terrorism can be extremely taxing for the democratic state to tackle. In particular, can the state remain benign, impartial and accountable when confronted with a sustained and violent challenge? And, above all, can it stay within the law? For if the state itself cannot abide by the law where is its legitimacy? And who can trust it? In turning to Northern Ireland as a test case for these questions we can draw the following conclusions about states and insurgency.

We plainly have the benefit of armchair scrutiny, but that can be employed to draw a number of key lessons:

- Firstly, the British state did not come up with an adequate political strategy for quite some time. As Boyle and Hadden (1985:66) express it, 'With hindsight it can be said that the main cause of the continuing violence in Northern Ireland has been the failure of the British Government to get to grips with the essentials of the political problem'. For perhaps 20 years there were largely reactive, opportunistic responses to what was seen as primarily a colonial, security situation. There appears to have been consistently poor assessments of the situation and a poverty of thinking on solutions. This failure to cope with the political dimensions of the conflict needlessly prolonged it.

- Secondly, the former shortcoming led, with the effective collapse of conventional law enforcement, to calling in the military and to trying to impose early on a military solution. With the Army in the driving seat there were a range of large-scale operations and controversial incidents that only served to alienate the minority population. The heavy-handed presence of the military sent out the message that this was an army of occupation. There could perhaps have been a UN peacekeeping force, but this would have been an admission that the UK could not solve its internal problems.

- Thirdly, and most importantly, *the state took sides*. And it did so aggressively and consistently. This was really a crucial factor in turning the minority population away from the British government and its rhetoric. When that partiality became indisputably apparent the state no longer had legitimacy and could not be trusted. This stance was a fatal error with the state committed to defending the indefensible, as it had done since the 1920s.

- Fourthly, and pivotally, the three factors above led the state to commit crimes and to cover them up. The mighty British state resorted to an 'operational code' in Northern Ireland that included crimes of a sort it was roundly condemning in its 'criminal' opponents. There was ambivalence in that it was fighting a 'war' yet insisted that it was combatting common 'criminals' while ostensibly employing conventional laws and procedures applicable in British society. Given the testing circumstances in Northern Ireland it was almost inevitable that practitioners would break those laws and procedures. But although the squaddy may have pulled the trigger in Crossmaglen, the real 'actus reus' has to be located in London with the 'mens rea' resting within a small group of decison-makers in Whitehall. Accountability should be drawn upwards; but that happens rarely in states which seek to avoid responsibility and evade accountability.

- Fifthly, that deviance of lower level operatives also fostered widespread deviance at diverse levels to cover up the misdeeds of the state. Behind the shootings was a hidden army of officials who in the interests of the state went about the business of gagging the press, smearing individuals, destroying documents, manipulating evidence, breaking into property and burglary, constructing false statements for the courts, lying under oath, destroying reputations by leaks and non-attributable interviews, labelling troublesome people mentally ill and revealing the identity of a whistleblower and hence endangering his life and that of his family. Collectively these shenanigans throughout the Troubles revealed the state to be not only cynically devious but also vindictive. This proved extremely damaging to the legitimacy and credibility of the British state.

- Sixthly, and finally, the most significant lesson to be learned from this material is that when state agencies constantly choose a deviant path in a security situation it can prove counter-productive. It may achieve results in the short term, but a state that allows abuses and excesses faces negative publicity and political opposition while handing ready-made propaganda victories to the opponent. Violence begets violence; and illegitimate state violence does more damage to the fabric of society both politically and morally than terrorist violence. Security forces in an emergency situation tend to respond, often with the encouragement or if not forceful demands from politicians, to hit back and score successes against the 'enemy'. But 'successes' gained in the short term are in the long run not particularly effective. Furthermore, it is a matter of enlightened self-interest that a state establishes its legitimacy and integrity by not going down the slippery slope into routine deviance (such as torture or extra-judicial executions). In the battle for hearts, minds, public opinion and international approval, the state that abandons the rule of law lowers itself to the level of those it vilifies as being beyond the law. And as the Police Ombudsman cogently puts it:

> ... one of the greatest dangers to any anti-terrorist work is that, if those charged with intelligence gathering and investigation do not abide by the rules, and if those who manage them do not operate effectively to ensure compliance with both law and policy, *the risk of terrorist attacks is enhanced, not reduced.* (OPONI 2007:145, my emphasis)

Drawing on the historical background of the Northern Ireland experience and the wider literature confirms that there is no quick fix when it comes to coping with insurgent terrorism. Furthermore, it is problematic to what extent states are capable of learning from experience elsewhere. However, the clear message from the above is for states to think in the long term and keep channels of communication open for possible negotiations. To anticipate a political solution and the necessity for compromise. Not to rely exclusively on a military strategy and avoid an excessive military presence. To endeavour rapidly to restore conventional law enforcement where that has become ineffective and/or illegitimate; to use as much as possible conventional law enforcement in combating insurgent terrorism;[4] and to minimise the impact of measures on the wider public. And be careful in the use and duration of emergency measures. But, above all, abide by the law. The 'Old' IRA of the 1920s (McGahern 2005:13) understood it was necessary to provoke the state into action that was, 'counter-productive in its harshness. The rule of law was crucial to the British administration. To provoke them into breaking their own laws was to subvert their most powerful weapon.' Indeed, this view became central to Marighela's (1970) *Mini-manual of the Urban Guerrilla* which influenced so many modern insurgent movements. In essence, a fundamental message emerging from this material is that overly repressive, counter-terrorism campaigns can rebound and foster more 'resilient, aggressive terrorist organizations' (Parker 2007:155).

Plainly this plea for state restraint is a counsel of perfection. But there is wide consensus among the aficionados of terrorism studies that maintaining the legitimacy of the state is vital; and hence that abusing the rule of law is self-defeating. Wilkinson (2005) in particular constantly hammers this principle home. For example, he refers to the campaign of assassinations by Mossad agents against Israel's enemies:

> There is a widespread misconception that using terror to defeat terror will ultimately work. On the contrary, the evidence is that this policy is counter-productive. Instead of suppressing terrorism against Israel these methods tend to reinvigorate the terrorist movements and gain them international sympathy. They have only tended to make it harder than ever to break the cycle of violence and sustain progress in the peace process. (Wilkinson 2005:69)

Indeed, one of the staples of insurgent identity and propaganda is the honouring of martyrs and the ritual of funerals. Wilkinson

(2005:15, 23) goes on to accentuate the following crystal clear position:

> It must be a cardinal principle of a liberal democracy in dealing with the problems of terrorism, however serious these may be, never to be tempted into using methods which are incompatible with the liberal values of humanity, liberty and justice. It is a dangerous illusion to believe one can 'protect' liberal democracy by suspending liberal rights and forms of government ... However hard the going gets in coping with severe internal terrorism or international terrorism, or both, a liberal democratic government has a primary duty to preserve constitutional government.

In the light of these insights from a leading authority in this field, it is painfully apparent that many of the main measures adopted in Northern Ireland proved counter-productive and played into the hands of the IRA. The insurgents deliberately set out to bait and provoke the state into a savage response. This produced an acute dilemma for all involved in counter-terrorism.

My thesis is that the British state failed in responding to that dilemma. The accountability trail for this runs through senior police and Army officers and government officials to the most senior representatives of the British state. It may not have been an explicit conspiracy and may perhaps have been a form of tacit conspiracy. It may also have been allied to fluctuating degrees of indifference, misjudgement, wilful blindness, recklessness or even lack of political and moral courage. But whatever the cause, the collective accountability has to be traced to some members of the Cabinet or inner-circle on whose watch it took place. Every individual within the security community who took part in illegality on behalf of the state during the Troubles carries a personal, moral and legal responsibility for his or her actions. But the footprints in the sand lead us to locate the ultimate accountability among the representatives of the state in Whitehall.

The importance of this tale of the Troubles is that the appalling extent of sacrifice demands that the state learns from these lessons. This is particularly urgent because there has been a rebranding of the counter-insurgency campaign in Northern Ireland as a 'success' and this version has been sold to the US for adoption in conflicts abroad (Campbell & Connolly 2003:341). That 'success' plainly needs to be modified in the light of the material and analysis above. But also importantly because counter-terrorism has come to dominate the security agenda in the US and UK in the last decade (Reiner 2010). In unravelling all this there are views of the state as powerful, especially from radical thinkers and academics, but also, in contrast, as increasingly feeble. Regarding the latter the perspective is that the nation state has been losing out to international and transnational entities (Loader & Walker 2007). Strong, weak, withering or fading, the state has overseen in recent years the fragmentation of criminal justice and law enforcement in several societies (Bayley & Shearing 2001); and also the 'blurring of boundaries' between them and the military and intelligence apparatus (Hoogenboom 2010a). In terms of democratic accountability and separation of agencies with the civil police holding primacy, this blurring is a potentially dangerous development given the dominance of that counter-terrorism agenda (Reiner 2007). It leads to that ominous CIA statement about the GWOT (Global War on Terrorism) being won, 'in large measure by forces you do not know about, in actions you will not see and in ways you may not want to know about' (Scahill 2007:254). This surely is one of the most indelible lessons from the Troubles, not to make law enforcement subordinate to a security agenda that subverts legality.

This viewpoint was well expressed by a Catholic priest who had consistently opposed IRA violence:

> Justice is the big thing, justice is the solution. Most of the problems in the 1980s were created by the British government. We could have wiped out the Provos [Provisional IRA] long ago if the Government had put proper discipline into the RUC, the British Army and the UDR. All we've ever asked for is for the security forces to act within the law. Don't torture. Don't shoot to kill. Don't unjustly harass people. The Provos rely on atrocities by the security forces to bail them out. The Provos love harshness and cruelty and misery ... The only way to beat the IRA is to be kind and just to the Catholic people and take them away from the Provos. Only the Catholic people will tell them to stop ... . (Geraghty 2000:112)

The problem was that British governments consistently proved incapable or unwilling to administer that 'proper discipline'. There was failure in 1972 with Bloody Sunday and failure again in 1982 after the Lurgan shootings. Stalker's investigation could have led to cleaning out the stables: but yet again a British government failed to take the necessary steps. Representatives of the state discredited

Stalker and undermined his investigation, which was professionally damaging for him but, far more importantly, it meant that there was no justice and no truth surrounding the Lurgan killings. Given the distorted system of 'justice' in Northern Ireland this only confirmed the pattern of providing rich propaganda for the opponent. Indeed, the fundamental issue was how that failure to investigate touched on fundamental principles of governance, accountablity and legitimacy. The British state's failure to react adequately to the Lurgan killings not only displayed its deviousness and hypocrisy but also prolonged the conflict for over another decade. Perhaps the real 'conspiracy'was the collective failure of those elected to serve the state to do what the state, and the public, demand of them; to solve problems rather than making them worse. The British state has, then, to carry a considerable measure of blame, but clearly not alone, for the suffering inflicted during the Troubles. Perhaps a British Prime Minister should go to Belfast and Dublin and offer apolgies on behalf of the British state to the people of all Ireland.[5]

Finally, much of history informs us that states cannot be trusted. Indeed, it could be said that the state has no memory and no conscience and hence can be vicious, vindictive and merciless without any agonising reflection. Also it tends to be a slow learner and hence it often goes on to repeat its mistakes. It also proves extremely difficult to get it convicted for its crimes; this means it keeps getting away with it, leaving a deep sense of injustice (Nollkaemper & van der Wilt 2009). And certainly in the conflict in Northern Ireland the British state revealed itself as not only devious and untrustworthy but also as a repeat offender.

Notes

CHAPTER 1

1. See Milgram (1974) for his renowned if not infamous experiment on obedience.
2. Northern Ireland is a constituent part of the UK; it is also called the 'Province' referring to the Province of Ulster (which is formally incorrect) while people also say 'North' and 'South' when referring to Northern Ireland and Ireland; in law the Republic of Ireland is not the state's official name, but many use 'Republic' to distinguish Ireland from Northern Ireland.
3. I shall use 'Derry' throughout; this Irish city was renamed 'Londonderry' by the British in 1613 but is now 'Derry City'. It was and is Derry to nationalists and Londonderry to loyalists and many Britons.
4. There is considerable material – reports, books, films, television footage, music, documentaries, newspaper articles and personal accounts – on Bloody Sunday including the play *Scenes from the Saville Inquiry* (Norton-Taylor 2005).
5. On one side in the conflict in Northern Ireland were 'nationalists', who were mostly Catholic and often republicans, and who wanted Irish unity in a republic free from Britain; on the other side were 'loyalists', who were mostly Protestants and typically unionists, in favour of the continued union of Northern Ireland with the UK and remaining loyal to the Crown. In relation to insurgent, paramilitary activity I shall refer to the two sides as nationalist and loyalist.
6. McGuinness was then active in PIRA and later admitted his presence as second in command of the Derry IRA; he became a leading member of *Sinn Fein*.
7. Many of the leading actors were conscious that military means alone were insufficient and that political change was needed; but they faced a deteriorating security situation that had to be tackled; moreover the changes required time as the government in Northern Ireland was having considerable difficulties delivering those reforms.
8. A former soldier with many tours of duty in the Province between 1969–88, rising to command rank, wrote that the conduct of many so-called 'green' (meaning conventional Army) soldiers, often teenagers, should be a 'source of pride' while they also, unlike the covert military units, took most of the 'incoming' fire and casualties. The Green Army mostly displayed a restraint which he believed 'would not have been matched by many, if any, contemporary armies' (personal communication). He was not uncritical of what took place, but this narrative would probably reflect the position of many of the thousands of military personnel who served in Northern Ireland.
9. In these areas the IRA set up roadblocks, controlled traffic and issued passes to journalists.
10. An account of Bloody Sunday was written by a para in 1975. He recalls that a lieutenant (Lt.) addressed his platoon stating that Derry had been severely bombed, hundreds of soldiers 'had been hospitalised' without any arrests while the Creggan Estate was 'an I.R.A. fortress, conning towers, machine guns and barbed wire as well as land mines guarding its approaches'. He adds, 'As I looked at my friends I could see that after all the abuse and nights without sleep, frustration and tension, this is what they had been waiting for. We were all in high

spirits and when our Lt. said "let's teach these buggers a lesson – we want some kills tomorrow", to the mentality of the blokes to whom he was speaking, this was tantamount to an order i.e. *an exoneration of all responsibility*' (Geraghty 2000:65; my emphasis). This rhetoric was reprehensible from an officer; the provocative 'briefing' was wildly inaccurate, exaggerating the level of danger.

11. There was dismay if not disgust among other soldiers concerning the paras conduct. The former soldier with wide experience in the Province had experienced the paras at first hand; he writes that they did little to 'dilute their undoubted aggression and physicality to an internal security environment' and 'they built up a reservoir of aggression'. He is convinced that the 'overwhelming majority of units' would not have opened fire on that day (personal communication).

12. The paras Commander admitted to the Inquiry that his earlier account of experiencing submachine gun fire and of seeing a gunman with a carbine was not 'accurate' and he had not personally witnessed them.

13. This is from a select version of Rolston's (2000) book, written with M. Gilmartin, reproduced on the CAIN website, dated 2006 with copyright to Rolston, which I have used.

14. The Lord Chief Justice was then the head of the judiciary and President of the Courts of England and Wales.

15. From CAIN website (2011a), 'Events: Bloody Sunday – Summary of Main Events'.

16. All these incidents will be dealt with in the text below.

17. The French withdrawal from Algeria, which formally was an integral part of France, was wrenchingly traumatic; France faced a long struggle against insurgents, a mutiny among its military, influential French intellectuals favouring Algerian independence, a right-wing terrorist campaign, and an influx of well over one million *pied noirs* (French settlers in Algeria) into France (Horne 1977).

18. The officer who led the paras on that fateful day in 1972, Colonel Wilford, was honoured with an OBE a year later.

19. In 1999 Colonel Wilford was still negatively labelling the relatives of the victims as representing 'republican organizations'.

20. The Abercorn Restaurant in the Belfast city-centre attracted shoppers, mostly young women and mothers with children. Two sisters went into Belfast to shop and suffered multiple injuries in the explosion; both had their legs amputated and one also lost an arm and an eye. There were 136 wounded with some gravely injured; two young women died and both were Catholic (English 2004:157).

21. Richardson (2006:84) states that an analysis of IRA violence reveals 'a chronic concern on their part to tailor their targeting strategies in a way as to inflict harm, gain attention and raise the costs for Britain of its presence in Northern Ireland, but not to alienate the Catholic population of the province'.

22. Only a thin coat of paint prevented the explosive device detonating inside the plane to London with over 80 people aboard including the Chief Constable, his wife, several MPs and two RUC officers going to receive gallantry awards (Ryder 2000:135).

23. The IRA bombers were viewed as innovative, adaptable and bright by the Army Bomb Disposal officers; they were 'first division', the bombs 'very well made' and the makers were cunning; 'I don't think there is any organization in the world as cunning as the IRA … We have a great deal of respect for their skills … not as individuals, but their skills' (Gorman 1992; Hoffman 2006:253).

24. Of 31 groups studied in Europe and North America, 20 had ceased to exist after around six and a half years (Gurr 1970:92).

25. The Troubles enriched the language with 'stiffing' (killing), 'spray job' (an attack by spraying bullets with an automatic weapon), 'rompering' (tormenting through prolonged violence), 'digging' (beating up), 'on the blanket' (refusing to dress in prison clothes and wearing only a blanket) and a 'Black and Dekker job' (knee-capping with an electric drill).

26. Richardson (2006:2) describes her Irish childhood in the 1960s when she had a 'passionate hatred of England' and where the morning school assembly was beneath a statue of Christ, the Declaration of Irish Independence and photos of the martyrs of the 1916 Easter Rising.

27. The first siege lasted 13 days and three hostages were killed, but it was ended by negotiations; the second siege lasted 20 days and, although no one was killed, negotiations failed; in an assault by Marine Commandos the insurgents and two hostages passengers were killed but the remaining hostages were freed (Bootsma 2001).

28. Although used as a synonym for Northern Ireland, especially by loyalists and unionists, the original Irish province of Ulster consists of nine counties and not the six of Northern Ireland. Some nationalists speak contemptuously of the 'Six County State' or 'British Occupied Northern Ireland'.

29. There are tributes to the courage, dedication and professionalism of RUC officers in various publications and while this is partly special pleading it is doubtless true of some officers. Dillon (1990), on the 'Shankill Butchers', portrays a detective working in exemplary fashion to solve these gruesome cases; the same is true of a scene of crime officer (SOCO), regarding the 'Miami Showband Massacre' (Travers & Fetherstonhaugh 2007). The latter also aided the authors years later by displaying that evidence which shed crucial light on the events of that dreadful night in 1975, which I shall deal with below.

30. Moloney (2007) writes of the re-branding of Adams after the GFA as a benign celebrity who denies direct involvement in any violence and of ever being a member of the IRA.

31. For instance, the widow of an unarmed IRA activist (McKerr) who was killed in the first of the RUC Lurgan shootings by the RUC (see Chapter 3), became involved in convoluted legal battles to discover the truth about his death including bringing the case to the ECHR in Strasbourg. Her determination and assertiveness were clearly not appreciated and elicited harassment; her sister stated: 'Her house was raided by the RUC and British Army on many occasions. During one of the raids, they suggested to her that she go to live in America. She was followed by the RUC and any car she was travelling in was stopped. Over the 12 years of legal action my sister continually asked the RUC for the return of her husband's car, the contents of the car and his clothes. All she received was a wallet and wedding ring'. She also attracted hate mail and abusive phone calls (Rolston 2006:30).

32. http://www.patfinucanecentre.org

CHAPTER 2

1. In 1968 American soldiers massacred some 300–500 villagers in Vietnam, according to diverse sources. When the soldiers faced prosecution in the US there was an upsurge of popular support for them that brought President Nixon to intervene. The main defendant, Lieutenant Calley, was the only one

convicted, yet he spent under four years under house arrest with President Nixon commuting his sentence. No other defendant was convicted including Captain Medina who led the operation (McCarthy 1973). The evidence was overwhelming that the US Army had murdered innocent civilians, but effectively all involved in the direction of the operation and the actual massacre were let off without being sanctioned – except for Calley, who never saw the inside of a prison after his conviction.

2. In his book on Blackwater, a Private Military Company, Scahill (2007) mentions private companies involved in 'extraordinary rendition' flights on behalf of the CIA taking illegally abducted suspects of terrorism to secret interrogation centres in countries with little concern for human rights where they are tortured into 'confessions'.

3. Indeed Glenny (2009:9) views terrorism as 'primitive' and 'insignificant' compared with the power, influence and violence of contemporary trans-national organised crime. Currently (in 2011) there is almost a state of war between rival drugs cartels, and between them and the federal government in Mexico, which is being fought with gruesome savagery and many casualties. The scale dwarfs much insurgent terrorism with some 30,000-dead reported in Mexico since a government crackdown in 2006; in one city, Cuidad Juarez, the death toll from the drug wars was some 3,000 in 2010 alone (*BBC World News* 2010).

4. The Iran-Contra scandal was a complex affair; exposed in 1986, it displayed abuse of the law within the administration of President Reagan. A group within the White House planned to sell weapons to 'moderates' in the Iran of the Islamic Ayatollahs using Israel as the go-between. The major motive was to affect the release of American hostages being held by the Islamist Hezbollah group in Lebanon. This covert operation broke both an international arms embargo against Iran and a Congressional ban on supplying government funds to the right-wing, anti-Sandinista Contras in Nicaragua. Part of the machinations was to use some of the money to support the Contras. Reagan subsequently took responsibility when the affair unfolded, accepted the sharp criticism but emerged largely unscathed. Several highly-placed officials resigned and some were prosecuted and convicted; but the convictions were overturned on appeal or the culprits were pardoned by Reagan's successor, President George Bush. No one ever served a custodial sentence.

5. There were 'numerous' shipments from Libya of which three were intercepted at sea (English 2004:249). The SAMs were never used. Semtex is a plastic explosive with qualities that make it ideal for terrorist groups. Large amounts have been exported from the Czech Republic since the 1960s, including a colossal 700 tonnes for Libya. Probably only 8 ounces of semtex-H was used in the bomb which exploded aboard flight Pan Am 103 above Lockerbie (Hoffman 2006: 264)

6. Later, Gaddafi sought improved relations with western countries and the US resumed full diplomatic relations with Libya in 2006, removing it from the list of lands that support terrorism. Earlier, Gaddafi allowed the extradition of two Libyans to face trial for the bombing; one was convicted but was released on 'medical grounds' in 2009. It is assumed that the Libyan secret service played a major role in the bombing; during the anti-regime turbulence in Libya in early 2011, a defector from the regime claimed that Gaddafi had personally ordered the Lockerbie bombing.

7. Farida (2010) explains Hizbollah's (her spelling) success and popularity through its recruitment strategy, hierarchical structure, historical background, its military activities and the various services it provides to members and their families.

8. Withholding the label can also have significance; for a long time the US did not classify the IRA as a 'terrorist' organisation, allowing American funds to be sent to republicans via the Irish Northern Aid Committee (Noraid); also, US courts were reluctant to extradite IRA suspects to the UK because the offences were viewed as 'political' and not 'criminal'; and in 1979 President Carter banned an export of firearms to the RUC.

9. Particularly since 1945, armed conflicts in general have increasingly targeted civilians or led to high civilian casualties (Wilkinson 2005:4).

10. Apparently an IRA marksman shot ten British soldiers at a considerable distance in 'bandit country' near Crossmaglen using a high-velocity Barret Light 50 sniping-rifle (Horgan 2005:14).

11. The 9/11 attacks in the US in 2001 cost an estimated $500,000 but caused $25–50 billion in damages paid out by insurance companies. The bomb which killed the MP Airey Neave within the Parliament compound at Westminster cost merely £5 (McDonald & Holland 2010:169).

12. The Maze Prison was also known as 'Long Kesh' or the 'H-Blocks'. There was an inmates' council comprising the groups interned and this communicated with the prison management about inmates' needs and wishes. This fostered a measure of fraternisation while there was an understanding that there would be no inter-group violence, which held for much of the time. During incarceration there were some radical changes of views with some hard-men turning to religion and some to ideas on peace and reconciliation. Also some unexpected relationships and even friendships developed between people from both sides (Moloney 2010).

13. During a car-check, an Army sniffer-dog had mistaken the smell of creosote used in farming for explosives. Collins, his brother and father were taken in for questioning; he was intimidated with firearms in the Army jeep with a rifle-barrel shoved in his mouth, was roughed up and repeatedly sworn at, and, when he returned from questioning, the soldiers had spent the night in his home with his mother and the other young children while the house was 'torn to pieces'.

14. A rogue Army squad that had been involved in a violent stabbing of two farmers as a reprisal for fatal attacks on fellow soldiers, although the victims were entirely innocent, returned to their field-camp at night and cleaned off the blood amid scenes of ribaldry in which many soldiers took part (Dillon 1991:124–60).

15. From a presentation of a Dutch police officer who had worked on IRA investigations activities in the Netherlands. Barker (2004:195) writes of a female IRA activist who would often become emotionally and sexually aroused during operations and on 'one occasion she had asked another volunteer for sex as they both sat in a hijacked vehicle'.

16. General Grivas, who led the EOKA independence movement in Cyprus, said of the British commander, 'Harding persisted in his error; he underestimated his enemy on the one hand and overrated his forces on the other. But one does not send a tank to catch field-mice – a cat will do the job better' (Richardson 2005:226).

CHAPTER 3

1. Geraghty (2000:366) states that this launching of major terrorist campaigns from a 'standing start' was a 'unique event in the history of guerrilla warfare'.

2. The reliable source on fatalities is the 'Sutton Index'; a revised, updated version of the original book (Sutton 1994) is available on the CAIN website, with copyright to Sutton.

3. These were informants with inside knowledge of insurgency from active participation in terrorist activities and a willingness to name names in return for a deal, such as immunity from prosecution.

4. The entire population is hardly more than a large city, roughly equivalent to Philadelphia in the US, while Greater Manchester in Britain has about a million more inhabitants than Northern Ireland.

5. In the 1998 Omagh bombing, the police had just received a warning and were directing people away from where the bomb was supposedly placed only to move them into the path of the devastating explosion (OPONI 2005).

6. One such suspected informant was Mrs McConville. She was a Protestant who became a Catholic on marrying her husband who had served as a British soldier; he died leaving her with ten children. She was also said to have helped a wounded British soldier and this seemed to have raised animosity against her. About 20 masked IRA members arrived and some entered her flat; they told the children that she would be back within hours and left them to fend for themselves. She was abducted, interrogated, accused of being an informer, shot in the head and buried at a secret location. Her remains were only recovered by accident over 30 years later. This was bullying, intimidating and inhumane treatment meted out to a vulnerable female, and the IRA refused to reveal the grave's location even after the GFA. The IRA activist Brendan Hughes claims that she was an informer for the British Army using a radio transmitter; this was uncovered, she had been let off with a warning but had re-offended leading to her 'execution' (Moloney 2010). This sounds unconvincing but everything is possible: however, the Police Ombudsman (OPONI 2006) found no evidence to substantiate this allegation.

7. This was carried out by the 'Glenanne Gang' who were members of the UVF with several in the UDR; it was implicated in some 100 murders and was linked to many other crimes including bombings in the South. Their aim that night was to pose as an UDR check-point; to plant a bomb in the group's van while the band's members were lined up on the road; and to blow up the van when it reached Ireland to implicate the musicians in transporting bombs for the IRA. But the bomb exploded prematurely killing two UVF men immediately; and the gang then pursued the fleeing musicians shooting them repeatedly; the lead-singer was shot 22 times in the face. But in the confusion two band-members survived; one escaped uninjured while the other survived terrible injuries (Travers & Fetherstonhaugh 2007). The UVF announced that a unit encountered an ambush in progress, came under fire and that several weapons were recovered making this 'justifiable homicide'. This was blatantly untrue.

8. The carnage at the Bus Station was appalling; limbs were blown off torsos, which were also stripped of clothes, and a head was stuck to a wall; a few days later, human remains were found on a roof because seagulls were diving on

them. The TV news briefly showed firemen shoveling body parts into plastic bags (Burleigh 2009).

9. Here, the label 'outrage' would have been applied principally by the British authorities, the Protestant majority in Northern Ireland and by majority public opinion in other countries. In contrast, IRA actions would have been seen as legitimate and even laudable in nationalist and republican circles in the UK, the Irish Republic and the US as part of the 'war' to rid Ireland of British troops and reunite the country.

CHAPTER 4

1. The term 'Special Branch' emerged during the Fenian terrorist campaign in England during the 1880s when the Met formed the 'Special Irish Branch', later 'Irish' was dropped from the name. Special Branch deals with 'politically' motivated crime and threats to state security (Allason 1983).

2. The IRA adopted the technique of the 'one shot sniper'; the sniper would fire only once and get away quickly before attracting return fire or risking apprehension (Crenshaw 1998:14).

3. A massive 800-pound (360-kilo) roadside bomb was exploded just as the soldiers' vehicles passed; the unit re-grouped at a nearby driveway to attend the wounded; predicting this, the IRA had placed a similarly large bomb close to that spot which caused more casualties. The second blast almost brought down a helicopter taking away the wounded from the first explosion.

4. A loyalist activist killed three mourners at the Belfast funeral of the 'Gibraltar Three' (who had been shot by the SAS on Gibraltar); at the funeral of these new victims, two British soldiers in plain-clothes were mistaken for loyalists when they pulled out their pistols but they were dragged out of their car by the mob, beaten, taken to waste ground, stripped and shot dead. This almost barbaric incident was filmed by an army helicopter.

5. The Army felt that the RUC was secretive, sometimes mediocre and generally mistrustful of outsiders. Also, SB officers were 'hugely overworked', under constant pressure and not always well supported in taking the mental strain. They faced severe restrictions on their private life with at home bulletproof windows and doors, electronic sensors and flood lights (Simpson 2010:250).

6. Perhaps McCauley was tipped off by an informant about the weapons because the 'open window' sounds an unlikely coincidence. McCauley was active in the IRA and some years later he was arrested in Colombia for aiding the FARC on the use of explosives.

7. There are several versions of the event. It may be there were no 'roadblocks' at all and the idea of an officer in the road waving down oncoming cars was simply invented to generate the alleged danger to the officers.

8. High-powered rifles, such as the Armalite AR-15, could be purchased in America as a hunting rifle. America was a source of weapons via Noraid, ostensibly for humanitarian aid to Northern Ireland, as well as through the pro-Irish contingent within the New York Police Department. This meant that American cops were financing the killing of UK police officers.

9. The SAS was then severely stretched and could only get about a dozen soldiers to the Province. By SAS, here I am referring specifically to its covert CIUs; the SAS as a regiment had earlier served openly in the Province with its uniformed units visibly on patrol (Asher 2004).

CHAPTER 5

1. An incident conveying the multi-level, dirty war occurred when an RUC Inspector was shot at close quarters and killed amidst a holiday crowd on Easter Monday 1987 at Newcastle, County Down. The IRA supplier of the firearm and one of the gunmen were both agents of the security services, according to Ingram and Harkin (2004:260).

2. The hit-squad had allegedly been given safe passage to and from the target, but this is discounted in the Cory Report (2004).

3. It was legal for a UDR soldier to be a member of the UDA until it was banned in 1992, and some were plainly involved with the banned UVF. When members of the Miami Showband were murdered they were stopped by what looked like UDR soldiers who actually were UVF members – a grisly but inconvertible piece of evidence after the premature bomb explosion in the musicians' van was a dismembered arm with 'UVF Portadown' tattooed on it – and the two killed in the explosion and two others in the UVF gang were also UDR members (Dillon 1991:209–30 & 248–77).

4. This code of 1033 for Nelson used by Davies differs from that used by Ingram, who refers to him as agent 6137.

5. There was also friction between Nelson and his handlers when an Army unit shot dead a loyalist gunman. A covert team from 14th Int. encountered a UVF hit-squad that had just shot dead an ordinary Catholic; the 14th Int. agents immediately intervened, killing one of the assailants and arresting the other (Davies 1999:194–50). Nelson was furious about this.

6. Cory had conducted two previous inquiries into possible collusion. Billy Wright (nicknamed 'Mad Dog') was a loyalist who joined the UVF but then split from it to found the Loyalist Volunteer Force (LVF); he was at odds with the UVF leadership and was assassinated inside the Maze Prison by three members of the INLA. The suspicious circumstances – how did they know of Wright's movements, and how did they gain access to the area where a minibus transporting Wright was stationary? – were such that there was at the least laxity within the prison and at worst police collusion to allow this to happen (McDonald & Cusack 2010:444–54). Following on from the work of Cory, the MacLean Report (2010) found no evidence of collusion in Wright's murder. It is possible that loyalists tipped off the INLA in order to rid the movement of Wright.

7. A CID officer said to Stevens that not to comply with SB's bidding might lead to a posting to the 'Outer Siberia of policing in some obscure department' (Simpson 2010:54).

8. Mrs. O'Loan is a Catholic woman from the mainland married to a nationalist politician, which amounts to a quadruple disqualification for some unionists. When the Ombudsman published a report on the Omagh bombing that was critical of the RUC leadership (OPONI 2005), she was called a 'suicide-bomber' by the unionist leader Ken Maginnis (no relation to Martin McGuinness).

CHAPTER 6

1. Being set free had a major impact on Collins; in prison he had distanced himself from violence and from the authoritarianism of the IRA. He was impressed that the judge had seriously applied the criterion of 'beyond reasonable doubt',

took account of confessions obtained under duress and granted him his freedom instead of sentencing him to a long period in jail. This positive experience of British justice reinforced his decision to reject violence (Collins 1998).

2. Someone with extensive military service in Northern Ireland maintained that in the early 'chaotic' days when soldiers faced 'extreme violence' and were often dismayed and bewildered to be asked to account for their actions in court, the work of Army lawyers was simply an ad hoc reaction to advise them how to conduct themselves before the law. It was not in his experience starting in 1969/1970 some sort of 'conscious attempt' to bend the facts; he is adamant on this and never felt it was an officially-sanctioned attempt at judicial cover-up (personal communication). But it is plain from a number of sources that it later became a more assertive form of witness preparation.

3. Before 1972 with the creation of the Crown Prosecution Service in Northern Ireland, the RUC was responsible for preparing prosecutions.

4. Even John Hume of the SDLP who was a strong advocate of the nationalist cause, with a good relationship with Gerry Adams, could at times fulminate against such excesses by the IRA (McKittrick & McVea 2001:186): 'They are the pure master race of Irish. They are the keepers of the holy grail of the nation. That deep-seated attitude, married to their method, has all the hallmarks of undiluted fascism. They have all the other hallmarks of the fascist – the scapegoat – the Brits are to blame for everything, even their own atrocities!'

CHAPTER 7

1. Thatcher also had many other battles to fight such as the Miners' Strike (1984) and not least the Falklands War (1982). A Northern Ireland insider told me she became obsessed with the border and proposed a Berlin-style wall across Ireland (360 kilometres, or 224 miles) to keep out the insurgents; this to the dismay of her security officials and financial advisors.

2. Gerry Adams was, however, elected to the *Dail* (the Irish Parliament) in early 2011 and Martin McGuinness is running for the Irish presidency.

3. Without explanation, army units would be asked to raid a house by SB and make drawings of the lay-out or to respect a temporary exclusion zone; this would provide a hit squad with a plan of the building as well as free access to and from a murderous raid. Also, CID and the Drug Squad had to bow without murmur to SB's whims (Mulcahy 2006:80).

4. In the mid-1970s Roy Mason as Secretary of State for Northern Ireland with two new Army chiefs began a no-nonsense and concerted effort to 'squeeze the IRA like a tube of toothpaste' by conventional methods of arrest, investigation, trial and conviction (Bishop & Mallie 1988:275). This almost beat the IRA with McGuinness admitting, 'Mason beat the shit out of us' (Wheatcroft 2004). The counter-terrorism campaign was also greatly aided by advances in forensic techniques and resources, in computerization with substantial, inter-linked data banks and in electronic monitoring at Government Communications Headquarters in Britain including that of mobile phones.

5. There has been debate about setting up a TRC to help exorcise the past and heal the wounds (there is one for Northern Ireland but only in fiction: Park 2010). One argument is that the divisions in Northern Ireland are still great so it might simply ignite conflict if past practices from the diverse groups were made public.

Bibliography

Allason, R. (1983) *The Branch* (London: Secker and Warburg).

Amnesty International (1978) *Report of an Amnesty International Mission to Northern Ireland* (London: Amnesty International).

Anderson, D. M. and Killingray, D. (1991) *Policing the Empire: Government, Authority and Control 1830–1940* (Manchester: Manchester University Press).

Appelbaum, A. (2003) *Gulag: A history of the Soviet camps* (London: Allen Lane).

Asher, M. (2004 [1990]) *Shoot to Kill* (London: Cassell).

—— (2008 [2007]) *The Regiment: The real story of the SAS* (London: Penguin Books).

Bandura, A. (1998) 'Mechanisms of moral disengagement', in *Origins of Terrorism*, W. Reich (ed.), (Washington, DC: Woodrow Wilson Center).

Barak, G. (1991) *Crimes by the Capitalist State: An Introduction to State Criminality* (Albany, NY: SUNY Press).

Barker, A. (2004) *Shadows: Inside Northern Ireland's Special Branch* (Edinburgh & London: Mainstream Publishing).

Barron Report (2003) *Report of the Independent Commission of Inquiry into the Dublin and Monaghan Bombings* (Dublin: Houses of Parliament).

—— (2005) *Report of the Independent Commission of Inquiry into the Murder of Seamus Ludlow* (Dublin: Houses of Parliament).

Bass, G. J. (2001) *Stay the Hand of Vengeance: The politics of war crimes tribunals* (Princeton, NJ: Princeton University Press).

Bayley, D. (2006) *Changing the Guard: Developing democratic police abroad* (New York & Oxford: Oxford University Press).

Bayley, D. H. and Shearing, C. D. (2001) *The New Structure of Policing: Description, conceptualization, and research agenda* (Washington, DC: National Institute of Justice).

BBC News UK (2007) 'Army paper says IRA not defeated', 6 July (web-service). Available at http://news.bbc.co.uk/2/hi/uk_news/northern_ireland/6276416.stm (updated 6 July 2007, accessed 14 November 2011).

—— (2009a) 'Real IRA was behind army attack', 8 March (web-service). Available at http://news.bbc.co.uk/2/hi/uk_news/northern_ireland/7930995.stm (updated 8 March 2009, accessed 14 November 2011).

—— (2009b) 'Continuity IRA shot dead officer,' 10 March (web-service). Available at http://news.bbc.co.uk/2/hi/uk_news/northern_ireland/7934426.stm (updated 10 March 2009, accessed 14 November 2011).

BBC World News (2010) 'Mexico's drug war: Number of dead passes 30,000', 16 December. Available at: http://www.bbc.co.uk/news/world-latin-america-12012425

Becker, J. (1978) *Hitler's Children: The story of the Baader-Meinhof gang* (London: Panther Books).

Belur, J. (2010) *Permission to Shoot: Police use of deadly force in democracies* (London: Springer).

Benn, S. I. and Peters, R. S. (1959) *Social Principles and the Democratic State* (London: Allen & Unwin).

Bennett Report (1979) *Report of the Committee of Inquiry into Police Interrogation Procedures in Northern Ireland* (London: HMSO).

Betancourt, I. (2011) *There is No Silence That Does Not End* (London: Virago).

Bishop, P. and Mallie, P. (1988) *The Provisional IRA* (London: Corgi).

Bootsma, P. (2001) *De Molukse acties* (Amsterdam: Boom).

Boraine, A. (2000) *A Country Unmasked* (New York & Oxford: Oxford University Press).

Bowcott, O. (2011a) 'Mau Mau victims seek compensation from UK for torture', *The Guardian*, 7 April.

Bowyer Bell, J. (1973) The escalation of insurgency: the Provisional IRA's experience. *The Review of Politics*, Vol. 36, No. 3, 398–411.

Boyle, K. and Hadden, T. (1985) *Ireland: A Positive Proposal* (Harmondsworth: Penguin).

Braithwaite, V. and Levi, M. (eds) (1998) *Trust & Governance* (New York: Russell Sage Foundation).

Bremner, C. (2005) 'Mitterand ordered bombing of Rainbow Warrior, spy chief says', *The Times*, 11 July.

Brock, G. (2008) 'Who really brought peace to Belfast?', *The Times Literary Supplement*, 27 February.

Brodeur, J.-P. (1981) 'Legitimizing police deviance', in *Organizational Police Deviance*, C. D. Shearing (ed.), (Toronto: Butterworth).

—— (1983) 'High and Low Policing; Remarks about the Policing of Political Activities,' *Social Problems*, Vol. 30, No. 5, 507–20.

Browning, C. R. (2001 [1992]) *Ordinary Men* (Harmondsworth: Penguin).

Burleigh, M. (2009) *Sacred causes* (web article). Available at http://www.wisertoday. blogspot.com/2009/02/Michael-burleigh.html (accessed 14 November 2011).

CAIN (2011a) *'Bloody Sunday', 30 January 1972 – Summary of main events* (Coleraine: CAIN Web Service). Available at http://www.cain.ulst.ac.uk/events/ bsunday/sum.htm (updated 17 June 2010, accessed 14 November 2011).

—— (2011b) *'Bloody Sunday', 30 January 1972 – A Chronology of Events* (Coleraine: CAIN Web Service). Available at http://www.cain.ulst.ac.uk/events/ bsunday/chron.htm (updated 17 June 2010, accessed 14 November 2011).

—— (2011c) *Sutton Index of Deaths*. Revised and updated extracts from Sutton, M. (1994) *'Bear in mind these dead': An Index of Deaths from the Conflict in Northern Ireland 1969–1993* (Dublin: Beyond the Pale). (Coleraine: CAIN Web Service). Available at http://www.cain.ulst.ac.uk/sutton/index.htm (accessed 14 November 2011).

Cameron Report (1969) *Disturbances in Northern Ireland: Report of the Commission Appointed by the Governor of Northern Ireland* (London: HMSO).

Campbell, C. and Connolly, I. (2006), 'Making War on Terror? Global Lessons from Northern Ireland', *Modern Law Review*, Vol. 69, No. 6, 935–57.

Channel 4 Television (1992) 'Secret History: Bloody Sunday', Interview with Bishop Daly, 22 January.

Clutterbuck, R. (1990) *Terrorism and Guerrilla Warfare* (London: Routledge).

Cobain, I. (2010a) 'Inside Castlereagh: "We got confessions by torture"', *The Guardian*, 11 October.

—— (2010b) 'Hundreds of Northern Ireland "terrorists" allege police torture', *The Guardian*, 11 October.

Cohen, S. (2001) *States of Denial: Knowing about Atrocities and Suffering* (Cambridge: Polity Press).

Collins, E. (1998) *Killing Rage* (London: Granta Books).

Collins, R. (2008) *Violence: A Micro-sociological Theory* (Princeton, NJ: Princeton University Press).

Compton Report (1971) *Report of an Enquiry into the Allegations against the Security Forces of Brutality in Northern Ireland Arising from the Events on the 9 August 1969* (London: HMSO).

Conquest, R. (2008) *The Great Terror: A reassessment* (New York & Oxford: Oxford University Press).

Coogan, T. P. (1993) *The IRA: A history* (Niwot, CO: Roberts Rinehart).

Cory Report (2004) *Cory Collusion Inquiry Report* (London: TSO).

Crawshaw, R., Cullen, S. and Holmström, L. (2006) *Essential Cases on Human Rights for the Police* (Leiden & Boston: Martinus Nijhoff).

Crenshaw, M. (1998) 'The logic of terrorism: Terrorist behaviour as a product of strategic choice', in *Origins of Terrorism*, W. Reich (ed.), (Washington, DC: Woodrow Wilson Center).

Cusack, J. and McDonald, H. (2008 [1997]) *UVF: The Endgame* (Dublin: Poolbeg Press).

Danner, M. (2004) *Torture and Truth: America, Abu Ghraib and the War on Terror* (New York, NY: The New York Review of Books).

Davenport, P. (1988) 'Spectrum: Stalker who became the prey', *The Times*, 9 February.

Davies, N. (1999) *Ten-Thirty Three: The Inside Story of Britain's Secret Killing Machine in Northern Ireland* (Edinburgh & London: Mainstream).

de Volkskrant (1998a) 'Ex-minister in Spanje kan 23 jaar cel krijgen,' 26 May.

—— (1998b) 'Spanje tegen Spanje,' 20 June.

—— (1998c) 'Ex-minister Spanje veroordeeld tot tien jaar cel,' 30 July.

Dillon, M. (1990 [1989]) *The Shankill Butchers: A case study of mass murder* (London: Arrow).

Dillon, M. (1991 [1990]) *The Dirty War* (London: Arrow).

Dixon, D. (ed.) (1999) *A Culture of Corruption* (Leichhardt, NSW: Hawkins Press).

Dixon, N. F. (1979 [1976]) *On the Psychology of Military Incompetence* (London: Futura Publications).

Doig, A. (2010) *State Crime* (Abingdon: Willan).

Dower, J. W. (1986) *War Without Mercy* (New York: Pantheon).

Downes, D. and Rock, P. (2007 [1972]) *Understanding Deviance*, 5th edn (Oxford: Oxford University Press).

Doyle, S. (ed.) (2010) *Policing the Narrow Ground: Lessons from the transformation of policing in Northern Ireland* (Dublin: Royal Irish Academy).

Ellis, J. (1982 [1980]) *The Sharp End of War* (London: Corgi).

Ellis, S. (1998) 'The historical significance of South Africa's Third Force,' *Journal of South African Studies*, Vol. 24, No. 2, 261–99.

Ellison, G. and Smyth, J. (2000) *The Crowned Harp: Policing in Northern Ireland* (London: Pluto Press).

Emsley, C. (1996) *The English Police: A Political and Social History* (London: Longman).

English, R. (2004 [2003]) *Armed Struggle: The History of the IRA* (London: Pan).

Ermann, M. and Lundman, R. J. (eds) (1982 [1978]) *Corporate and Governmental Deviance*, 2nd edn (New York & Oxford: Oxford University Press).

Farida, M. (2010) 'Field notes on Hizbullah's recruitment, training and organisational structure', *Journal of Policing, Intelligence and Counter Terrorism*, Vol. 5, No. 2, 71–7.

Ferracutti, F. (1998) 'Ideology and repentance: Terrorism in Italy', in *Origins of Terrorism*, W. Reich (ed.), (Washington, DC: Woodrow Wilson Center).

Geraghty, T. (2000 [1998]) *The Irish War* (London: Harper Collins).

Glenny, M. (2009) *McMafia: Seriously organized crime* (London: Vintage Books).

Gobert, J. and Punch, M. (2000) 'Whistleblowers, Public Interest and the Public Interest Disclosure Act 1998', *The Modern Law Review*, Vol. 63, No. 1, 25–54.

Gorman, E. (1992) 'Bomb Disposers Mark 21 years in Ulster', *The Times*, 7 November.

Gourevitch, P. and Morris, E. (2008) *Standard Operating Procedure: A War Story* (New York: Picador).

Green, P. and Ward, T. (2004) *State Crime: Governments, Violence and Corruption* (London: Pluto Press).

Gross, N. (1980) 'Organization Structure and Organizational Crime,' in *White Collar Crime*, G. Geis and E. Stotland (eds), (Beverly Hills, CA: Sage).

Grossman, D. (1995) *On Killing* (Boston: Little Brown).

Grossman, P. (2002) 'India's Secret Armies', in *Death Squads in Global Perspective*, B. B. Campbell and A. D. Brenner (eds), (Basingstoke: Macmillan), 261–312.

Gurr, T. R. (1970) *Why Men Rebel* (Princeton: Princeton University Press).

Gurr, T. R. (1998) 'Terrorism in Democracies: Its social and political bases' in W. Reich (ed.) *Origins of Terrorism: Psychologies, ideologies, theologies, states of mind* (Washington, DC: Woodrow Wilson Center), 86-102

Hainsworth, P. (1987) 'The Stalker Affair and the Administration of Justice in Northern Ireland', *Corruption and Reform*, Vol. 2, No. 3, 195–214.

Hamm, M. S. (2002) *In Bad Company: America's terrorist underground* (Boston, MA: North Eastern University Press)

Harding, T. (2002) 'Heath "told Army it had legal right to shoot rioters"', *Telegraph*, 25 November.

Hermann, M. G. and Hermann, C. F. (1998) 'Hostage taking, the presidency, and stress', in *Origins of Terrorism*, W. Reich (ed.), (Washington, DC: Woodrow Wilson Center).

Hillyard, P. (1987) 'The normalization of special powers: from Northern Ireland to Britain', in *Law, Order and the Authoritarian State*, P. Scraton (ed.), (Milton Keynes: Open University Press).

—— (2003) 'Imaginative Crimes or Crimes of the Imagination: Researching the Secret State', in *Unmasking the Crimes of the Powerful*, S. Tombs and D. Whyte (eds), (New York: Peter Lang Publishing).

Hinton, M. S. (2005) *The State on the Streets* (Boulder/London: Rienner).

Hinton, M. S. and Newburn, T. (eds) (2009) *Policing Developing Democracies* (Abingdon: Routledge).

Hoffman, B. (2006) *Inside Terrorism* (New York: Columbia University Press).

Hoogenboom, A. B. (2010a) *The Governance of Policing and Security: Ironies, Myths and Paradoxes* (Basingstoke: Palgrave).

—— (2010b) 'The Jack Bauer culture: Imbalance between publicity, privacy and secrecy', in *Ethics and Security*, M. den Boer and E. Kolthoff (eds), (The Hague: Eleven International Publishing).

Horgan, J. (2005) *The Psychology of Terrorism* (London & New York: Routledge).

Horne, A. (1979 [1977]) *A Savage War of Peace: Algeria 1954–1962* (Harmondsworth: Penguin).

Huggins, M. K. (ed.) (1991) *Vigilantism and the state in modern Latin America: essays on extralegal violence* (New York: Praeger).

Hughes, E. (1963) 'Good People and Dirty Work', in *The Other Side*, H. S. Becker (ed.), (Glencoe: Free Press).

Human Rights Watch (2007) *Annual Report* (New York: Human Rights Watch).

Hunt Report (1969) *Report of the Advisory Committee on Police in Northern Ireland* (London: HMSO).

Ingram, M. and Harkin, G. (2004) *Stakeknife: Britain's secret agents in Ireland* (Dublin: O'Brien Press).

Ireland v United Kingdom (1978) 5310/71, 18 January). European Court of Human Rights (Strasbourg: ECHR).

Jackall, R. (1988) *Moral Mazes* (New York & Oxford: Oxford University Press).

Jamieson, R. and McEvoy, K. (2005), 'State Crime by Proxy and Juridical Othering', *British Journal of Criminology*, Vol. 45, No. 4, 504–27.

Janis, (1972) *Victims of Groupthink* (Boston: Houghton Mifflin).

Jenkins, B. (1975) *International Terrorism: A new mode of conflict* (Santa Monica, CA: California Seminar on Arms Control and Foreign Policy).

Johnson, P. (1980) *Ireland: Land of troubles* (London: Eyre Methuen).

Katz, J. (1988) *The Seductions of Crime* (New York: Basic Books).

Kellen, K. (1998) 'Ideology and Rebellion: Terrorism and in West Germany', in *Origins of Terrorism*, W. Reich (ed.), (Washington, DC: Woodrow Wilson Center).

Kelman, H. C. (2009) 'The policy context of international crimes', in *System Criminality in International Law*, P. A. Nollkaemper and H. van der Wilt (eds), (Cambridge: Cambridge University Press).

King, M. (1986) *Death of the Rainbow Warrior* (Auckland: Penguin).

Kitson, F. (1989) *Low Intensity Operations: Subversion, insurgency and peacekeeping* (London: Faber and Faber).

Kleinig, J. (1996) *The Ethics of Policing* (Cambridge: Cambridge University Press).

Klockars, C. B. (2005) 'The Dirty Harry problem', in T. Newburn (ed.) *Policing: Key readings* (Cullompton: Willan Publishing).

Kramer, M. (1998) 'The moral logic of Hizballah', in W. Reich (ed.), *Origins of Terrorism* (Washington, DC: Woodrow Wilson Center).

Krisberg, B. (1975) *Crime and Privilege: Toward a New Criminology* (Englewood Cliffs, NJ: Prentice-Hall).

Lacquer, W. (1987) *The Age of Terrorism* (Boston, MA: Little Brown).

Lerner, M. J. (1980) *The Belief in a Just World* (New York & London: Plenum Press).

Loader, I. and Walker, N. (2007) *Civilizing Security* (Cambridge: Cambridge University Press).

Luban, D. (2011) 'Risk Taking and Force Protection'. In *Reading Walzer* (I. Benbaji and N. Sussman, eds), forthcoming; Georgetown Public Law Research Paper No. 11–72. Available at SSRN: http://ssrn.com/abstract=1855263.

MacLean Report (2010) *The Billy Wright Inquiry: Report* (London: TSO).

Margalit, A. (2010) *On Compromise And Rotten Compromises* (Princeton, NJ: University Press).

Markham, G. and Punch, M. (2007a) 'Embracing Accountability: The Way Forward – Part One', *Policing: Journal of Research and Practice*, Vol. 1, No. 3, 300–08.

—— (2007b) 'Embracing Accountability: The Way Forward – Part Two', *Policing: Journal of Research and Practice*, Vol. 1, No. 4, 485–94.

Marighela, C. (1970) *Mini-manual of the Urban Guerrilla* (Havana: Tricontinental).

Marx, G. T. (1988) *Undercover: Police Surveillance in America* (Berkeley, CA: University of California Press).

McAlpine, K. (2009) *We Died With Our Boots Clean* (Stroud: History Press).

McCann and Others v United Kingdom (1995) Series A, No 324, Application No 18984/91(1995). European Court of Human Rights (Strasbourg: ECHR).

McCarthy, M. (1973) *Medina* (London: Wildwood House).

McDonald, H. (2010) 'Bloody Sunday Report', *The Guardian*, 15 June.

McDonald, H. and Holland, J. (2010 [1994]) *INLA: Deadly Divisions* (Dublin: Poolbeg).

McGahern, J. (2003) 'Make them criminals: A classic of Ireland's wars', *The Times Literary Supplement*, 17 June.

McKerr v The United Kingdom (2002) Application No. 28883/95, Judgement of 4 May 2001. European Court of Human Rights (Strasbourg: ECHR).

McKittrick, D., Kelters, S., Feeney, B., Thornton, C. and McVea, D. (2007 [1999]) *Lost Lives: The stories of the men, women and children who died as a result of the Northern Ireland Troubles* (Edinburgh: Mainstream).

McKittrick, D. and McVea, D. (2001 [1999]) *Making Sense of the Troubles* (London: Penguin).

Merari, A. (2005) 'Social, organizational and psychological factors in suicide terrorism', in *Root Causes of Terrorism*, T. Bjørgo (ed.), (Abingdon: Routledge).

Milgram, S. (1974) *Obedience to Authority* (New York: HarperCollins).

Moloney, E. (2007 [2002]) *A Secret History of the IRA* (Harmondsworth: Penguin).

—— (2008) *Paisley: From Demagogue to Democrat?* (Dublin: Poolbeg Press).

—— (2010) *Voices from the Grave: Two Men's War in Ireland* (London: Faber & Faber).

Montefiore, S. (2003) *Stalin: The Court of the Red Tsar* (London: Weidenfeld and Nicolson).

Moysey, S. P. (2007) *The Road to Balcombe Street* (London: Haworth Press).

Mulcahy, A. (2006) *Policing Northern Ireland: Conflict, legitimacy and reform* (Cullompton: Willan).

Murphy, D. (1992) 'The Stalker Affair', *Corruption and Reform*, Vol. 7, No. 1, 19–40.

Newburn, T. (1999) *Understanding and preventing police corruption: Lessons from the literature* (London: Home Office).

Newsinger, J. (1997) *Dangerous Men: The SAS and popular culture* (London: Pluto Press).

Ni Aoláin, F. (2000) *The Politics of Force: Conflict management and state violence in Northern Ireland* (Belfast: Blackstaff).

Nollkaemper, P. A. and van der Wilt, H. (eds) *System Criminality in International Law* (Cambridge: Cambridge University Press).

Norton-Taylor, R. (ed.) (2005) *Scenes from the Saville Inquiry* (London: Oberon Books).

Operation Banner (2006) *An Analysis of Military Operations in Northern Ireland* (London: Ministry of Defence).

OPONI (2005) *Omagh Bomb Report: Statement by the Police Ombudsman for Northern Ireland on matters relating to the Omagh bombing of 15 August 1998* (Belfast: OPONI).

—— (2006) *Report into the complaint by James and Michael McConville regarding the police investigation into the abduction and murder of their mother Mrs Jean McConville* (Belfast: OPONI).

—— (2007) *Statement by the Police Ombudsman for Northern Ireland on her Investigation into the circumstances surrounding the death of Raymond McCord Junior and related matters* (Belfast: OPONI).

—— (2010) *Police Ombudsman's Claudy Report* (Belfast: OPONI).

Orde, H. (2003) 'Working with an Independent Investigation Agency', presentation at OPONI conference, *Policing the Police* (Belfast: OPONI).

Pakenham, T. (1992 [1979]) *The Boer War* (London: Abacus).

Park, D. (2010) *The Truth Commissioner* (London: Bloomsbury).

Parker, T. (2007) 'Fighting an Antaean Enemy: How Democratic States Unintentionally Sustain the Terrorist Movements They Oppose', *Terrorism and Political Violence*, Vol. 9, No. 2, 155–79.

Patten Report (1999) *A New Beginning: Policing in Northern Ireland. Report of the Independent Commission on Policing for Northern Ireland* (London: Home Office).

Pearce, F. (1976) *Crimes of the Powerful* (London: Pluto Press).

Penglase, B. (1996) *Final Justice: Police and death squad homicides of adolescents in Brazil* (New York: Human Rights Watch).

Polk, K. (1994) *When Men Kill: Scenarios of masculine violence* (Cambridge: Cambridge University Press).

Post, J. M. (1998) 'Terrorist psycho-logic: Terrorist behaviour as product of strategic choice', in *Origins of Terrorism*, W. Reich (ed.), (Washington, DC: Woodrow Wilson Center).

Prados, J. (1996) *Presidents' Secret Wars* (Lanham, MD: Ivan R. Dee).

Prince, R. and Leach, B. (2010) 'Bloody Sunday: Soldiers criticise Saville report findings', *The Telegraph*, 16 June.

Punch, M. (1979) *Policing the Inner City* (London: Macmillan).

—— (1985) *Conduct Unbecoming: The social construction of police deviance and control* (London: Tavistock).

—— (1996) *Dirty Business* (London: Sage).

—— (2003) 'Rotten Orchards: "Pestilence", Police Misconduct and System Failure', *Policing and Society*, Vol. 3, No. 2, 171–96.

—— (2005) 'The Belgian Disease: Dutroux, Scandal and "System Failure" in Belgium', in *Policing Corruption: International perspectives*, R. Sarre, D. Das and H. J. Albrecht (eds), (Langham, MD: Lexington Books).

—— (2008) 'The Organization Did It: Individuals, Corporations and Crime', in *Corporate and White-Collar Crime*, J. Minkes and L. Minkes (eds), (London: Sage).

—— (2009) *Police Corruption* (Cullompton: Willan).

—— (2010) *Shoot to Kill: Police accountability, firearms and fatal force* (Bristol: Policy Press).

Quinney, R. (1970) *The Social Reality of Crime* (Boston, MA: Little Brown).

Rawlinson, P. (2010) *From Fear to Fraternity: A Russian tale of crime, economy and modernity* (London: Pluto Press).

Rapoport, D. C. (1998) 'Sacred terror: A contemporary example from Islam' in *Origins of Terrorism*, W. Reich (ed.), (Washington, DC: Woodrow Wilson Center).

Reed, B. (1985) *Contra Terror in Nicaragua* (Boston, MA: South East Press).

Reich, W. (ed.) (1998) *Origins of Terrorism: Psychologies, ideologies, theologies, states of mind* (Washington, DC: Woodrow Wilson Center).

Reiner, R. (1997) 'Policing and the Police' in *The Oxford Handbook of Policing*, 2nd edn, M. Maguire, R. Morgan and R. Reiner (eds), (Oxford: Clarendon Press):

—— (2007) *Law and Order* (Cambridge: Polity Press).

—— (2010 [1984]) *The Politics of the Police*, 4th edn (Oxford: Oxford University Press).

Reisman, D. (1979) *Folded Lies* (New York, NY: Free Press).

Richardson, L. (2006) *What Terrorists Want: Understanding the terrorist threat* (London: John Murray).

Rolston, B. (2005), '"An effective mask for terror": Democracy, death squads and Northern Ireland', *Crime, Law and Social Change*, Vol. 44, No. 2 (September), 211–3.

—— (2006 [2000]) *Unfinished Business: State killings and the quest for truth* (Coleraine: CAIN Web Service).

—— (2010) 'The Saville Report: A Personal Reflection', *International State Crime Initiative*, King's College London. Available at: http://statecrime.org/component/content/article/61-bloody-sunday/203-the-saville-report-a-personal-reflection

Rozenberg, J. (2002) 'Bloody Sunday para admits telling lies', *The Telegraph*, 18 October.

Ryder, C. (2000 [1989]) *The RUC* (London: Arrow).

Sands, P. (2009) *Torture Team: Uncovering war crimes in the land of the free* (London: Penguin).

Saville Report (2010) *Report of the Bloody Sunday Inquiry* (London: TSO).

Scahill, J. (2007) *Blackwater: The rise of the world's most powerful mercenary army* (New York, NY: Nation Books).

Scarman Report (1972) *Violence and Civil Disturbances in Northern Ireland in 1969: Report of a tribunal of inquiry* (London: HMSO).

Schmid, A. (1992) 'Terrorism and Democracy', *Terrorism and Political Violence*, Vol. 4, No. 4, 14–25.

Schmid, A. P. and Jongman, A. J. (1988) *Political Terrorism* (Amsterdam: North Holland Publishing).

Shover, N. (1978) 'Organizations and inter-organizational fields as criminogenic behaviour settings,' unpublished paper (Knoxville, TN: University of Tennessee).

Simpson, A. (2010) *Duplicity and Deception* (Dingle & London: Brandon).

Smith, M. L. R. and Neumann, P. R. (2005) 'Motorman's Long Journey: Changing the Strategic Setting in Northern Ireland', *Contemporary British History*, Vol. 19, No. 4, 413–35.

Solomons, E. (1966) *Portraits of Patriots* (Dublin: Allen Figgis & Co.).

Sprinzak, E. (1998) 'The psychopolitical formation of extreme left terrorism in a democracy: The case of the Weathermen', in *Origins of Terrorism*, W. Reich (ed.), (Washington, DC: Woodrow Wilson Center).

Stalker, J. (1988) *Stalker: Ireland, 'Shoot to Kill' and the 'Affair'* (Harmonsdworth: Penguin).

Stevens, J. (2003) *Stevens Enquiry 3: Overview and recommendations* (London: Home Office).

Sutton, M. (1994) *'Bear in Mind these Dead'... An index of deaths from the conflict in Northern Ireland 1969–1993* (Dublin: Beyond the Pale).

Sykes, G. and Matza, D. (1957) 'Techniques of Neutralization', *American Sociological Review*, Vol. 22, December, 664–70.

Taylor, P. (1987) *Stalker* (London: Faber).

—— (1998) *Provos: The IRA and Sinn Fein* (London: Bloomsbury).

—— (2000) *Loyalists* (London: Bloomsbury).

—— (2001) *Brits: The war against the IRA* (London: Bloomsbury).

Thatcher, M. and Dale, I. (2010) *Margaret Thatcher in Her Own Words* (London: Biteback).

Thames Television (1988) 'Death on the Rock', 28 April.

Tóibín, C. (1994) *Bad Blood: A walk along the Irish border* (Basingstoke: Picador).

Tombs, S. and Whyte, D. (eds) (2003) *Unmasking the Crimes of the Powerful* (New York, NY: Peter Lang).

Travers, S. and Fetherstonhaugh, N. (2007) *Miami Showband Massacre* (Dublin: Hodder Headline Ireland).

United Nations (2010) *Report of the Special Rapporteur on Extrajudicial, Summary or Arbitrary Executions*, Philip Alston August 2004 to July 2010 (New York: United Nations).

Urban, M. (1993 [1992]) *Big Boys' Rules* (London: Faber & Faber).

Walker, C. and Starmer, K. (1999) *Miscarriages of Justice: A review of justice in error* (London: Blackstone).

Waddington, P. A. J. (1991) *The Strong Arm of the Law* (Oxford: Oxford University Press).

Gerth, H. H. and and Wright Mills, C. W. (1948) *From Max Weber: Essays in Sociology* (London: Routledge and Kegan Paul)

Walsh, J. (2009) 'Sinn Fein is walking a tightrope', *The Guardian*, 9 March.

Wheatcroft, G. (2004) 'A happy 80th birthday to IRA's most deadly foe', *The Telegraph*, 16 April.

Weitzer, R. (1990) *Transforming Settler States: Communal conflict and internal security in Zimbabwe and Northern Ireland* (Berkeley, CA: University of California Press).

—— (1995) *Policing Under Fire* (Albany, NY: SUNY Press).

White, R. W. (1989) 'From Peaceful Protest to Guerrilla War: Micromobilization of the Provisional Irish Republican Army', *American Society of Sociology*, Vol. 94, No. 6, 1277–1302.

Widgery Report (1972) *Report of the Tribunal into the events on Sunday, 30 January 1972* (London: HMSO).

Wilkinson, P. (1986) *Terrorism and the Liberal State* (Basingstoke: Macmillan).

—— (2005) *Terrorism versus Democracy: The Liberal State Response* (London & New York: Frank Cass).

—— (2010) *State Terrorism and Human Rights* (Abingdon: Routledge).

Williams, M. (1989) *Murder on the Rock* (London: Larkin).

Wilson, R. A. (2001) *The Politics of Truth and Reconciliation in South Africa* (Cambridge: Cambridge University Press).

Woodward, R. (2006) *State of Denial* (New York: Simon & Schuster).

Woodworth, P. (2002) *Dirty War, Clean Hands: ETA, the GAL and Spanish Democracy* (New Haven CT: Yale University Press).

Wright, S. A. (2007) *Patriots, Politics, and the Oklahoma City Bombing* (Cambridge & New York: Cambridge University Press).

Zimbardo, P. G. (2008) *The Lucifer Effect: Understanding how good people turn evil* (New York: Random House).

Index

Compiled by Sue Carlton

Names in inverted commas are pseudonyms